Understanding

STATISTICS

for the Social Sciences, Criminal Justice, and Criminology

Jeffery T. Walker, PhD
Department of Criminal Justice
University of Little Rock
Little Rock, AR

Sean Maddan, PhD
Department of Criminology and Criminal Justice
University of Tampa
Tampa, FL

JONES & BARTLETT
LEARNING

World Headquarters
Jones & Bartlett Learning
5 Wall Street
Burlington, MA 01803
978-443-5000
info@jblearning.com
www.jblearning.com

Jones & Bartlett Learning books and products are available through most bookstores and online booksellers. To contact Jones & Bartlett Learning directly, call 800-832-0034, fax 978-443-8000, or visit our website, www.jblearning.com.

Substantial discounts on bulk quantities of Jones & Bartlett Learning publications are available to corporations, professional associations, and other qualified organizations. For details and specific discount information, contact the special sales department at Jones & Bartlett Learning via the above contact information or send an email to specialsales@jblearning.com.

Production Credits
Publisher: Cathleen Sether
Acquisitions Editor: Sean Connelly
Editorial Assistant: Caitlin Murphy
Director of Production: Amy Rose
Production Assistant: Alyssa Lawrence
Marketing Manager: Lindsay White
Manufacturing and Inventory Control Supervisor: Amy Bacus
Cover Design: Timothy Dziewit
Composition: Northeast Compositors, Inc.
Cover Image: © fivespots/ShutterStock, Inc.
Printing and Binding: Malloy, Inc.
Cover Printing: Malloy, Inc.

To order this product, use ISBN: 978-1-4496-4922-7

Library of Congress Cataloging-in-Publication Data
Walker, Jeffery T.
   Understanding statistics for the social sciences, criminal justice, and criminology / Jeffery T. Walker and Sean Maddan.
       p. cm.
   Includes index.
   Adapted from: Statistics in criminology and criminal justice / Jeffery T. Walker, Sean Maddan. 3rd ed. c2009.
   ISBN-13: 978-1-4496-3403-2 (pbk.)
   ISBN-10: 1-4496-3403-6 (pbk.)
1. Criminal statistics--Textbooks. 2. Social sciences--Statistical methods--Textbooks. I. Maddan, Sean. II. Walker, Jeffery T. Statistics in criminology and criminal justice. III. Title.
   HV6030.W335 2013
   364.01'5195--dc23
                            2011033491

6048

Printed in the United States of America
16 15 14 13 12   10 9 8 7 6 5 4 3 2 1

Contents

Preface

Other than pure math classes, few courses elicit the antipathy that statistics courses in the social sciences suffer. Students approach statistics courses with a mix of reactions ranging from hating math, to trepidation, to a general perception that statistics are difficult, to a failure to understand how statistics will help them in their academic or professional careers. Additionally, while there are plenty of rules associated with statistics, oftentimes there are multiple ways to attempt to answer questions through statistical analyses. A certain sense of vertigo in student learning ensues. Any one of these barriers makes it more difficult for students to learn the material.

The role of the textbook in statistics courses is key. Many introductory statistics textbooks in the social sciences do a poor job when it comes to describing the mechanics associated with the underpinnings of statistical analysis. As such, students, who may already have a negative mindset towards statistics, oftentimes have difficulty connecting information in lectures with information in the book—especially when it comes to working through equations.

This book provides a simplified approach for professors and students teaching and taking statistics courses in the social sciences. It addresses all of the basics of statistical analysis while still providing students with the larger view of statistics. While focusing on the substance of statistics at a simplistic, basic level of understanding, the book also provides information on deciding when to use particular statistical analyses, how to input and analyze data through programs such as Microsoft Excel and SPSS, the interpretation of statistical output, and making conclusions based on those results. After completing this book, students will have a strong basis in statistics—conceptually and pragmatically.

Acknowledgments

We would like to thank the individuals listed below for their thoughtful reviews of our original manuscript. We would also like to thank Sean Connelly and all the fine folks at Jones & Bartlett Learning for their diligence in seeing this project through to the end.

Reviewers

Mark R. Baird, *Clackamas Community College*

Kevin M. Beaver, *Florida State University*

J. Pete Blair, *Texas State University*

Peggy Bowen-Hartung, *Alvernia University*

Clairissa Breen, *Gannon University*

Kevin D. Cannon, *Southern Illinois University, Edwardsville*

Michael Costelloe, *Northern Arizona University*

Melchor C. de Guzman, *The College at Brockport, SUNY*

M. George Eichenberg, *Tarleton State University*

Qinghai Gao, *SUNY at Farmingdale*

Lisa M. Graziano, *California State University, Los Angeles*

Lisa M. Lancaster, *Tennessee State Univeristy*

Joseph LeFevre, *University Wisconsin–Platteville.*

Raymond V Liedka, *Oakland University*

Billy Long, *Ferrum College*

Barbara May, *Mercer County Community College*

Virginia McGovern, *Mount Saint Mary's University*

J. Mitchell Miller, *University of Texas San Antonio*

Geoffrey Moss, *Temple University*

Jennifer Murphy, *California State University, Sacramento*

John L. Padgett, *Capella University*

Nicholas L. Parsons, *Eastern Connecticut State University*

Michelle Y Richter, *St. Edward's University*

Dennis B. Roderick, *UMass Dartmouth*

Daniel Simone, *Saint Peter's College*

Ron Thrasher, Stillwater Police Department; *Oklahoma State University*

Finally, special thanks go to Tak-Shing Harry So at the University of Indiana for lending another set of eyes with a thorough technical review of the statistical work found in this textbook.

About the Authors

Jeffery T. Walker is a professor of Criminal Justice and Criminology and Chair of the Department of Criminal Justice at the University of Arkansas, Little Rock, where he has worked since 1990. Dr. Walker has written 7 books and over 50 journal articles and book chapters. He has obtained over $9 million in grants from the Department of Justice, National Institute of Drug Abuse, and others. His areas of interest are social/environmental factors of crime and the study of non-linear dynamics as they relate to crime. He is a past President of the Academy of Criminal Justice Sciences. Editorial experience includes service as Editor of the *Journal of Criminal Justice Education*, *Journal of Critical Criminology*, and *Crime Patterns and Analysis*. Previous publications include articles in *Justice Quarterly*, *Journal of Quantitative Criminology*, and *Journal of Criminal Justice Education*, and the books *Leading Cases in Law Enforcement* (8th Edition), *Statistics in Criminal Justice and Criminology: Analysis and Interpretation* (4th Edition) and *Myths in Crime and Justice* (2nd Edition).

Sean Maddan is Associate Professor in the Department of Criminology and Criminal Justice at the University of Tampa. His research areas include criminological theory, statistics, research methods, and the efficacy of sex offender registration and notification laws. Dr. Maddan has authored over a dozen articles, which have appeared in many outlets including *Justice Quarterly, Crime and Justice*, and the *Journal of Criminal Justice*. Dr. Maddan has also authored/co-authored several books. The most recent is *Criminology and Criminal Justice: Theory, Research Methods, and Statistics*.

Chapter 1
The Foundations of Statistics: Theory, Methods, and Measurement

Learning Objectives

- Understand the difference between statistics and math.
- Explain the role of statistics in the process of scientific inquiry.
- Discuss the relationship among theory, research methods, and statistics.
- Identify the steps in the research process.
- Understand the relationship among primary questions, research questions, null hypotheses, and research hypotheses.
- Explain the differences among nominal, ordinal, interval, and ratio level data.
- Determine the level of measurement for data in exercises.

Key Terms

bivariate statistics
concept
descriptive statistics
discovery
inferential statistics
interval
level of measurement
multivariate statistics
nominal
null hypothesis
observation
operationalization
ordinal
primary question

process of inquiry
ratio
research
research design
research hypothesis
research methods
research question
scientific inquiry
statistical analysis
statistics
theory
true zero
univariate statistics
variable

People often think statistics is a math class. It is true that statistics involves math—sometimes a lot of math. But statistics is more than just getting the right answer to a problem. Statistics is about *discovery*—discovery of something previously unknown or something we thought we knew but were not sure. For example, it is commonly believed that poverty causes crime. While there may be some relationship between the two, research has shown that poverty by itself does not cause crime. So what does?

Statistics, as a part of a research project, could help us figure this out—or at least know more about it. The process of *scientific inquiry* provides a method of examining things that interest us in a systematic manner. This process generally requires evidence to support an argument. One of the clearest methods of establishing evidence is by examining numbers associated with the objects being studied. That examination takes place through *statistical analysis*.

The purpose of this book is to further your knowledge of statistical analysis—and to do it in a way that makes sense and calms the fears of those who hate math. We will walk you through commonsense discussions of statistical procedures, introduce you to how to talk about statistics and the results of statistical analyses, and show you how to do statistical analyses in ways that are not as math heavy as many think necessary. We also want to give you some background on statistics so you may better understand where it came from and why it is important. It is to that history that we now turn.

1-1   Some Statistical History

The earliest form of what is now considered statistical analysis was developed by Pythagoras in the 6th century B.C. This was the forerunner of *descriptive statistics*. The other type of statistical analysis—*inferential statistics*—is thought to have first developed in the Orient around 200 B.C. in attempts to predict whether an expected child was likely to be male or female. Probability theory, as it would come to be known, was born in the form of gambling mathematics in the works of people such as Pascal (1623–1662). Many of the other descriptive statistics were developed in the late 1800s and early 1900s by mathematicians and scientists such as Galton (1883) and Pearson (1895).

Statistics moved beyond gambling and purely mathematical concepts through what was called political arithmetic, developed by John Graunt in 1662 to study London's death rates. Although there is fierce debate concerning the original use of the term *statistics*, the greatest support is that it was coined by Eberhard August Wilhelm von Zimmerman in 1787.

1-2   Statistics and the Process of Scientific Inquiry

Statistics as you will come to know them are methods used to examine data collected in the process of scientific inquiry. These methods allow researchers to think logically about the data and to do one of two things:

- To come to some succinct and meaningful conclusions about the data (descriptive statistics), or
- To determine—or infer—characteristics of large groups based on the data collected on small parts (samples) of the group (inferential statistics).

For example, data could be gathered on all children in all middle schools in the state for a research project to determine their breakdown according to sex and race. This would be a descriptive analysis. Alternatively, data from a sample of middle school students from one school district could be collected and the data from the sample used to make statements about all middle school children in the state. This would be drawing conclusions (inferences) about a large group based on information about a sample of the group.

But *statistics* is just one part of the process of scientific inquiry. The other two critical components are *theory* and *research methods*. Let's talk about these two briefly before we get into the concept of statistical analysis.

Theory

At the most basic level, theory consists of statements concerning the relationship among the characteristics of people or things. For example, in criminology, there are theories addressing how people learn to be criminal. In these theories, statements are constructed that deal with the role of peers in a person's learning of criminal behavior, how the rewards from a crime can influence behavior, and what influence punishment can have on the decision to commit a crime. The goal of these statements is to develop explanations of why things are as they appear and to try to explain their meaning.

We often have ideas about the causes of events and why things work the way that they do. The problem with these explanations, however, is that they are often too simplistic to be of any real value. Theory attempts to provide a stronger foundation for these ideas by asking questions such as:

- What is the point of all this?
- What does it mean?
- Why are things this way?

Without theory, there is often only conjecture and war stories. With theory, we may begin to develop statements or ideas that are based on sound observation and thought.

Research Methods

Theory cannot stand alone, however. Theory must also have research methods to give structure to the inquiry and *statistical analysis* to back it up. Theory without research and statistical analysis to back it up is little more than fable. Research methods without *theory* are like a house without plans. And research without statistical analysis is like building a house without nails.

Research methods are a scientific, systematic way of examining and testing theory. They are a systematic way of turning observation and statistical analysis into theory (induction) or testing theory through statistical analysis (deduction). Although there are no exact, cookbook steps that must be followed in conducting a study, there are some general guidelines that should be followed to ensure nothing is left out or done improperly. These are discussed next.

The Process of Conducting Research

The process of scientific inquiry (using a deductive method) is shown in **Figure 1-1**. This is a typical process of research, and it shows where statistics fits into the process. As shown in this diagram, theory and methods are at the starting point of the process. Many steps flow from theory and methods and where they meet. Each part of this figure and where it fits within the process of conducting research are discussed in the sections that follow.

Observation and Inquisitiveness

The first step in the process of scientific inquiry, and one of the most important, is often overlooked: *observation* and inquisitiveness. Many research projects are never begun because the researcher was not aware of his or her surroundings or did not recognize something as a topic worthy of research. As you go through school and read research and material you find interesting, you will sometimes think you have a better way to do something, or what you read may stimulate you to further examine a topic. This observation and curiosity is what starts the scientific process.

Primary Question

A *primary question* is the one driving thought behind a research project. It should represent the entire reason for the study. The primary question should be a carefully worded phrase that states exactly the focus of the study. For example, in research on

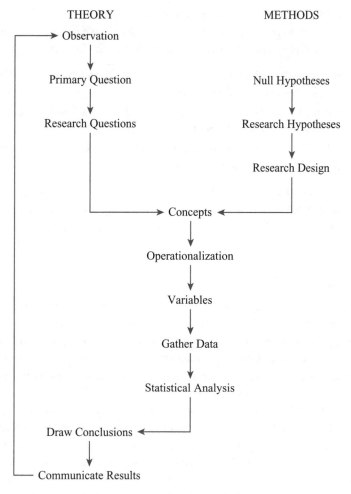

Figure 1–1   Process of Scientific Inquiry Using a Deductive Method

what political parties people become involved in, a possible *primary question* might be, What factors most influence a person to participate in a specific political party?

Often, the primary question will be theoretical, vague, and perhaps not directly addressable through research. For that reason, *research questions* are the next step in the research process.

Research Questions

Research questions break down the primary question into subproblems that are more manageable and make the primary question testable through research. If the primary question establishes the goal of the research, the research questions suggest ways of achieving that goal. In our earlier example concerning people participating in political parties, some possible *research questions* might include the following:

■ What is the relationship between a person's family background and whether she or he is active in her or his political party?

■ What is the relationship between a person's educational level and whether he or she is more likely to be a Republican or a Democrat?

■ How does the economy influence both which political party a person belongs to and how active the person is in the party?

These research questions break down the primary question into smaller parts that can be examined more easily. The answers to these questions are derived from the research process and statistical analysis and allow the researcher to answer the primary question.

Hypotheses

Once the research questions have been developed, you must decide what the research is attempting to determine. This moves into the process of methods on the right side of Figure 1-1. Hypotheses are questions or statements whose answers will support or refute the theoretical questions of the research. Hypotheses are generally broken down into *null hypotheses* and *research hypotheses*. These match to the primary question and the research questions on the theory side of Figure 1-1. Null and research hypotheses are introduced here and discussed more fully in Chapters 9 and 10.

One of the often difficult to understand but vital aspects of research is that research alone cannot prove anything. Even when researchers find a great deal of support for an association between two variables, these results may occur because information is missing or the research is somehow flawed. Other researchers may be able to disprove these findings by conducting additional research. If research cannot *prove* anything, what can it do?

Research can be used to disprove something or to eliminate alternatives. For example, even though research cannot prove that more-educated people will be active in their political parties, it may disprove that there is no relationship between education and political activism. This is accomplished with a null hypothesis, which generally takes the form of one of the following examples:

■ There is no statistically significant difference between the groups being compared.

■ There is no statistically significant difference between a group being studied and the population.

■ The differences between the groups are due to random errors.

This is an example of a null hypothesis:

There is no statistically significant difference between a person's education level and his or her probability of being active in a political party.

The null hypothesis is a broad hypothesis covering all of the research, much as a primary question does.

Like the primary question, the null hypothesis should be broken down into a number of research hypotheses. A research hypothesis is a statement, similar to a research question, that indicates the expected outcome of a part of a research project. If a research question in a project asks, "What is the relationship between a person's educational level and whether the person is more likely to be a Republican or Democrat?" then the research hypothesis might be, "There is a statistically significant correlation between a person's educational level and whether the person is more likely to be a Democrat."

In using research hypotheses, the researcher turns the relatively abstract wording of theory development into a more concrete, testable form appropriate for statistical analysis. Only after a clear picture of the theory to be tested has been developed through questions and hypotheses should the way of testing the theory be developed. This is critical. Many people want to first develop a survey and then determine what they can find out from it. Surveys should be developed far into the process of research, after a complete understanding of the theory and methods is developed.

Research Design

Once a decision is made of what will be studied, planning the research may begin. As a researcher, you should be cautious not to jump ahead of this step to other steps in the research process. You would not start building a house without first looking at other houses and thinking about what you want your house to look like; why would you start a research project without thorough consideration of what you want to do and find?

Activities in developing the *research design* include determining the method to be used (experiment, survey, or other method) and generally deciding how to approach the research. If the researcher has to collect the data, decisions must be made concerning how to collect it, what group it will be collected from, and other parameters.

Concepts

Once research questions and hypotheses have been developed, they must be broken down into more manageable parts. This is accomplished by drawing out the *concepts* from the questions and hypotheses. Concepts are terms that are generally agreed upon as representing a characteristic or a phenomenon. For example, *poverty* and *prejudice* are fairly abstract concepts. You know immediately what each of these means, but it would probably be difficult for you to write a concise description of what they mean and even more difficult to get a consensus among the class members of what the terms mean.

The use of concepts allows researchers to break down questions and hypotheses but to retain the flexibility, for now, of not having to describe specifically what is being studied. In the example above concerning political activism, the concepts to be addressed are person, educational level, economic conditions, and party affiliation.

Operationalization and Variables

To be able to address concepts in terms of statistical analysis, the concepts must be placed in a form that can be analyzed mathematically. This is accomplished through *operationalization*. This is a process of translating a concept, which is abstract and verbal, into a *variable*, which can be seen and tested, by describing how the concept can be measured. The process of converting the abstract to the concrete can be seen in the example of political activism. In cases like this, the difference between a concept and a variable may be determined by asking if the word is specific enough to be able to find data on it. *Democrat* is a fairly clear term, but for the purposes of research it is still a concept that needs to be operationalized. Questions to be answered include the following:

■ Will all people who have registered to vote as a Democrat be used, or just people who voted in the last election?

■ Will people who only vote Democrat be selected, or will people who generally vote Democrat but sometimes vote Republican be included?

The answers to these questions and others will operationalize the somewhat vague concept of a Democrat into someone who can be classified as an object of the research.

The process of transforming concepts into variables demonstrates a critical point in operationalization: Operationalized definitions used in research are the researcher's definitions and do not have to match the definitions others might use or definitions the same researcher might use in other research. For example, in this research project, the term *Democrats* might be operationalized as only people who voted strictly Democrat in the last election. Others could define the term *Democrat* differently by including people who self-identify themselves as Democrats, even if they did not vote in the last election.

Gathering Data

Gathering the data is the step in the research process where most people want to begin, and it is nearly the last place they should begin. Returning to the example of building a house, to begin by gathering data would be like deciding to build a house and, without developing any plans, ordering a truckload of 2 × 4s, 1,000 lbs of nails, and five bags of concrete and then going to work. You might actually get the house built this way, especially if you are an expert, but it would be better to begin with carefully developed plans.

Gathering the data should be a simple process if it is done properly. All you have to do is to look at the variables that have been operationalized from the concepts and gather the data you said you needed, following the rest of the research design created in that step.

Statistical Analysis

The next step in the research process is statistical analysis. Statistical analysis is the nuts-and-bolts work that gives researchers the information needed to determine the success or failure of the research. Statistical analysis deals specifically with the art of making comparisons, and it will be the focus of the rest of the chapters, so the discussion of statistical analysis is abbreviated here.

Drawing Conclusions

Mistakenly, many people believe the process of statistical analysis, and even scientific inquiry, stops at the end of the analysis. Nothing could be further from the truth. Statisticians and researchers distinguish themselves in the interpretation of analyses and in the conclusions that can be drawn. This is also generally the most difficult part of research.

This step involves determining if the results of the statistical analysis support the hypotheses developed at the beginning of the research process. At this step, the research process leaves statistical analysis and methodological issues and returns to theory. If the researcher is using a deductive process, this is the point at which the theory outlined in the first steps is compared to the results and a decision is made concerning whether the theory is supported or refuted.

Communicating Results

The final step in the process of scientific inquiry is to communicate the results of the research. This step is also often overlooked. Beyond just making sure people know of the findings of the research, it can also aid in the process of scientific inquiry, as discussed at the beginning of the chapter, by stimulating others to undertake research.

This concludes the research process. There is one more topic of research methods that needs to be addressed before we get completely into the art of statistics: levels of measurement of data.

1-3   Levels of Measurement

To be able to discuss the characteristics of our surroundings in terms of statistics, these characteristics must be in a form suitable for statistical analysis. A critical component of examining data is to determine the proper *level of measurement* of the data that has been (or will be) collected. This is important because the level of measurement of data is a determining factor in the type of statistical analyses that can be used. Incorrectly identifying the level of measurement of a variable can be disastrous to research because statistical analyses that are not appropriate for the data could mistakenly be used, which would give erroneous results.

Measurement itself is a way of assigning numbers, or numbered symbols, to characteristics (people, social phenomena, etc.), using certain rules and in such a way that the relationships between the numbers reflect the relationships between the characteristics or variables being studied. In fields such as physics or engineering, determining the level of measurement is easy. A person conducting research on the Space Shuttle can operate in terms of the speed of the Space Shuttle, height above Earth, and so on, which are already in the form of numbers. In social sciences, determining the level of measurement is not always so simple.

Every variable can be put into one of four categories: *nominal, ordinal, interval,* and *ratio*. Each of these levels of measurement has different characteristics that must be considered when deciding on a statistical procedure. Let's look at the different levels of measurement and what makes them special for certain types of statistical analysis.

Nominal Level Data

The lowest level of data in terms of levels of measurement is *nominal*. Nominal level data is purely qualitative in nature, meaning that the variables are typically found as words, as opposed to quantitative data, which is number-oriented. Variables in this category might include race, occupation, and hair color.

By assigning numbers to these characteristics, thereby making them useful for statistical analysis, we are doing nothing more than renaming them in a numeric format, and words or letters would serve just as well. For example, the categories of the variable "gender" could be classified as either male or female; or these categories could be abbreviated as M or F; or numbers could be substituted for these classifications, making them 1 and 2. The numbers are simply labels or names that can indicate how the groups differ; but the numbers have no real numeric significance that can tell magnitudes of differences or how the numbers are ordered. Additionally, they could be switched around such that female/male, F/M, and 2/1 also mean the same as in the first three instances. The only reason to use numbers rather than letters is to make mathematical operations possible.

The primary difference between nominal level data and other levels of measurement is that nominal level data cannot be ordered. Since values are arbitrarily assigned, it cannot be argued that one value is greater than or less than another value. For example, coding blue eyes as 2 and brown eyes as 1 does not mean that blue eyes are better than brown eyes, and we could just as easily label blue eyes as 1 and brown eyes as 2. The variable *eye color* cannot be ordered on the characteristic being studied. It is very important, then, to establish the ordering (or lack thereof) of the categories. You should be very specific as to why the categories can or cannot be ordered. Failure to be very clear concerning the ability to order categories will almost always result in misclassification of the level of measurement. For example, you may have data such as patrol district number, which you obtained from the local police agency. These patrol district numbers may look as follows:

1

2

3

4

5

These are certainly ordered, right? Wrong. If you examined them closely, you would see that the numbers can be ordered but what they represent (patrol districts) is not ordered. You could just as easily have labeled them patrol districts A, B, C, D, E.

Ordinal Level Data

Ordinal level data is similar to nominal level data in that it is often made up of words that we place with numbers to use in math. For example, you might say a shirt comes in small, medium, and large. To use shirt size in research, however, you would need to assign it numbers; so you could assign them as small = 1, medium = 2, and large = 3.

The difference between nominal and ordinal level data is that ordinal level data can be ordered. In ordinal level data, the order of the numbers reflects the order of the relationship between the characteristics being studied. This order in the categories is such that one may be said to be less than or greater than another, but it cannot be said by how much. This ordering is similar to having a footrace without a stopwatch. It is possible to determine who finished first, but it is difficult to determine exactly by how much that runner won. In the example above, it is easy to see that a medium shirt is larger than a small shirt and smaller than a large shirt. But it is not possible to determine by how much each is different, and there may be differences between different types of shirts. So the best we can do is to order the shirt sizes here. More precise measurement requires a higher level of data, as discussed next.

Interval Level Data

Interval level data builds on ordinal level data because the data may be ranked or ordered; but with interval level data, there are also equal intervals between categories. With ordinal level data it is not possible to know exactly what the interval is between, for example, shirt sizes of small, medium, and large; but with interval level data it can be established that there are equal intervals between, for example, miles per gallon in fuel economy (where the interval between each point is 1 mi/gal).

Ratio Level Data

Ratio level data is considered the highest order of data. It is interval level data with a *true zero*, where there is the possibility of a true absence of the characteristic in the variable. For example, income is generally considered to be a ratio level variable. You can certainly have zero income! Ratio data includes things that can be counted such as dollars, eggs, and people. Anything that is present and can be counted generally can have an absence of that item, so the data is ratio.

A very important thing to remember about levels of measurement is that a set of data has to meet *all* of the characteristics of the level of measurement, not just some of them. For example, it is possible to have something with a true zero. Suppose you are measuring social security numbers. It is possible for a person to not have a social security number, so there is the possibility of an absence of the number. However, social security numbers are not ordered in a meaningful way; so since they cannot be ordered, they are nominal even though they may have a true zero.

Practical Process for Determining Level of Measurement

As discussed above, properly identifying data and classifying it into its correct level of measurement are a vital part of the research process. A practical process for determining the level of measurement is shown in **Figure 1-2**.

The first step in this process is to determine if the data can be ordered. If the data cannot be ordered, or if the categories can be switched around such that the ordering does not matter, then the data is considered nominal level. If the data can be ordered, it is at least ordinal level and requires further examination. The next step in this process is to determine if there are equal intervals between data points. Note here that equal intervals need not be present—just the possibility of equal intervals. For example, when people are surveyed about their age, there are definite gaps in the data. This is so because there are usually not enough people surveyed to have someone at every possible

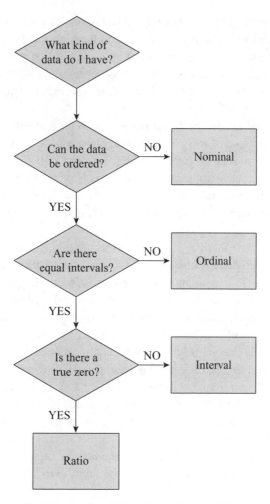

Figure 1–2   Process for Determining Level of Measurement

age. This does not mean the data is not interval, though, simply because there are not perfect intervals in the collected data. If there is no possibility of equal intervals but the data is ordered, then the data is ordinal. If there is the possibility of equal intervals between the data points, such as age in years or months (where the interval between each data point is one year or one month, respectively), then the data is at least interval level and requires further examination. The final step in this process is to determine if there is a true zero, whether clearly identifiable or implied. If there is no true zero, the data is interval; otherwise, the data is ratio level.

There are a few important points to remember when you use this process to determine the level of measurement. These will not make the process of determining the level of measurement easier, but they will make it more accurate. First, it is important to be specific about the data. It is not enough to think abstractly about the variable. You have to ask how the data is arranged *in this case*. This is particularly important in establishing whether the data is ordered. It is not sufficient simply to state that the data can be ordered. How can it be ordered? What specifically supports an argument that it can be ordered?

In addition, look at how the data is being used in the research. Age, for example, can be used in a number of ways in the research process—ways that can change the level of measurement. If age is categorized into groups (0–10, 11–20, etc.), it is probably ordinal level, whereas someone's age in years is probably interval level. Do not simply assume that all variables are measured at the same level all the time. Check the specifics of the research before you jump to conclusions about the level of measurement.

It is also imperative that you look beyond the numbers in a frequency distribution and look at the underlying dimension to understand whether there are equal intervals. For example, if you are examining how long in months prisoners have been incarcerated, the underlying dimension is time in prison in months. In this case, the interval is always months, regardless of what actually is displayed in a frequency distribution. In measuring the taste of doughnuts on a scale of 1 to 10, however, the underlying dimension is taste. The interval is how one doughnut tastes compared to another. Here, the interval will probably be different. For example, the difference between a 5 and a 6 may be quite different from that between a 1 and a 2, because when you move from a 5 to a 6, you are saying that the doughnut tastes good rather than just okay; thus the interval that may take a doughnut from a 5 to a 6 is probably larger than that to get from a 1 to a 2. The jump to get from a 9 to a perfect 10 may be the largest of all because it takes a great doughnut to be perfect. The bottom line here is that the intervals between different categories of taste are not the same, even though the difference in the numbers is 1.

Finally, it is imperative to work through the process outlined in Figure 1-2 until a "no" answer is reached. Ordering must be shown for a variable before equal intervals matter. There are many variables that have a true zero but cannot be ordered. Having a true zero does not matter if the data cannot be ordered; it is still nominal level data. To state that a variable is measured at the ratio level, it is necessary to show all of the following:

1. The data can be ordered.
2. There are equal intervals.
3. There is a true zero.

Also, do not succumb to the temptation to find that a variable can be ordered and then quit, stating that it is ordinal. Find out first if there are equal intervals. If there are no equal intervals, the variable is ordinal; if there are equal intervals, the process continues.

1-4   For Further Reading

Behan, F. L., & Behan, R. A. Football numbers. *American Psychologist*, 1954, *9*, 262.

Duncan, O. D. *Notes on measurement: Historical and critical.* New York: Russell Sage Foundation, 1984.

Glaser, B. G., & Strauss, A. L. *The discovery of grounded theory.* Chicago: Aldine Publishing Company, 1967.

Kuhn, T. S. *The structure of scientific revolutions* (2d ed.). Chicago: University of Chicago Press, 1970.

Reynolds, P. D. *A primer in theory construction.* Indianapolis, IN: Bobbs-Merrill Educational Publishing, 1971.

Stevens, S. S. On the theory of scales of measurement. *Science*, 1946, 103 (2684), 677.

Stevens, S. S. Mathematics, measurement and psychophysics. In S. S. Stevens (Ed.), *Handbook of experimental psychology*. New York: Wiley, 1951.

—. Measurement, statistics and the schemapiric view. *Science*, 1968, *161*(3844), 849.

Wallace, W. L. *The logic of science in sociology.* New York: Aldine Publishing Company, 1971.

Chapter 2
Measures of Central Tendency

Learning Objectives

- Understand how frequency tables are used in statistical analysis.
- Explain the conventions for building distributions.
- Understand the mode, median, and mean as measures of central tendency.
- Identify the proper measure of central tendency to use for each level of measurement.
- Explain how to calculate the mode, median, and mean.

Key Terms

bivariate	median
central tendency	mode
frequency distribution	multivariate
mean	univariate

Now we begin statistical analysis. Statistical analysis may be broken down into three broad categories:

- Univariate analyses
- Bivariate analyses
- Multivariate analyses

These divisions are fairly straightforward. *Univariate* analyses deal with one variable at a time. *Bivariate* analyses compare two variables to each other to see how they differ or if they are the same. In statistical analysis this could take the form of association or correlation. *Multivariate* analyses compare three or more variables to one another, or compare more than two variables (called *independent variables*) in how they influence a variable we are interested in knowing something about (called a *dependent variable*).

The focus of this chapter and of Chapter 3 is on univariate analysis. Univariate descriptive statistics are used to describe and interpret the meaning of a distribution. These statistics tell a lot about a data set by revealing a few critical characteristics. You should always undertake this process before doing any bivariate or multivariate analyses; but you can do sound research just using the analyses we will address in these chapters. Univariate descriptive statistics make compact characterizations of distributions in terms of three properties of the data: *central tendency*, which translates to the average, middle point, or most common value of the distribution; *dispersion*, which relates to how spread out the values are around the central measure; and the *form* of the distribution, which relates to what the distribution would look like if it were displayed graphically.

2-1   Frequency Distributions

Most statistical analyses are displayed through tables (and sometimes charts). Throughout these chapters, you will see different kinds of tables and graphs displaying various types of data. At the most basic level, data is displayed through a frequency distribution (which often contains univariate statistics displayed with the data). Frequency distributions are helpful in summarizing data (scores) because they provide a visualization of how scores are spread over categories. The most common type of distribution for current statistical packages is a combination distribution. This is the type of distribution shown in **Table 2-1**. In SPSS a combination distribution includes percentage, valid percentage, and cumulative percentage. A lot can be learned from these frequency distributions, but we want to focus on the univariate descriptive statistics that usually are a part of these printouts.

Conventions for Building Distributions

Within statistical analysis, there are conventions and standards for presenting tables and distributions. You will soon realize that many people do not follow these conventions; however, if you adhere to these guidelines when building your own tables and distributions, they will be clearer and the results will be easier to interpret.

First, the title of the table or distribution should clearly explain the contents. It should contain the variables included in the table and any variable label or explanation

EDUCATION What is your highest level of education?					
Value Label	**Value**	**Frequency**	**Percent**	**Valid Percent**	**Cumulative Percent**
Less than High School	1	16	4.6	4.8	4.8
GED	2	59	17.0	17.6	22.3
High School Graduate	3	8	2.3	2.4	24.7
Some College	4	117	33.7	34.8	59.5
College Graduate	5	72	20.7	21.4	81.0
Postgraduate	6	64	18.4	19.0	100.0
Total		336	96.8	100.0	
System	Missing	11	3.2		
	Total	347	100.0		

Table 2-1   Combination Table for Education from 1993 Little Rock Community Policing Survey

EDUCATION What is your highest level of education?					
Value Label	**Value**	**Frequency**	**Percent**	**Valid %**	**Cum %**
Less than High School	1	16	4.6	4.8	4.8
GED	2	59	17.0	17.6	22.3
High School Graduate	3	8	2.3	2.4	24.7
Some College	4	117	33.7	34.8	59.5
College Graduate	5	72	20.7	21.4	81.0
Postgraduate	6	64	18.4	19.0	100.0
System	Missing	11	3.2		
		347	100.0		

Table 2-2   Constructed in Excel

of the variable that makes it clear what data the distribution contains. In Table 2-1, the variable is *education*, and the explanation is the wording from the survey from which the variable was drawn: "What is your highest level of education?" If the origin of the data is not expressed clearly in the discussion, the title should also contain this information. This may include the year the data was collected, the geographic region of collection, and any specific information about how the data was gathered.

Possibly more important than the title is proper labeling of the columns and categories. The categories of the data should be clearly identified in the left column, called the *stub* of the table or distribution. These categories should be labeled even if the values are included. In Table 2-1, simply including the values 1 to 6 does not help the reader interpret the table unless he or she has the categories (less than high school, GED, high school, etc.) that correspond to the values. The words that represent the numbers in the stub are called the *value labels*. Each column should also be clearly labeled with its heading.

All relevant columns should be totaled. These totals are called *marginals*. This is important information for summary analysis, and it prevents the reader from having to make independent calculations. It is also important to provide the reader with information on how the table or distribution was developed. In Table 2-1, for example, the frequency and percent totals are based on 347 responses. Valid percent and cumulative percent, however, are based on the total minus the missing responses (11).

Finally, footnotes should be added to tables and distributions when more information is needed, when clarification is necessary, or when there is something unusual about the table or distribution. If not included in the title, the source of the information should be presented in a footnote. This is particularly important when the data in the table or distribution is not collected by the presenter.

Box 2-1   How Do You Do That?

Throughout this text, we will present boxes that show you how to obtain the results or output discussed in the chapter. Often, both SPSS and Excel methods will be demonstrated. For more advanced analyses, only SPSS will be shown. This box shows you how to obtain *frequency distributions*.

SPSS

1. Open a data set.
   a. Start SPSS.
   b. Select File, then Open, then Data.
   c. Select the file you want to open, then select Open.
2. Once the data is visible, select Analyze, then Descriptive Statistics, then Frequencies.
3. Make sure that Display Frequency Tables is checked.
4. Select the variables you wish to include in your distribution, and press the ▶ between the two windows.

5. For now, do not worry about the option boxes at the bottom of the window, and just press OK.

6. An output window should appear that contains a distribution similar in format to Table 2-1.

Excel

Excel does not build tables for you. To complete a table in Excel, follow the instructions for building a table described above, filling in the proper cells with the values and/or data.

1. Start in the second row and fill in the column headings. Block the cells, select the Bold button, and then then select the Center button to make the text boldface and to center it.

2. Block the cells above the headings, right-click the mouse and select Format Cells, select the Alignment tab, and check the box marked Merge Cells. Type in the heading of the table and select the Center button to center the text.

3. Type in the value labels. Note that you may have to expand the cell width to get all of the text in the cell.

4. Type in the data values and the frequencies. You might place the word *Missing* in the cell identifying missing data so you know immediately what that is.

5. Now Excel will do calculations for you. To total the frequencies, click on the Σ in the Home toolbar. Block the cells you want to add and press Return.

6. To calculate the Percent, click on the Σ in the Home toolbar, then select the first frequency (16), type in a / in the formula bar next to the cell value (C3), then type in the frequency total (347), then press Return. You will need to right-click the cell, select Format Cells, select the Number tab, select Percentage from the list, then make sure it is 1 decimal place. To calculate the percentages for the other cells, simply block the cell and then drag down to copy. To make sure you have 100%, simply add the column as described in step 5.

7. Calculating the Valid Percent is done in much the same way as calculating the Percent. The difference here is using $347 - 11$ to divide each cell by the total minus the missing values.

8. To calculate the Cumulative Percent, copy and paste the value in the first cell in the Valid Percent column (4.8%). Click on the Σ in the Home toolbar, then select the value above the empty cell (4.8%), then type a + into the formula bar, then select the cell next to the empty cell, then press Return. This will give the next value in Cumulative Percent. You can fill in the rest of the cells by copying and pasting this cell.

> The result of this work will look like **Table 2-2**. Save this table once you have created it. It is a simple matter to replace these values with others to quickly make additional frequency tables in Excel.

2-2   Measures of Central Tendency

Measures of central tendency examine where the distribution's central—or most typical—value is located. There are three common measures of central tendency, one for each level of measurement. These are the *mode* for nominal level data, the *median* for ordinal level data, and the *mean* for interval and ratio level data.

Mode

At the lowest level of sophistication is the *mode* (symbolized by Mo). The mode is used primarily for nominal data to identify the category with the greatest number of cases. The mode is the most frequently occurring value, or case, in a distribution. It is the tallest column on a histogram or the peak on a polygon or line chart. The mode has the advantage of being spotted easily in a distribution, and it is often used as a first indicator of the central tendency of a distribution.

The mode is the only measure of central tendency appropriate for nominal variables because it is simply a count of the values. Unlike other measures of central tendency, the mode explains nothing about the ordering of variables or variation within the variables. In fact, the mode ignores information about ordering and interval size even if it is available. So it is generally not advised to use the mode for ordinal or interval level data (unless it is used in addition to the median or mean) because too much information is lost.

There is no formula or calculation for the mode. The procedure is to count the scores and determine the most frequently occurring value. Consider the data set in **Figure 2-1**, which show the number of prisoners who escaped from 15 prisons over a 10-year period. Two prisons had 7 escapes, one had 6 escapes, three had 5, two had

7	5	4	3	2
7	5	4	3	1
6	5	3	3	1

Figure 2-1   Number of Escapes from 15 Prisons, 2000–2010

4, four had 3, one had 2, and two had 1 escape. The mode in this data set would be 3 escapes, since there are more 3s than any other value.

For data that is already in a frequency table, determining the mode is even easier because the numbers are already counted. In Table 2-1, you can easily see that Some College (value 4) has the greatest number of people (117). This means that 4 or Some College is the mode.

One caution when discussing the mode. The mode is *not* the frequency of the number that occurs most often but is rather the category (or class) itself. It is tempting to state that the mode in Table 2-1 is 117 because that is the frequency that is highest. This is not the mode, however; the mode is the *category* of the value that has the highest frequency—in this case, 4, or Some College.

A distribution is not confined to having only one mode. There are often situations in which a distribution will have several categories that have the same or similar frequencies. In these cases, the distribution can be said to be *bimodal* or even *multimodal*. It is also possible for a distribution to have no mode if the frequencies are the same for each category.

Box 2-2   Obtaining Univariate Descriptive Measures in SPSS

You can obtain all of the univariate descriptive statistics within the same procedure in SPSS, and it is just an extension of the same procedure used above to obtain a frequency distribution. Follow these steps:

1. Open a data set such as one provided at go.jblearning.com/Walker.
   a. Start SPSS.
   b. Select File, then Open, then Data.
   c. Select the file you want to open, then select Open.
2. Select Analyze, then Descriptive Statistics, then Frequencies.
3. Make sure that Display Frequency Tables is checked.
4. Select the variables you wish to include in your distribution and press the > between the two windows.
5. Select the Statistics button at the bottom of the window.
6. Check the boxes of any of the univariate measures you want to include.
7. Select Continue, then OK.
8. An output window should appear containing a distribution similar in format to **Table 2-3**.

Median

If the data is at least ordinal level, the median (symbolized by Me) may be a better choice for examining the central tendency of the distribution. The *median* is the point of the 50th percentile of the distribution. This means that the median is the exact mid-point of a distribution, or the value that cuts the distribution into two equal parts.

For the simple distribution 1, 2, 3, the median is 2 because it cuts this distribution in half. Note that 2 is not the most frequently occurring value or the product of some formula, but is simply the value in the middle. The median will always be the middle value, but sometimes it will be necessary to resort to math to determine the exact middle value.

EDUCATION What is your highest level of education?					
Value Label	Value	Frequency	Percent	Valid Percent	Cumulative Percent
Less than High School	1	16	4.6	4.8	4.8
GED	2	59	17.0	17.6	22.3
High School Graduate	3	8	2.3	2.4	24.7
Some College	4	117	33.7	34.8	59.5
College Graduate	5	72	20.7	21.4	81.0
Postgraduate	6	64	18.4	19.0	100.0
Total		336	96.8	100.0	
System	Missing	11	3.2		
	Total	347	100.0		

N	Valid	336
	Missing	11
Mean		4.08
Median		4.00
Mode		4
Std. Deviation		1.460
Variance		2.131
Skewness		−0.477
Std. Error of Skewness		0.133
Kurtosis		−0.705
Std. Error of Kurtosis		0.265
Range		5

Table 2-3   SPSS Output of Univariate Descriptive Statistics

The median is used with ordinal level data because it does not imply distance between intervals, only direction—above the median or below it. Recall from Chapter 1 that the nature of ordinal level data is that you can determine which category is greater than or less than another category; but there are not equal intervals, so there is no way to determine how much greater or lesser the category is. The median also works on this principle, determining the midpoint of a distribution such that a category can be said to be less than or greater than the median, but there is no way to tell by how much. For example, take the following two distributions:

$$1, 2, 3, 3, 4, 4, 5 \qquad 1, 1, 1, 3, 10, 50, 100$$

Each has the same number of values, 7, although each has very different numbers. In this case, the modes are different: 3 and 4 in the first; 1 in the second. Also, as discussed below, the means are different: 3.14 in the first, 23.71 in the second. The median for both of these distributions, however, is 3, the middle value in the distribution. In both distributions, there are three values below the median and three values above the median.

Calculation of the median is relatively simple. All that is needed is N for the distribution. If N is not given, simply count the number of scores (remember—do *not* add the scores, *count* them). Then the value of N is placed in the formula $(N + 1)/2$. Once you have this value, if the scores are not arranged in order, you should do so. Then simply count up the data until you reach the value obtained in the formula (the 12th value in **Figure 2-2**). This is the median. In this case, if we count to the 12th score, we get a score of 3. An example of how to make the same calculations in Excel is shown in Box 2-3.[1]

7	5	4	2	2
6	5	3	2	1
6	5	3	2	1
6	5	3	2	
6	4	2	2	

$$\frac{N + 1}{2} = \frac{23 + 1}{2} = \frac{24}{2} = 12$$

Figure 2-2   Calculating the Median

Box 2-3   Using Excel to Calculate the Median

1. If the data is not sorted, do so by clicking on the column heading for the data you want to sort, clicking on Data, then clicking on the button to Sort Descending.
2. Since there are 23 rows, this is *N*.
   a. *N* + 1 = 24.
   b. 24 / 2 = 12.
3. Count up (or down) in the data until you reach the 12th number. This is 3, which is the median.

There are several issues to note about the median. These should be considered any time you use the median for analysis. First, you must be careful when you calculate the median because there are two different numbers you must deal with. To begin, you get a number from the formula. This is not the median; it is simply the number of values to count up in the distribution to find the median. The median is the score that contains the number from the formula. Also, if there is more than one of the same score in the median class (there are three 3s in Figure 2-2), the median is still that score even though it occurs more than once. Finally, unlike the mode, the median does not have to be a value that is in the distribution. For an odd number of scores (such as in Figure 2-2), the median will be one of the scores because it is the point that cuts the distribution in half. If there are an even number of scores, however, the median will fall in between two of the scores. For example, in the distribution

$$3, 4, 5, 6, 7, 8, 9, 10$$

the formula $(N + 1)/2$ gives a value of 4.5. This puts the median between 6 and 7. When this occurs, the median is a value that is halfway between the two scores. In this case, the median is 6.5. This is even more complicated if the two numbers do not have an interval of 1. For example, in the distribution 5, 6, 8, 10, 11, 12, the number from the formula puts the median between the score of 8 and the score of 10; therefore the median is 9.

Mean

The most popular measure of central tendency is the *mean*. The mean is primarily used for interval and ratio level data. Because it assumes equality of intervals, the mean is generally not used with nominal or ordinal level data. The mean is very important to statistical analysis because it is the basis (along with the variance) of many of the formulas for higher-order statistical procedures.

The symbolic notation for the mean is different than others that have been used to this point. The mean is symbolized either by μ or $\overline{X}$, depending on whether the data is a population or sample estimate (this distinction will be discussed when we get to inferential statistics). It is interesting that descriptive statistics deals with a population, but it has become convention that the mean most commonly used in descriptive statistics is actually the symbol for the sample mean ($\overline{X}$). Since most texts use this notation for the mean in descriptive analyses, it will also be used here, even though the more proper notation is the population mean (μ).

The mean is simply the average of the values in the distribution. To obtain the mean, add the scores in a distribution and divide by N (it is just like calculating an average). In statistical terms, the mean is calculated as

$$\overline{X} = \frac{\Sigma fX}{N}$$

If we grouped the data from Figure 2-2, it would look like that in **Table 2-4**. Here, all we did is to take the numbers and add a column called f. This column is the number of times that value occurs in our data set. In this table, we also added a column called fX, where fX is calculated by multiplying X by the frequency f for each value. If we add the numbers in the fX column, we get 84. If we add the numbers in the f column, we get 23, which is the same as N. So the sum of f is the same as N. Now we have all of the numbers we need for the formula. Plugging the numbers into the formula, we get $84 \div 23$, or 3.65.

The mean has some advantages over other measures of central tendency. From a practical standpoint, the mean is preferred because it is standardized, allowing for it to be compared across distributions. This is beneficial when you are comparing similar

X	f	fX
7	1	7
6	4	24
5	4	20
4	2	8
3	3	9
2	7	14
1	2	2
N	23	
ΣfX		84

Table 2-4   Calculating the Mean

data from different sources. For example, we could compare the mean number of calls for service among several police agencies because we can directly compare their mean values and tell which agency had more calls for service on average.

The greatest problem with the mean is that it is highly affected by extreme scores in the distribution. In the following data

$$1, 1, 3, 3, 4, 4, 100$$

the median is 3, which is reasonable given this data. The mean, however, is 16.57. This number is not even close to most of the numbers in the data set; but because one of the numbers is 100, it draws the mean away from the other numbers. That is why the median is used in cases where data is skewed, as discussed in Chapter 3.

2-3 Selecting the Most Appropriate Measure of Central Tendency

As with levels of measurement, the most important part of measures of central tendency is the selection of the proper one for the data. Selection of the most appropriate measure of central tendency depends on several factors, including the level of data, the nature of the data, and the purpose of the summarization.

The level of data has a substantial influence on which measure of central tendency should be used. As discussed above, each measure is most appropriate for a particular level of data. The mode is most appropriate for nominal level data, and its use with ordinal and interval level data results in a loss of power in terms of the information that could be gained from the data. The median is most appropriate with ordinal level data; and although it can be used with interval level data (especially skewed distributions), it should not be used with nominal level data because the rankings assumed in the median cannot be achieved with nominal level data. Finally, the mean should only be used with interval and ratio level data because it assumes equal intervals of the data that cannot be achieved by nominal and ordinal level data.

Selection of the most appropriate measure of central tendency is also sometimes based on the nature of the distribution. As will be discussed more fully in Chapter 3, if a distribution is highly skewed, the median should be used rather than the mean for interval and ratio level data.

The final criterion for choosing a measure of central tendency is the purpose of summarization, typically in terms of what you are trying to predict. Imagine that you are asked to state one measure that will best capture the nature of the distribution. How do you go about that? To put it another way, you might bet $100 that you could guess a number drawn at random from a distribution. Which one do you choose? One way to address these questions is to find the score at the "heart" of the distribution—the most common score, the one that cut the distribution in half, the average score. That is the goal and role of measures of central tendency.

If you know all the values in the distribution, you can easily and quickly calculate the mode. If you are interested in predicting an exact value, you should probably use the mode since it has the highest probability of occurring in any given distribution. Both the median and the mean have the possibility to return values that are not in the distribution; so if you must guess and be absolutely right on the number, use the mode.

If, on the other hand, you want to maximize your prediction by getting closest to the number over several tries, thereby minimizing your error, then the median may be a better choice. Here, whether you chose too high or too low is irrelevant; what is important is the size of the error. In a popular game show, contestants are given $7 and required to guess the exact numbers included in the price of a car. For each number they are off, they lose $1. If they have money left over after making all of the guesses, they win the car; if they run out of money, they lose. Probability of response plays a big part in the first two or three numbers (you would not want to guess 9 for the first number, for example). If you are at the fourth or fifth number, however, and still have money left, you may want to choose the median value (probably a 5) to minimize the error (loss of dollars). The median is both good and bad in this instance. It is good in that, since it is the middle value, it will produce the smallest absolute error from any value you choose. There is, however, an equal chance of its being high or low on any given value chosen.

Finally, if you have the opportunity to average your misses over several guesses and the signs do matter (high guesses can offset low guesses), then the mean is the best choice. The mean is good in that if you don't know a value, it is often best to choose the average.

This chapter addressed constructing and understanding frequency distributions and measures of central tendency. These skills will be necessary in Chapter 3 as the next two univariate descriptive statistics are discussed.

2-4 Equations in This Chapter

Mean:

$$\overline{X} = \frac{\sum fx}{N}$$

Median:

$$Me = \frac{N + 1}{2}$$

2-5   Note

1. Note that it is possible to calculate the median and other statistics directly in Excel. This approach has received some criticism from the American Statistical Association and others. As such, this text will use Excel to aid in calculations, but will not utilize its formulas or pivot table options. These procedures may be taught in class, however.

2-6   For Further Reading

Edwards, W. J., White, N., Bennett, I., & Pezzella, F. Who has come out of the pipeline? African Americans in criminology and criminal justice. *Journal of Criminal Justice Education*, 1998, 9(2), 249–266.

Galton, F. *inquiries into human faculty and its development.* London: MacMillan, 1883.

Pearson, K. Classification of asymmetrical frequency curves in general. Types actually occurring. *Philosophical Transactions of the Royal Society of London*, series A, vol. 186. London: Cambridge University Press, 1895.

2-7   Exercises

The exercises for this chapter and for Chapter 3 will use the same examples. This will allow you to work through problems using all three types of univariate descriptive statistics.

1. For the set of data below, calculate the
   a. Mode
   b. Median
   c. Mean

$$6, 7, 8, 10, 10, 10, 12, 14$$

2. For the set of data below, calculate the
   a. Mode
   b. Median
   c. Mean

$$7, 4, 2, 3, 4, 5, 8, 1, 9, 4$$

3. For the set of data below, calculate the
   a. Mode
   b. Median
   c. Mean

Value (X)	Frequency (f)
90	6
80	8
70	4
60	3
50	2

4. For the set of data below, calculate the
   a. Mode
   b. Median
   c. Mean

Value (X)	Frequency (f)
90	5
80	7
70	9
60	4

5. Using the following frequency tables, discuss the three measures of central tendency.

HOME What type of house do you live in?					
		Frequency	**Percent**	**Valid Percent**	**Cumulative Percent**
Valid		1	.3	.3	.3
House	1	279	81.3	82.1	82.4
Duplex	2	3	0.9	0.9	83.2
Trailer	3	34	9.9	10.0	93.2
Apartment	4	21	6.1	6.2	99.4
Other	5	2	0.6	0.6	100.0
	Total	340	99.1	100.0	
Missing	System	3	0.9		
Total		343	100.0		

N	Valid	340
	Missing	3
Mean		1.41
Std. Error of Mean		0.051
Median		1.00
Mode		1
Std. Deviation		0.945
Variance		0.892
Skewness		2.001
Std. Error of Skewness		0.132
Kurtosis		2.613
Std. Error of Kurtosis		.264
Range		5

ARREST How many times have you been arrested?		Frequency	Percent	Valid Percent	Cumulative Percent
Valid	0	243	70.8	86.2	86.2
	1	23	6.7	8.2	94.3
	2	10	2.9	3.5	97.9
	3	3	0.9	1.1	98.9
	5	2	0.6	0.7	99.6
	24	1	0.3	0.4	100.0
	Total	282	82.2	100.0	
Missing	System	61	17.8		
Total		343	100.0		

N	Valid	282
	Missing	61
Mean		0.30
Std. Error of Mean		0.093
Median		0.00
Mode		0
Std. Deviation		1.567
Variance		2.455
Skewness		12.692
Std. Error of Skewness		0.145
Kurtosis		187.898
Std. Error of Kurtosis		0.289
Range		24

TENURE How long have you lived at your current address (months)?					
		Frequency	**Percent**	**Valid Percent**	**Cumulative Percent**
Valid	1	14	4.1	4.3	4.3
	2	6	1.7	1.8	6.1
	3	4	1.2	1.2	7.3
	4	4	1.2	1.2	8.6
	5	6	1.7	1.8	10.4
	6	6	1.7	1.8	12.2
	7	1	0.3	0.3	12.5
	8	3	0.9	0.9	13.5
	9	2	0.6	0.6	14.1
	10	1	0.3	0.3	14.4
	11	1	0.3	0.3	14.7
	12	11	3.2	3.4	18.0
	14	1	0.3	0.3	18.3
	18	5	1.5	1.5	19.9
	21	1	0.3	0.3	20.2
	24	30	8.7	9.2	29.4
	30	1	0.3	0.3	29.7

| TENURE | How long have you lived at your current address (months)? | | | | |
		Frequency	Percent	Valid Percent	Cumulative Percent
Valid	31	1	0.3	0.3	30.0
	32	1	0.3	0.3	30.3
	36	22	6.4	6.7	37.0
	42	1	0.3	0.3	37.3
	48	12	3.5	3.7	41.0
	60	24	7.0	7.3	48.3
	72	14	4.1	4.3	52.6
	76	1	0.3	0.3	52.9
	84	8	2.3	2.4	55.4
	96	18	5.2	5.5	60.9
	108	4	1.2	1.2	62.1
	120	9	2.6	2.8	64.8
	132	11	3.2	3.4	68.2
	144	21	6.1	6.4	74.6
	156	13	3.8	4.0	78.6
	168	11	3.2	3.4	82.0
	170	5	1.5	1.5	83.5
	180	7	2.0	2.1	85.6
	182	2	0.6	0.6	86.2
	186	1	0.3	0.3	86.5
	192	14	4.1	4.3	90.8
	198	1	0.3	0.3	91.1
	204	24	7.0	7.3	98.5
	216	3	0.9	0.9	99.4
	240	2	0.6	0.6	100.0
	Total	327	95.3	100.0	
Missing	System	16	4.7		
Total		343	100.0		

N Valid		327
Missing		16
Mean		88.77
Std. Error of Mean		3.880
Median		72.00
Mode		24
Std. Deviation		70.164
Variance		4,923.055
Skewness		0.365
Std. Error of Skewness		0.135
Kurtosis		−1.284
Std. Error of Kurtosis		0.269
Range		239

SIBS How many brothers and sisters do you have?					
		Frequency	**Percent**	**Valid Percent**	**Cumulative Percent**
Valid	0	39	11.4	11.5	11.5
	1	137	39.9	40.5	52.1
	2	79	23.0	23.4	75.4
	3	39	11.4	11.5	87.0
	4	17	5.0	5.0	92.0
	5	13	3.8	3.8	95.9
	6	6	1.7	1.8	97.6
	7	4	1.2	1.2	98.8
	9	1	0.3	0.3	99.1
	10	1	0.3	0.3	99.4
	12	1	0.3	0.3	99.7
	15	1	0.3	0.3	100.0
	Total	338	98.5	100.0	
Missing	System	5	1.5		
Total		343	100.0		

N	Valid	338
	Missing	5
Mean		1.94
Std. Error of Mean		0.098
Median		1.00
Mode		1
Std. Deviation		1.801
Variance		3.245
Skewness		2.664
Std. Error of Skewness		0.133
Kurtosis		12.027
Std. Error of Kurtosis		0.265
Range		15

Chapter 3
Measures of Dispersion and Form

Learning Objectives

- Understand the difference between dispersion and deviation.
- Understand the range, variance, and standard deviation as measures of dispersion.
- Identify the proper measure of dispersion for analyzing data.
- Explain how to calculate the range, variance, and standard deviation.
- Understand the number of modes, skewness, and kurtosis as they relate to explaining a data set.
- Explain the difference between the mode and the number of modes.
- Interpret the values of skewness and kurtosis as they relate to univariate analysis.
- Discuss the importance of the normal curve in statistics.
- Describe the properties of the normal curve.

Key Terms

absolute deviations
dispersion
deviation
form
index of dispersion
kurtosis
leptokurtic
mesokurtic
negatively skewed
normal curve

number of modes
platykurtic
positively skewed
range
skew
standard deviation
sum of squares
variance
Z score

This chapter adds to your ability to describe data by discussing procedures to determine how values differ from one another within a single variable. In this chapter, measures of dispersion and measures of form are discussed, along with some simplified ways of calculating them. The discussion of the variance and standard deviation sets the stage for their use in later chapters as well as their use in measuring dispersion. You will also learn how to determine both the form of a distribution from the values provided in SPSS and the acceptable limits of skewness and kurtosis. The chapter finishes with a discussion of the normal curve, which will be needed for the chapters on inferential statistics.

3-1   Measures of Dispersion

It is important to know the central value of a distribution, but it is just one characteristic of the distribution. We also need to know how spread out the values are, along with the central value, because it is possible to have two data sets with the same central value but with very different distributions. For example, two tests were given, and the results are listed below. Each test has a mean of 75. The scores of test 1 range from 0 to 100, while all of the scores for test 2 are 75.

Test 1	0	80	85	90	95	100
Test 2	75	75	75	75	75	75

Both of these distributions have the same mean but very different spreads of scores. If you did not know your score and had to choose which group you were going to be in, you would want to know the spread of scores. If you were a weak student, it might be better to go with the all-75 group, whereas if you were a good student, you would definitely want to go with the spread-out group. This is why we need to know the dispersion of the distribution along with the measure of central tendency.

3-2   Deviation and Dispersion

Before we get into the measures of dispersion, we want to address a common misperception about dispersion versus deviation. Dispersion and deviation are largely synonymous. The only practical difference is that *deviation* typically refers to the difference between a single value or case and the measure of central tendency, whereas *dispersion* is used more to refer to the overall difference between all cases or values and the measure of central tendency.

Dispersion and deviation are important to research. All variables have dispersion. Otherwise, they would not be variables (values that change from case to case); they would be constants (a constant value no matter what the case is). Take juvenile delinquency, for example. Some juveniles do not commit any delinquent acts during their teenage years (at least theoretically), some juveniles commit a few delinquent acts, and some juveniles commit many delinquent acts. This is what makes *delinquency* a variable: The number of delinquent acts varies among juveniles. This also means there is dispersion among the number of juvenile acts committed. If a researcher determined how many delinquent acts juveniles committed on average, the answer would represent the central value of juvenile delinquency. That does not tell the entire story, however. The researcher also needs to know how the juveniles differ from one another in their delinquency. This is the measure of dispersion.

3-3   Types of Measures of Dispersion

Measures of dispersion indicate how narrow or how spread out the values are around the central value. Unlike the measures of central tendency, there is not a measure of dispersion for each level of measurement. Although some measures of dispersion are more appropriate for certain levels of measurement, it is not as clear-cut as for the measures of central tendency. The dispersion of nominal level data is typically best analyzed with the *range*. The range or average *absolute deviations* from the median can be used with ordinal level data. Interval and ratio data can be examined with the variance or standard deviation. Furthermore, there are only a few measures of dispersion that are commonly used. SPSS does not include the *index of dispersion* or average absolute deviations from the median in its analyses. Since these are seldom used measures, this chapter will focus on only the range, standard deviation, and variance.

Range

The simplest measure of the dispersion of a distribution is the range. The range is generally used with nominal and partially ordered ordinal variables, although it is sometimes included as an additional measure of dispersion for higher-level variables. The *range* is simply the difference between the highest and lowest values in a distribution. For example, if the spread of ages in a class were from 18 to 35, the range would be 17. Although the range is generally stated in terms of a single figure, it is sometimes stated simply as the two extreme values ("the range of scores is from 18 to 35").

The range is useful in that it is a quick and easily calculated measure of dispersion. Although most statistical packages include the range as a measure of dispersion, it is generally not necessary to use this feature except when you are examining a very large data set where the number of values might make it time-consuming to determine the highest and lowest values. In the SPSS printout in **Table 3-1**, the range would be simple to calculate even if we did not know the value from the descriptive statistics.

What is your highest level of education?					
Value	**Value Label**	**Frequency**	**Percent**	**Valid Percent**	**Cumulative Percent**
1	Less than High School	16	4.6	4.8	4.8
2	GED	59	17.0	17.6	22.3
3	High School Graduate	8	2.3	2.4	24.7
4	Some College	117	33.7	34.8	59.5
5	College Graduate	72	20.7	21.4	81.0
6	Postgraduate	64	18.4	19.0	100.0
	Total	336	96.8	100.0	
Missing	System	11	3.2		
Total		347	100.0		

N	Valid	336
	Missing	11
Mean		4.08
Median		4.00
Mode		4
Std. Deviation		1.460
Variance		2.131
Skewness		−0.477
Std. Error of Skewness		0.133
Kurtosis		−0.705
Std. Error of Kurtosis		0.265
Range		5

Table 3-1   SPSS Output of Dispersion

Table 3-1 is the same as Table 2-3. The important part of this table for the discussion here is the bottom part. Here, you can see the mean, median, and mode, as discussed in Chapter 2. Also included here are the range, standard deviation, and variance, along with other values that will be addressed later in this chapter. For our purposes here, we can easily find the range by looking at the value for the range in this table, or just calculate it by looking at the Value column in the top table and subtracting the smallest value from the largest value. Here, the range of values is 5 (= 6 − 1).

Even though the range is a quick and easy measure of dispersion, it is limited for three reasons. First, it only gives a general indication of the variability of the values in the distribution. For example, if the range is reported as a 5, you must still examine the data to understand what that means. It could mean the data ranges from 1 to 6, or it could mean that the data ranges from 101 to 106, for example. Second, the range does not account for intracategory variation, or the way the scores are distributed between the extremes. Stating that the range is 5 provides little information about how the data is arranged within the range. Look at **Table 3-2**. This is a distribution of the number of absences between the freshman class and the senior class at a high school. Here, you can see that for both groups, the number of absences ranged from 0 to 5, so the range is 5 for both. However, the intracategory variation is quite different. There could be a relatively equal number in each category, as in the freshman class, or there could be only a few values in all but one category, as in the senior class.

Number of Absences	Freshman Class	Senior Class
0	25	99
1	20	0
2	18	0
3	15	0
4	12	0
5	10	1
Total	100	100

Table 3-2   Distribution of Absences for Two Classes

Third, the range is heavily influenced by extremely high or low values in a distribution which may be atypical of the distribution. Take, for example, the distribution of inmate deaths in two different prisons in a state, shown in **Table 3-3**. In this table, both prison A and prison B have similar records of inmate deaths. In fact, only one year is different between the two prisons; in 1990, prison B had a riot, and 26 prisoners were killed. This will heavily influence the range for this prison. The range for prison A is 3 (= 3 − 0) or 0–3, while the range for prison B is 26 (= 26 − 0) or 0–26. This demonstrates the problems with using the range as a measure of dispersion.

Year	Prison A	Prison B
1990	0	26
1991	0	0
1992	1	1
1993	3	3
1994	1	1
1995	2	2

Table 3-3   Number of Inmate Deaths 1990-1995

Variance

At the opposite end of the scale of sophistication are the variance and standard deviation. The standard deviation is simply the square root of the variance, so these measures are often spoken of together. These two measures of dispersion are most appropriate for interval and ratio level data, although they are often used with ordinal (especially fully ordered ordinal) level data because of their power over other measures of dispersion. The variance and standard deviation do not work well with nominal and partially ordered ordinal level data because they measure the deviation about the mean; so if the mean is not appropriate for nominal and ordinal level data, then measures of dispersion based on the mean would not be either.

The *variance* (represented by s^2 for samples or σ^2 for populations) measures the average of squared deviations of scores around the mean (the difference between the mean and each score). The formula for the variance is

$$\sigma^2 = \frac{\Sigma(X - \overline{X})^2}{N}$$

This formula begins by calculating the difference between each value in the distribution and the mean. Then each difference is squared. Next, the squared differences are summed, and this is called the *sum of the squares*. The result will be the smallest distance from any given value to the mean. Dividing the sum by N results in a formula that is the mean of the squared deviations, just as when we calculate the mean of any variable.

The calculations in Excel that will give the numbers needed for the formula are shown in **Table 3-4**. In this table, X and f are the values from Figure 2-2. Calculating the variance requires three pieces of information: the mean, the difference between the mean and each value (X or midpoint), and the square of the differences. Then the square of the differences is divided by N. Here, the mean is 3.65 (84/23). The third column represents calculations that subtract the mean from each value of X. For example, the first value is 7. Since the mean is 3.65, this value is 3.35 greater than the mean. This can be repeated for each of the scores, where each score can be seen as greater than, less than, or the same as the mean. Notice also that the sum of the third column is 0. The fourth column takes each of these values and squares them [for example, $(3.65)^2 = 3.65 \times 3.65 = 11.21$]. The sum of the calculations in the fourth column equals 75.22. It is then simply a matter of dividing this value by N (23), which is the same as calculating the mean (average) of the squared deviations. The result is 3.27, so the mean of deviations is 3.27 (this is the variance).

Recall that this section of the text is dealing with descriptive statistics. That means that we are assuming that the data being analyzed represents a population. If the data were considered a sample of a population, the formula for the variance would change, and the denominator would be $N - 1$.

X	f	$X - \overline{X}$	$(X - \overline{X})^2$
7	1	3.35	11.21
6	1	2.35	5.51
6	1	2.35	5.51
6	1	2.35	5.51
6	1	2.35	5.51
5	1	1.35	1.82
5	1	1.35	1.82
5	1	1.35	1.82
5	1	1.35	1.82
4	1	0.35	0.12
4	1	0.35	0.12
3	1	−0.65	0.43
3	1	−0.65	0.43
3	1	−0.65	0.43
2	1	−1.65	2.73
2	1	−1.65	2.73
2	1	−1.65	2.73
2	1	−1.65	2.73
2	1	−1.65	2.73
2	1	−1.65	2.73
2	1	−1.65	2.73
1	1	−2.65	7.03
1	1	−2.65	7.03
84	23	0	75.22

Table 3-4   Calculation of the Variance

In interpreting the variance, if all of the values in a distribution are the same (the value of the mean), the value of the variance will be 0. In this case, if all of the values of X had been 3.65, the mean would have been 3.65 and the variance would have been 0.

The variance will be at a maximum when all of the scores are grouped in the extremes of the distribution (the highest and lowest values in the distribution). For example, if the data from Table 3-4 were altered so that each value was either a 7 or a 1, it would look like that in **Table 3-5**. Here, although the sum of *f* remains 23, the mean

X	f	$X - \overline{X}$	$(X - \overline{X})^2$
7	1	2.87	8.2369
7	1	2.87	8.2369
7	1	2.87	8.2369
7	1	2.87	8.2369
7	1	2.87	8.2369
7	1	2.87	8.2369
7	1	2.87	8.2369
7	1	2.87	8.2369
7	1	2.87	8.2369
7	1	2.87	8.2369
7	1	2.87	8.2369
7	1	2.87	8.2369
1	1	−3.13	9.7969
1	1	−3.13	9.7969
1	1	−3.13	9.7969
1	1	−3.13	9.7969
1	1	−3.13	9.7969
1	1	−3.13	9.7969
1	1	−3.13	9.7969
1	1	−3.13	9.7969
1	1	−3.13	9.7969
1	1	−3.13	9.7969
1	1	−3.13	9.7969
95	23	0.1	206.61

Table 3-5   Calculation of the Maximum Variance

will be different because the sum of X has changed to 95 rather than 92. Additionally, although the sum of differences from the mean remains 0 (actually 0.1 because of rounding), the sum of the squared values is much larger (206.61 rather than 68).

This would be the first indicator that the variance is going to be much larger. Indeed, the calculation of the variance for this data set produces a variance of 8.98, almost 3 times as large as the variance in Table 3-4. Said another way, the variance is important in describing data because it gives weight to extreme values. For example, a deviation of 2 from the mean has greater weight than two deviations of 1 each

($2^2 = 4 > 1^2 + 1^2 = 2$). Because of this characteristic, data sets with many small deviations will show smaller variance than data sets with fewer but larger deviations.

The squaring of deviations presents problems for the variance, however. Since all values are squared, the units of measurement are no longer the same as the original values, which makes the variance difficult to interpret. For example, it is difficult or impossible to interpret a value of 8.98 from our example when the values range only from 1 to 7. This is the reason the standard deviation has become important.

Standard Deviation

The *standard deviation* resolves this problem of the variance by putting the dispersion in the same units as the distribution. The standard deviation is calculated by taking the square root of the variance. Since the differences from the mean were squared to account for the sign (thus putting the values on a scale different than the data), it is a simple mathematical procedure to take the square root of the sum of those values and put the sum back on the same scale as the original data.

The calculation of the standard deviation is both simple and complex. The simple part is that if the variance is known, simply take the square root of that value. If the variance is not known, however, that value must be determined prior to calculating the standard deviation. The formula for calculating the standard deviation without knowing the variance beforehand is

$$\sigma = \sqrt{\frac{\Sigma (X - \bar{X})^2}{N}}$$

This, of course, is the square root of the variance.

In the example from Table 3-5, the standard deviation is the square root of 8.98, which is 2.99. This value is much easier to interpret in terms of the range of scores in this distribution. It is also important to note that any score can be interpreted in terms of the number of standard deviations from the mean, which is called the *Z score*. This is important in discussions of the normal curve and inferential statistics.

3-4   Measures of the Form of a Distribution

The final univariate descriptive statistic ties together the central tendency and the dispersion of the data. This is the *form* of the distribution. Three characteristics make up the form of a distribution—the number of modes, the symmetry, and the kurtosis. In discussing the form of a distribution, we often use a polygon to visually represent these characteristics. Several polygons are shown in the rest of this chapter to help you understand elements of the form of a distribution.

Number of Modes

The first measure of the form of a distribution is the *number of modes*. The number of modes is important to higher-order analyses because it is indicative of the normality of the distribution (which is discussed when we get to inferential statistics). To use many bivariate and multivariate statistical procedures, a unimodal distribution is preferred.

In determining the number of modes, a slight deviation from determining the mode may be necessary. Recall from the discussion of central tendency that it is common to count only the highest frequency in a distribution as the mode, even though some argue that all peaks of a distribution should be considered. For determining the number of modes in an analysis of form, it may be more beneficial to look at peaks than to find the one, highest value. Consider, for example, the distribution in **Figure 3-1**. Even though there is only one highest value, there are three peaks in the distribution. Multiple peaks may make the data unsuitable for certain statistical procedures unless transformations are made.

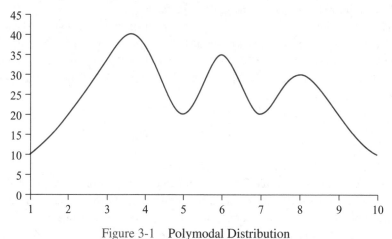

Figure 3-1   Polymodal Distribution

Skewness

The next characteristic of the form of the distribution is the degree of symmetry (skewness) of the distribution. This measure of the form of a distribution has three categories: symmetrical, positively skewed, and negatively skewed.

A fully symmetrical distribution has mirror-image sides such that the distribution could be split at the mean and the sides folded over each other for a perfect match. In **Figure 3-2**, it is easy to see the symmetry in the distribution. The frequencies displayed in this distribution are very balanced: Categories 1 and 7 have the same frequency, as do 2 and 6, and 3 and 5. Category 4 has the highest frequency. It is easy to see that this distribution could be folded in half and the two sides would match perfectly. This distribution, therefore, is a perfectly symmetrical distribution.

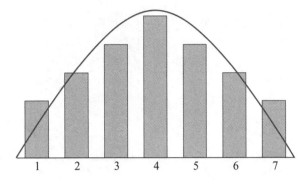

Figure 3-2   Histogram and Normal Curve for a Symmetrical Distribution

In actual research, however, it is not common to see a perfectly symmetrical distribution. More typically, the distribution either will be only close to symmetrical or will be not symmetrical at all. Note that the number of modes does not necessarily affect the *skew* of the distribution. A distribution that is bimodal could still be cut in half where the distribution mirrors itself. The only difference in this case is that the mode and the other measures of central tendency would not be the same. If a distribution is such that one side is different from the other, it is said to be *skewed*. In skewed distributions, there is no point that can be drawn in the polygon where it could be divided into two similar halves.

If the tail of the curve is to the left of the graph, it is said to be *negatively skewed* (the tail of the graph points to the negative end of the scale, or the smaller positive numbers). In **Figure 3-3**, "children" is an example of a negatively skewed distribution. If the tail of the curve is to the right of the graph, it is said to be *positively skewed* (the tail of the graph points toward the positive end of the scale, or larger positive numbers). In Figure 3-3, "gun-wher" is an example of a positively skewed distribution.

SPSS provides the measure of skewness in descriptive statistics output. A value of 0 means there is no skew to the data. Skewness values of 0 are rarely obtained; however, a common rule is that a distribution can be considered symmetrical if the skewness value reported in SPSS output is between -1 and 1. A distribution is generally considered skewed if it has a skewness of greater than 1.00 or less (a greater negative number) than -1.00. The magnitude of the number represents the degree of skew. In Table 3-1, the value of skewness is -0.477. This means that the distribution is not perfectly symmetrical, but it is within the acceptable range of 0 to -1.00, which means that it exhibits an acceptable level of skew. There is some negative skew to this distribution, as exhibited by the negative value, but it is not enough to warrant additional analyses or cause for concern. If this value had been less than -1.00 (for

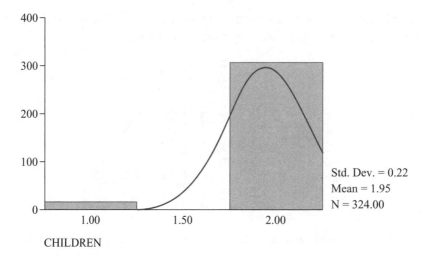

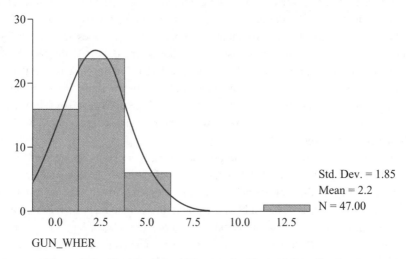

Figure 3-3   Positively and Negatively Skewed Distributions

example, −2.77), then additional analyses might be required, and it might be necessary to transform the distribution.

In conducting research, it is desirable to obtain a distribution that has a skewness as close to 0 as possible. If the skewness is outside the range of +1 to −1, the distribution may be too skewed to work with in its original scale, and efforts should be made to get the distribution closer to normal.

Kurtosis

The last characteristic of the form of a distribution is the *kurtosis*. For kurtosis, think of stacking blocks (or cases of beer cans) on top of one another to represent the frequency of a category in a histogram. The kurtosis is the extent to which cases are piled up around the measure of central tendency or piled up in the tails of the distribution. If most of the values in the distribution are very close to the measure of central tendency, the distribution is said to be *leptokurtic* (as shown in the leftmost curve of **Figure 3-4**). If most of the values in the distribution are out in the tails, the distribution is said to be *platykurtic*, as shown in the rightmost curve of Figure 3-4. If the values in the distribution are such that they represent a distribution like that shown in Figure 3-2, the distribution is said to be *mesokurtic*, as shown in the center curve of Figure 3-4. It is desirable to have a mesokurtic distribution in research; otherwise, the data may have to be transformed.

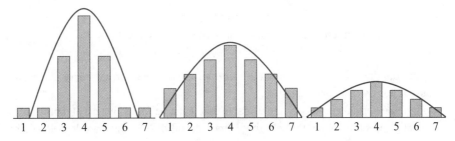

Figure 3-4   Leptokurtic, Mesokurtic, and Platykurtic Distributions

Kurtosis is measured the same as skewness in SPSS. A value between −1 and 1 represents a mesokurtic distribution. Positive numbers greater than 1 represent leptokurtic curves. Negative numbers less than (a greater negative number) −1 represent platykurtic curves. As with skewness, it is desirable to get the kurtosis as close as possible to 0.

Examining the kurtosis value in Table 3-1 shows that the distribution is mesokurtic because the value −0.705 is between −1.00 and 0. If this value had been −1.705, the distribution would have been platykurtic.

3-5   The Normal Curve

Knowing the shape of the distribution allows us to talk about a very important concept in statistical analysis called the normal curve. An example of a normal curve can be shown in grades in a course (see **Figure 3-5**). Say that most people in the course scored a C on the first test. This would be the modal grade, which would be the top part of the curve. There are those who received high A's; but there would be only a few of these, and they would be at the positive end of the curve. There are also those who received very low F's; but these are also few, and they would be at the negative end of the curve. Most people would be in between these two extremes, with more people making around C's than other grades, and more people making B's and D's than A's and F's. For the sake of argument, though, say that no one received a 100 and there were a few people who did not take the test. Therefore, the ends of the tails will never completely touch the baseline.

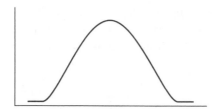

Figure 3-5   Normal Curve of Grades in a Class

This distribution of data is called a *normal curve*. The normal curve is special because it has certain characteristics.

First, the normal curve is symmetrical in that it can be folded in half and both sides are exactly the same. Note, though, that some normal distributions are leptokurtic or platykurtic. As long as they are symmetrical, they may be normal. This was shown in Figure 3-3 where each of those distributions was symmetrical even if it was kurtose.

Also, a normal curve is unimodal; there is one, and only one, peak. This peak is at the maximum frequency of the data distribution so that the mean, median, and mode are all the same value. From the peak, the tails of a normal curve fall off on both ends and extend to infinity, always getting closer to the baseline but never touching it. This is shown in Figure 3-5, where the bottom part of the curve straightens out and runs relatively parallel to the horizontal axis.

A final characteristic of the normal curve merits discussion: The area under a normal curve is always the same, regardless of the data set. The area under the normal curve is 1.00, or 100% of all values in the distribution. This will become extremely important when we talk about inferential analyses because of its importance in estimating the placement of a sample distribution within a population or another sample. The area under the normal curve also offers the opportunity to put the variance and standard deviation into practice. As discussed earlier, the variance and standard deviation dictate the shape of the distribution. In the leptokurtic distribution, the variance and standard deviation would be smaller than in the mesokurtic distribution. The variance and standard deviation of the platykurtic distribution would be larger than in either the mesokurtic or the leptokurtic distribution.

Now let's put that in practice. Say, for example, that a researcher is examining the time prisoners were out on parole before they committed another crime or returned to prison on a technical violation. If the time each parolee took before being reincarcerated is plotted, it might look like that in **Figure 3-6**. There were a few people who returned to prison right away, most of the parolees who returned to prison did it within 2 to 4 years, and some parolees took longer. Some had not recidivated at the time of the research, so the end of the distribution is open.

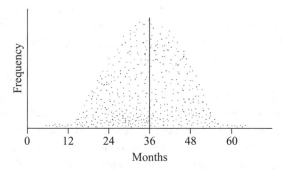

Figure 3-6   Distribution of Time to Reincarceration for Parolees

An analysis of the central tendency puts the mean of this distribution at 36 months, which is represented by the vertical line. This is good information: the average length of time for parolees to be reincarcerated is 3 years. It is obvious from this distribution, however, that not all of the parolees were reincarcerated at the same time. The span of time runs from a couple of months to more than 5 years. To get a more accurate picture of the distribution of parolees, we might want to know, on average, how far each is from the mean.

To calculate this, the procedure is to determine how far each person (each dot in Figure 3-6) is from the mean. This could be completed by actually measuring the distance with a ruler; but since this is a numeric scale, it could also be completed by subtracting each value from the mean. This operation is denoted as $X - \overline{X}$. Summing all of these values, represented by $\Sigma(X - \overline{X})$, gives us the total of the distance from each value to the mean. But remember that the sum of each value subtracted from the mean equals 0, so that does not help any. A solution to this is to square each value before summing it. This calculation, $\Sigma (X - \overline{X})^2$, will give a positive value. Knowing the total squared distance between the mean and each value is good, but a simpler value would be the average of the squared distance from each value to the mean. To do this, we simply divide by the total number of cases (N). Of course, you recognize this is the procedure for calculating the variance and ultimately the standard deviation for the distribution.

Although this procedure can be completed for any distribution, it is particularly important for a normal curve because of what the standard deviation represents. Because the area under the normal curve is always 100% and since standard deviations represent standard distances in relation to the mean of the distribution, standard deviations can be used to calculate the area under the normal curve for particular values. For example, between the mean and 1 standard deviation under a normal curve lies 34.13% of all of the data. Between the mean and 2 standard deviations contains 47.72% of all of the data. Between the mean and 3 standard deviations is 49.87% of all of the data. That covers 49.87% of the possible 50% of one-half of the curve.

Since the normal curve is symmetrical, the same values can be obtained whether one is counting from the left of the mean or the right. This also means that the values could be doubled from one side and the area under the whole normal curve could be determined for values plus or minus a certain number of standard deviations from the mean. If the figures above are doubled, the result is 68.26% of the data between -1 and 1 standard deviation; 95.44% of the data between -2 and 2 standard deviations; and 99.74% of the data between -3 and 3 standard deviations. Two of these scores that will become important later when we talk about inferential statistics are 1.96 and 2.58. These correspond to 95% and 99% of the area under the normal curve, respectively. These are important because researchers often want to know where 95% or 99% of the values in the distribution fall, or researchers may want to compare two values and see if they fall within 95% or 99% of the values in the distribution.

3-6   Conclusion

This chapter completes the description of one variable at a time from a distribution—univariate descriptive analysis. You have learned how to describe a variable such that it can be relayed to another person with some accuracy and in a form that allows the person to get a mental image of the distribution. The descriptions of single variables can take many forms: frequency distributions and graphs, measures of central tendency, measures of dispersion, and the form of the distribution. These all have the goal of describing the attributes of the distribution and determining if a variable is suitable for further analyses. In the next chapters, we put together two variables—bivariate descriptive analyses—and describe what relationship might exist between them. The success of those analyses depends on the successful univariate description of data.

3-7   Equations in This Chapter

Variance:

$$\sigma^2 = \frac{\Sigma(X - \overline{X})^2}{N}$$

Standard deviation:

$$\sigma = \sqrt{\frac{\Sigma(X - \overline{X})^2}{N}}$$

3-8   For Further Reading

Galton, Francis. *Inquiries into human faculty and its development.* London: Mac-Millan, 1883.

MacGillivray, H. L. The mean, median, mode inequality and skewness for a class of densities. *Australian Journal of Statistics*, 1981, *23*, 1981, 247.

Pearson, K. Classification of asymmetrical frequency curves in general. Types actually occurring. *Philosophical Transactions of the Royal Society of London*, series A, vol. 186. London: Cambridge University Press, 1895.

3-9   Exercises

1. For the following set of data, calculate the

    a. Range

    b. Variance

    c. Standard deviation

$$6, 7, 8, 10, 10, 10, 12, 14$$

2. For the following set of data, calculate the

    a. Range

    b. Variance

    c. Standard deviation

$$7, 4, 2, 3, 4, 5, 8, 1, 9, 4$$

3. For the following data set, calculate the

   a. Range
   b. Variance
   c. Standard deviation

Value (X)	Frequency (f)
90	6
80	8
70	4
60	3
50	2

4. For the following set of data, calculate the

   a. Range
   b. Variance
   c. Standard deviation

Value (X)	Frequency (f)
90	5
80	7
70	9
60	4

5. Using the frequency tables below,

   a. Discuss the measures of dispersion that would be appropriate for each.
   b. Discuss the number of modes.
   c. Determine the skewness and kurtosis and discuss whether the distribution is positively skewed or negatively skewed and whether it is leptokurtic, mesokurtic, or platykurtic.

HOME	What type of house do you live in?				
		Frequency	**Percent**	**Valid Percent**	**Cumulative Percent**
Valid		1	0.3	0.3	0.3
House	1	279	81.3	82.1	82.4
Duplex	2	3	0.9	0.9	83.2
Trailer	3	34	9.9	10.0	93.2
Apartment	4	21	6.1	6.2	99.4
Other	5	2	0.6	0.6	100.0
	Total	340	99.1	100.0	
Missing	System	3	0.9		
Total		343	100.0		

	N	Valid	340
		Missing	3
	Mean		1.41
	Std. Error of Mean		.051
	Median		1.00
	Mode		1
	Std. Deviation		.945
	Variance		.892
	Skewness		2.001
	Std. Error of Skewness		.132
	Kurtosis		2.613
	Std. Error of Kurtosis		.264
	Range		5

ARREST How many times have you been arrested?					
		Frequency	**Percent**	**Valid Percent**	**Cumulative Percent**
Valid	0	243	70.8	86.2	86.2
	1	23	6.7	8.2	94.3
	2	10	2.9	3.5	97.9
	3	3	0.9	1.1	98.9
	5	2	0.6	0.7	99.6
	24	1	0.3	0.4	100.0
	Total	282	82.2	100.0	
Missing	System	61	17.8		
Total		343	100.0		

N	Valid	282
	Missing	61
Mean		0.30
Std. Error of Mean		0.093
Median		0.00
Mode		0
Std. Deviation		1.567
Variance		2.455
Skewness		12.692
Std. Error of Skewness		0.145
Kurtosis		187.898
Std. Error of Kurtosis		0.289
Range		24

TENURE How long have you lived at your current address (months)					
		Frequency	**Percent**	**Valid Percent**	**Cumulative Percent**
Valid	1	14	4.1	4.3	4.3
	2	6	1.7	1.8	6.1
	3	4	1.2	1.2	7.3
	4	4	1.2	1.2	8.6
	5	6	1.7	1.8	10.4
	6	6	1.7	1.8	12.2

		Frequency	Percent	Valid Percent	Cumulative Percent
	7	1	0.3	0.3	12.5
	8	3	0.9	0.9	13.5
	9	2	0.6	0.6	14.1
	10	1	0.3	0.3	14.4
	11	1	0.3	0.3	14.7
	12	11	3.2	3.4	18.0
	14	1	0.3	0.3	18.3
	18	5	1.5	1.5	19.9
	21	1	0.3	0.3	20.2
	24	30	8.7	9.2	29.4
	30	1	0.3	0.3	29.7
	31	1	0.3	0.3	30.0
	32	1	0.3	0.3	30.3
	36	22	6.4	6.7	37.0
	42	1	0.3	0.3	37.3
	48	12	3.5	3.7	41.0
	60	24	7.0	7.3	48.3
	72	14	4.1	4.3	52.6
	76	1	0.3	0.3	52.9
	84	8	2.3	2.4	55.4
	96	18	5.2	5.5	60.9
	108	4	1.2	1.2	62.1
	120	9	2.6	2.8	64.8
	132	11	3.2	3.4	68.2
	144	21	6.1	6.4	74.6
	156	13	3.8	4.0	78.6
	168	11	3.2	3.4	82.0
	170	5	1.5	1.5	83.5
	180	7	2.0	2.1	85.6
	182	2	0.6	0.6	86.2
	186	1	0.3	0.3	86.5
	192	14	4.1	4.3	90.8
	198	1	0.3	0.3	91.1

		Frequency	Percent	Valid Percent	Cumulative Percent
	204	24	7.0	7.3	98.5
	216	3	0.9	0.9	99.4
	240	2	0.6	0.6	100.0
	Total	327	95.3	100.0	
Missing	System	16	4.7		
Total		343	100.0		

N	Valid		327
	Missing		16
Mean			88.77
Std. Error of Mean			3.880
Median			72.00
Mode			24
Std. Deviation			70.164
Variance			4,923.055
Skewness			0.365
Std. Error of Skewness			0.135
Kurtosis			−1.284
Std. Error of Kurtosis			0.269
Range			239

SIBS	How many brothers and sisters do you have?				
		Frequency	Percent	Valid Percent	Cumulative Percent
Valid	0	39	11.4	11.5	11.5
	1	137	39.9	40.5	52.1
	2	79	23.0	23.4	75.4
	3	39	11.4	11.5	87.0
	4	17	5.0	5.0	92.0
	5	13	3.8	3.8	95.9
	6	6	1.7	1.8	97.6
	7	4	1.2	1.2	98.8
	9	1	0.3	0.3	99.1
	10	1	0.3	0.3	99.4

		Frequency	Percent	Valid Percent	Cumulative Percent
	12	1	0.3	0.3	99.7
	15	1	0.3	0.3	100.0
	Total	338	98.5	100.0	
Missing	System	5	1.5		
Total		343	100.0		

N	Valid	338
	Missing	5
Mean		1.94
Std. Error of Mean		0.098
Median		1.00
Mode		1
Std. Deviation		1.801
Variance		3.245
Skewness		2.664
Std. Error of Skewness		0.133
Kurtosis		12.027
Std. Error of Kurtosis		0.265
Range		15

Chapter 4
Bivariate Tables and Analysis

Learning Objectives

- Describe the purpose of a bivariate table.
- Explain how to construct a bivariate table.
- Describe how to determine the cell number of a bivariate table.
- Properly fill in a blank bivariate table with correct elements.

Key Terms

bivariate

cell

cell frequency

column percentage

crosstab

direction

existence

marginals

nature

relationship

row percentage

strength

total percentage

variance

In previous chapters, frequency tables were discussed as a method of examining the characteristics of a particular variable. It is possible to use those frequency tables to examine the *relationship* between two or more variables. As an example, take the two variables *sex* and *type of victimization*. The combination tables from SPSS for each variable are shown in **Table 4-1**.

Sex of Respondent					
Value		**Frequency**	**Percent**	**Valid Percent**	**Cumulative Percent**
1	Male	99	28.5	29.1	29.1
2	Female	241	69.5	70.9	100.0
	Total	340	98.0	100.0	
Missing	System	7	2.0		
Total		347	100.0		
Valid cases	340	Missing cases	7		

Have you been a victim of any of these crimes in the last 6 months?					
Value		**Frequency**	**Percent**	**Valid Percent**	**Cumulative Percent**
0	No Response	7	2.0	5.9	5.9
1	Burglary	30	8.6	25.4	31.4
2	Vandalism	28	8.1	23.7	55.1
3	Car Theft	14	4.0	11.9	66.9
4	Robbery	9	2.6	7.6	74.6
5	Assault	3	.9	2.5	77.1
6	Rape	22	6.3	18.6	95.8
7	Other	5	1.4	4.2	100.0
	Total	118	34.0	100.0	
Missing	System	229	66.0		
Total		347	100.0		
	Valid cases	118	Missing cases	229	

Table 4-1   Combination Tables for Sex and Victimization

The univariate statistics of each of these variables can be determined from these frequency tables. These show that there are more than double the number of female respondents than male and that the most frequent victimization was for burglary, closely followed by vandalism and then rape. The table for victimization also contains seven people who indicated on a previous question that they had been victimized but who did not respond as to the actual crime in this question. It is difficult, however, to make any determinations about the possible sex of victims from these tables. For instance, it is impossible to determine from these tables how many males and how many females were victims of burglary.

With some additional work and analyses, however, the tables can be arranged by the sex of the respondent. This allows statements to be made about male victims and female victims. The results are shown in **Table 4-2**. Here, it can be shown that females had a higher number and percentage of vandalism, car theft, assault, and rape; and that males had a higher percentage of burglaries, robberies, and other victimizations (although there were still more females in each of these categories except burglary, which had the same number of males and females, and no response). This is a somewhat complicated process, however, and requires looking back and forth between each table. It would be much easier if we could make more direct, or side-by-side, comparisons of the variables.

Male Victim		
	Freq	**Percent**
No response	1	2.9%
Burglary	15	42.9%
Vandalism	5	14.3%
Car theft	3	8.6%
Robbery	3	8.6%
Assault	0	0%
Rape	5	14.3%
Other	3	8.6%

Female Victim		
	Freq	**Percent**
No response	4	5.1%
Burglary	15	19.0%
Vandalism	21	26.6%
Car theft	11	13.9%
Robbery	6	7.6%
Assault	3	3.8%
Rape	17	21.5%
Other	2	2.5%

Table 4-2   Tables for Male and Female Victims of Crime

A bivariate table does just that. A *bivariate* table displays the joint frequencies of two variables and attempts to show an association between the variables by determining how many times they have paired occurrences, such as females who have been victims of burglary, in their categories versus the differences in those categories. This table is commonly referred to as a *cross-tabulation table*, or *crosstab* for short.[1] A crosstab from SPSS for type of the victimization and sex is shown in **Table 4-3**. This table presents the categories—frequencies and/or percentages—of one variable compared to the categories of another variable. This is usually presented in a format such as females who have been victims of a crime versus males who have been victims of a crime.

4-1 Constructing Bivariate Tables

Now let us talk about constructing bivariate tables. You will not have to construct a bivariate table from scratch often, but you do need to know what a good one looks like, and you may have to make some decisions or modifications to statistical software printouts to make sure your tables are correct.

The basic format of a bivariate table is to put the variables in rows and columns where the dependent variable is in the *rows* and the independent variable is in the *columns*. Although this ordering can be reversed, some bivariate procedures assume this ordering, and consistency does make analysis easier. In Table 4-3, type of victimization is the dependent variable and sex is the independent variable. The probability of persons becoming victims of a certain crime may be affected by whether they are male or female. Whether a person is a victim of a crime has no influence on determining whether the person is male or female at birth.

A bivariate table is classified by the number of rows and columns, using $Y \times X$ as the model. For example, a 4×3 table is a bivariate table with the dependent variable, Y, divided into four categories and the independent variable, X, divided into three categories. The table in Table 4-3 is a 7×2 table; that is, there are seven categories of the dependent variable (Y) and two categories of the independent variable (X).

Each of the boxes of a table is called a *cell*. The frequency of a cell is determined by calculating the number of occurrences of a pair of values from the independent and dependent variables. This is called the *cell frequency* and is usually denoted by the symbol n_{ij} or n_{rc}, where *ij* or *rc* stands for the row and column in which the cell is located. For example, in Table 4-3, the cell that contains the joint frequencies for males who have had a response of Other is cell 1-1 (row 1, column 1). The frequency for this cell is 3, which means that there were three males who had a response other than the other categories listed. In written form, this frequency might be represented in the form $n_{11} = 3$.

Have you been a victim of any of these crimes in the last 6 months? * Sex of Respondent Crosstabulation				
VICTIM Have you been a victim of any of these crimes in the last 6 months?		**SEX** Sex of respondent		**Total**
		1 Male	2 Female	
7 Other	Count	3	2	5
	Expected Count	1.5	3.5	5.0
	% within VICTIM	60.0	40.0	100.0
	% within SEX	8.6	2.5	4.4
	% of Total	2.6	1.8	4.4
6 Rape	Count	5	17	22
	Expected Count	6.8	15.2	22.0
	% within VICTIM	22.7	77.3	100.0
	% within SEX	14.3	21.5	19.3
	% of Total	4.4	14.9	19.3
5 Assault	Count	0	3	3
	Expected Count	0.9	2.1	3.0
	% within VICTIM	0.0	100.0	100.0
	% within SEX	0.0	3.8	2.6
	% of Total	0.0	2.6	2.6
4 Robbery	Count	3	6	9
	Expected Count	2.8	6.2	9.0
	% within VICTIM	33.3	66.7	100.0
	% within SEX	8.6	7.6	7.9
	% of Total	2.6	5.3	7.9
3 Car Theft	Count	3	11	14
	Expected Count	4.3	9.7	14.0
	% within VICTIM	21.4	78.6	100.0
	% within SEX	8.6	13.9	12.3
	% of Total	2.6	9.6	12.3
2 Vandalism	Count	5	21	26
	Expected Count	8.0	18.0	26.0
	% within VICTIM	19.2	80.8	100.0
	% within SEX	14.3	26.6	22.8
	% of Total	4.4	18.4	22.8
1 Burglery	Count	15	15	30
	Expected Count	9.2	20.8	30.0
	% within VICTIM	50.0	50.0	100.0
	% within SEX	42.9	19.0	26.3
	% of Total	13.2	13.2	26.3
0 No Response	Count	1	4	5
	Expected Count	1.5	3.5	5.0
	% within VICTIM	20.0	80.0	100.0
	% within SEX	2.9	5.1	4.4
	% of Total	0.9	3.5	4.4
	Count	35	79	114
	% within VICTIM	30.7	69.3	100.0
	% within SEX	100.0	100.0	100.0
	% of Total	30.7	69.3	100.0

Figure 4-3   Crosstab of Victim by Sex

The type of bivariate table is taken from the type of data it contains, the same as with identifying the type of frequency table. If the values in the cells are data values, the table is called a frequency table; if the values are percentages, the table is called a percentage table; if there are both, it is called a combination table.

The level of the bivariate table is taken from the level of data it contains; that is, ordinal level tables contain ordinal level variables, and nominal level tables contain nominal level variables. The level of data in the table, and thus the table itself, is an important consideration in analysis because the level of data will determine the type of statistical procedures used to analyze the data.

Ordinal Level Table Construction

Because the development of an ordinal level table is somewhat more structured, we discuss it in detail first. Then we cover construction of a nominal level table based on the understanding of ordinal level table design.

For use of ordinal measures of association, both variables must be ordinal, dichotomized nominal such as male/female, or categorized interval level variables (which is interval level data such as income that has been placed into categories after data collection to ease analysis or presentation).

The first step in constructing an ordinal level table is to set up the title. The title is created in the form of *dependent variable (Y) by independent variable (X)*. As shown in **Table 4-4**, the title is Crosstab of Walking at Night by Perceptions of Crime Problem where *walking at night* is the dependent variable and *perceptions of crime problem* is the independent variable.

The next step is to set up the column and row headings. Columns contain independent variables, so the independent variable title is across the top of the table. Column headings should be arranged in ascending order (from low to high) as you move from left to right across the table. In the example in Table 4-4, the categories of *crime problem* move from No Problem (category 1) to Big Problem (category 3) as you move across the top of the table. Rows contain the dependent variables, so the dependent variable title is to the left of the table. Row headings should be arranged in descending order (from high to low), as you move from the top to the bottom of the table. In the example in Table 4-4, the rows for *walking at night* move from Often (category 3) to Never (category 1) as you move from top to bottom. Arranging the dependent variable so it moves from high values at the top of the table to low values at the bottom of the table will ensure the signs of analyses will be correct and the direction is visually attainable by how the values are arranged.

To fill out the table, place the proper numbers in each cell by counting how many times each pair occurs. For each of the two variables, the cell frequencies are determined by taking each pair of scores and hash-marking them in the appropriate cell.

How often do you walk in your neighborhood at night? * How big a problem is crime?
Crosstabulation

| | | | CRIME
How big a problem is crime? | | | |
			No Problem	Small Problem	Big Problem	Total
WALK How often do you walk in your neighborhood at night?	**Often**	Count	2	2	0	4
		Expected Count	2.7	1.2	0.2	4.0
		% within WALK	50.0	50.0	0.0	100.0
		% within CRIME	1.2	2.8	0.0	1.6
		% of Total	0.8	0.8	0.0	1.6
	Occasionally	Count	20	13	3	36
		Expected Count	23.9	10.4	1.7	36.0
		% within WALK	55.6	36.1	8.3	100.0
		% within CRIME	12.1	18.1	25.0	14.5
		% of Total	8.0	5.2	1.2	14.5
	Never	Count	143	57	9	209
		Expected Count	138.5	60.4	10.1	209.0
		% within WALK	68.4	27.3	4.3	100.0
		% within CRIME	86.7	79.2	75.0	83.9
		% of Total	57.4	22.9	3.6	83.9
Total		Count	165	72	12	249
		Expected Count	165.0	72.0	12.0	249.0
		% within WALK	66.3	28.9	4.8	100.0
		% within CRIME	100.0	100.0	100.0	100.0
		% of Total	66.3	28.9	4.8	100.0

Table 4-4   Crosstab of Walking at Night by Perceptions of Crime Problem

It is often difficult to compare two or more variables using just their frequencies because frequency values are difficult to interpret. It is a good practice, therefore, to convert frequencies to percentages so the variables can be more easily compared. This is accomplished by dividing each cell frequency by its column total, row total, or N, and then multiplying by 100. SPSS does this for you. When you check the box indicating *Row*, *Column*, and/or *Total* in SPSS, it will calculate the *row percentages*, *column percentages*, and/or *total percentages* of the data. These are listed in the printouts as "% within" the variable in the row or column, or as "% of total." For example, in row 2, cell 2-3 has a row percentage of 8.3% (3/36); cell 2-2 has a row percentage of 36.1% (13/36); and cell 2-1 has a row percentage of 55.6% (20/36). You know these are row percentages because they are labeled "% within WALK", which is the variable in the rows.

The same can be done for *column percentages*. In column 1 of Table 4-4, cell 1-1 has a column percentage of 1.2% (2/165); the column percentage of cell 2-1 is 12.1%

(20/165); and the column percentage of cell 3-1 is 86.7% (143/165). You know these are column percentages because they are labeled "% within CRIME?" which is the variable in the columns.

Finally, the *total percentages* can be calculated. This entails taking each cell and dividing by *N*. For example in column 2, the total percentage for cell 1-2 is 0.8% (2/249); the total percentage for cell 2-2 is 5.2% (13/249); and the total percentage for cell 3-2 is 22.9% (57/249).

Box 4-1   How Do You Do That? Bivariate Tables in SPSS

Although Excel can create bivariate tables (they are called *pivot tables*), the creation and analysis of them begin to get complicated. Here we show how to construct bivariate tables in SPSS. Just follow the examples below and the discussion in this chapter, and you should be fine.

1. Open a data set such as that provided at go.jblearning.com/Walker.
   a. Start SPSS.
   b. Select File, then Open, then Data.
   c. Select the file you want to open, then select Open.
2. Once the data is visible, select Analyze, then Descriptive Statistics, then Cross-tabs.
3. Select the variable you wish to include as your dependent variable, and press the next to the Row(s) window.
4. Select the variable you wish to include as your independent variable, and press the ▶ next to the Column(s) window.
5. For now, do not worry about the Exact and Statistics boxes at the bottom of the window.
6. Select the Cells button and check any of the boxes for information you may want in your crosstab. For a crosstab with full information, select Observed, Expected, Row, Column, and Total; then press Continue.
7. *Important:* Select the Format button, and check the box marked Descending. If you do not do this, your table will not be formatted as discussed in this chapter. An output window should appear containing a distribution similar in format to Table 4-4.

The numbers on the outside of the table are called the *marginals*. These are simply the total frequency counts or percentages of the data in the rows or columns. For example, *row total* contains the total cell frequency for all scores in that row, and the same is true for the *column total*. In Table 4-4, the row total for row 1 is 4 because there were two cells with frequencies of 2 and one cell with a frequency of 0. Likewise, the column total for column 3 is 12 because there were three cells with frequencies of 0, 3, and 9. The percentage values in the marginals are the contribution of that row or column to the total. For example, in Table 4-4, the value of 1.6% in row 1 means that the score *Often* contributes 1.6% of the total scores for all values of crime problem, (with *Occasionally* and *Never* contributing the other 98.4%). If these marginals were compared to the original frequency or percentage tables, the numbers would match for each category.

The values in the bottom right-hand corner of the table represent the totals for the table. In Table 4-4, the total frequency (*N*) is 249, and the 100% represents 100% of the row totals and 100% of the column totals.

Nominal Level Table Construction

If one of the variables to be studied is nominal (excluding dichotomized nominal), a nominal table and nominal statistics should be used to measure the association. The statistics associated with nominal tables provide less information than ordinal level tables because of the type of data.

As will be discussed in Chapter 5, nominal level tables can provide information on the existence and the strength of the relationship. If there are enough categories in each variable, nominal level tables can provide some information about the nature of the relationship. No determination can be made concerning the direction of the data because nominal level data cannot be ordered.

A nominal level table is created in the same way as an ordinal level table. The only difference is that the ordering of categories is not important. For these tables, the variable categories should be arranged in a way that makes the most logical sense. Even though no direction can be determined from a nominal level table, any ordinal level variables or any categorized interval level variables used should be put in order according to the directions for an ordinal level table. This assists in examining the data and standardizes the way tables are constructed.

4-2   Analysis of Bivariate Tables

Constructing bivariate tables is often the first step in bivariate analyses, but it is only the beginning of bivariate analysis. Bivariate analyses are covered in the next three chapters, but a short introduction is included here to show the link with table construction.

Bivariate tables and the statistics associated with them are one of the most common forms of analysis for nominal and ordinal data. These tables are seldom used, however, for interval and ratio data because there are often so many categories with this level of data that the table would be too large and complex to be useful. Furthermore, the statistics for interval and ratio level data are much stronger if the data is not categorized, so the data is usually left in raw form rather than put in tables.

Bivariate analyses examine the relationship between two variables, or the differences between categories of one variable as they relate to categories of a second variable. There are four steps involved in bivariate analysis. These steps examine or determine the characteristics of an association. For nominal and ordinal level data, these analyses are conducted using bivariate tables and the statistical procedures that go with them. For interval and ratio level data, the analyses are generally conducted without the use of bivariate tables.

The first step in a bivariate analysis is to test for the *existence* of an association, which will be covered in Chapter 5. An association is said to exist between two variables if the distribution of one variable differs in some respect between categories of the other variable. The next step is to measure the *strength* of an association. If an association exists, this determines how closely the two variables are associated. The third step is to determine the *direction* of an association. If the higher values of one variable are associated with higher values on the other, the association is said to be positive. If the higher values of one variable are associated with lower values on the other, the association is said to be negative. The final step is to determine the *nature* of an association. Patterns of an association may be irregular. If an increase in one increment in one variable is always related to a constant increase or decrease of a certain number of increments in the other variable, the nature of the association is said to be *linear*. Some patterns are curvilinear or nonlinear, however, and may influence other analyses of the variables.

Not all of these determinations can be made with the statistics available to all levels of data. For example, since nominal level data has no ordering, there is no way to determine direction. Proper bivariate analysis strives, however, to provide indicators of each of these steps so a complete summarization of the data and relationship is made. This process is discussed more fully in Chapters 5, 6, and 7.

4-3 Note

1. Crosstabs are also sometimes referred to as *contingency tables* in some disciplines.

4-4 Exercises

1. For the variables sex (male, female) and victim (yes, no):

   a. Fill in the information in the blanks to properly format the table.

	_____ by _____		
_____	1	2	_____
_____			
_____ 2	20	37	57
_____ 1	27	48	75
_____	47	85	132

   b. Is this a nominal or an ordinal table? Why?

2. From the following information, construct the appropriate table for use in a bivariate analysis.

   a.

Fear of Walking Alone during the Day	How Well Police Perform Their Duties
Great fear	Very Well
Medium fear	Average
Small fear	Below Average
No fear	Not At All

   b. Is this a nominal or ordinal level table? Why?

3. A survey of prison inmates in Oklahoma was conducted in which inmates were asked about their criminal careers and their incomes at the time of arrest. Below are the results of the survey.

Crimes per Month	Income, $
15	18,000
5	21,000
15	23,000
10	22,000
10	25,000
5	14,000
20	23,000
20	46,000

Crimes per Month	Income, $
5	15,000
5	17,000
15	24,000
15	18,000
15	21,000
15	31,000
20	52,000
7	21,000
7	17,000
20	48,000
20	45,000
10	19,000

a. In the spaces below, construct an ordinal bivariate table for *crimes per month* (dependent variable) and *income* (independent variable). For crimes per month, use the categories "10 and less" and "greater than 10." For income level, use the categories "$21,000 and more" and "less than $21,000."

_____   by   _____

_____   _____

_____ _____   _____ _____

_____ _____   _____ _____

_____   _____ _____

b. Is this a nominal or ordinal table? Why?

4. For the table below, do the following.

   a. Tell whether it is a nominal or ordinal level table and why.

   b. Identify the row percentage of cell 2-3.

   c. Identify the column percentage of cell 1-2.

   d. Identify the total percentage of cell 2-2.

   e. Identify the row percentage for row 1.

   f. Identify the column percentage for column 2.

Is crime a serious enough problem that you have considered moving in the past 12 months? * How much has fear of crime affected your decision to walk during the daytime? Cross-tabulation

Is crime a serious enough problem that you have considered moving in the past 12 months?			How much has fear of crime affected your decision to walk during the daytime?			Total
			1 No Effect	2 Small Effect	3 Great Effect	
	2 Yes	Count	83	48	22	153
		% within Is crime a serious enough problem that you have considered moving in the past 12 months?	54.2	31.4	14.4	100.0
		% within How much has fear of crime affected your decision to walk during the daytime?	69.2	44.0	24.7	48.1
		% of Total	26.1	15.1	6.9	48.1
	1 No	Count	37	61	67	165
		% within Is crime a serious enough problem that you have considered moving in the past 12 months?	22.4	37.0	40.6	100.0
		% within How much has fear of crime affected your decision to walk during the daytime?	30.8	56.0	75.3	51.9
		% of Total	11.6	19.2	21.1	51.9
Total		Count	120	109	89	318
		% within Is crime a serious enough problem that you have considered moving in the past 12 months?	37.7	34.3	28.0	100.0
		% within How much has fear of crime affected your decision to walk during the daytime?	100.0	100.0	100.0	100.0
		% of Total	37.7	34.3	28.0	100.0

Table 4-5   Crosstab of Whether a Person Considered Moving in the Previous 12 Months by the Perception of Fear of Crime during the Day.

Chapter 5
Measures of Existence and Statistical Significance

Learning Objectives

- Understand the existence of a relationship.
- Identify and discuss nominal level measures of existence.
- Explain how a percentaged table can be used in determining existence.
- Calculate and interpret an epsilon and a delta.
- Understand the use of chi-square in determining existence.
- Calculate and interpret chi-square.
- Explain the requirements for using chi-square.
- Explain the limitations of chi-square.
- Identify and discuss ordinal and interval level measures of existence.
- Interpret Spearman's rho and Pearson's *r* as measures of existence.

Key Terms

association	expected frequency
chance	Fisher's exact test
chi-square	model of no association
column percentaged table	observed frequency
degrees of freedom	row percentaged table
delta	statistically significant
epsilon	total percentaged table
existence	Yates correction

Once data has been put into a bivariate table, typically the next step is to determine if there is any real relationship between the variables or if the relationship could have occurred by chance. This is a process of determining the *existence* of a relationship, which is an important step because it may prevent needless effort being expended on other bivariate analyses. If there is no relationship between the variables, or if that relationship is probably occurring by chance, then there may be no need to conduct other analyses.

In this chapter we discuss how to determine the existence of a relationship and whether such existence might be due to chance. Again, we are describing here a population using descriptive statistics. If we wanted to make inferences to a larger group from our analyses, we would use inferential statistics, discussed in later chapters.

At the most basic level, an association is said to exist between two variables when the distribution of the categories of one variable differs from some of the categories of the other variable. The greater the difference, the stronger the *association* will be. This may sound counterintuitive; it may seem to make more sense that if two variables are associated, they should have the same values rather than different values. What you must keep in mind is that bivariate analyses look for *change* in one variable that may be associated with *change* in the other variable.

In a perfect world, an increase of one unit in an independent variable would be associated with a one unit increase (or decrease) in the dependent variable. For example, if we were studying drug use and crime, ideally we would like to see that for every instance of drug use, the probability of committing a crime rose by 1%. If changes in the independent variable reflect no changes in the dependent variable (that is increases in categories of one variable show no change in the categories of the other variable), then nothing has been gained by including the independent variable. In drug use and crime, for example, if criminal behavior did not increase no matter how much a person's drug use increased (or if the changes were so random you could not tell if an increase in drug use would produce an increase or decrease in crime), there would be no value in collecting data on drug use to explain criminal behavior. The way this change is examined is through bivariate tables, bivariate analyses, and the establishment of the statistical significance of the relationship.

5-1   Nominal Level Measures of Existence

We begin by examining how to determine the statistical significance of a relationship by looking at percentage tables. We then add on to the sophistication of the analysis step by step until we get to the measure of statistical analysis we will use for nominal and ordinal level data—chi-squared.

One of the best ways to make preliminary comparisons between variables, especially if they have different *N* values, is to convert the frequencies to percentages. This translates to bivariate analysis by constructing a *percentaged table*. A percentaged table allows direct comparison between categories of the variables. There are three types of percentaged tables (corresponding to the percentages contained in the crosstabs discussed in Chapter 4). A *row percentaged table* is based on the rows. This means that the rows will equal 100%, but the columns may not. A *column percentaged table*, on the other hand, is based on the columns, so the columns will total 100%, but the rows will not. A *total percentaged table* is constructed by dividing each cell frequency by *N*. Here, the total percentages of rows and columns will be 100%, but none of the individual rows or columns will. Each of these is shown in a single table in **Table 5-1**.

Recoded VICTIM to yes and no * Sex of Respondent Crosstabulation					
			Sex of respondent		
			Male	**Female**	**Total**
Recoded VICTIM to yes and no	**No**	Count	68	168	236
		Expected Count	68.7	167.3	236.0
		% within Recoded VICTIM	28.8	71.2	100.0
		% within Sex of respondent	68.7	69.7	69.4
		% of Total	20.0	49.4	69.4
	Yes	Count	31	73	104
		Expected Count	30.3	73.7	104.0
		% within Recoded VICTIM	29.8	70.2	100.0
		% within Sex of respondent	31.3	30.3	30.6
		% of Total	9.1	21.5	30.6
Total		Count	99	241	340
		Expected Count	99.0	241.0	340.0
		% within Recoded VICTIM	29.1	70.9	100.0
		% within Sex of respondent	100.0	100.0	100.0
		% of Total	29.1	70.9	100.0

Table 5-1   Crosstab of Victimization by Sex of Respondent

The type of table that is constructed is important in determining the existence of a relationship between two variables because *comparisons are made in the opposite direction from the way percentages are calculated*. If rows are used as the base of percentages (a row percentaged table), comparisons will be made on the dependent variable. If columns are used as the base of percentages (a column percentaged table), comparisons will be made on the independent variable.

A column percentaged table is the desired way to make comparisons because the goal is to determine what influence the independent variable is having on the dependent variable. To accomplish this requires examining the effect of the independent variable on the dependent variable. This requires removing the effect of the different frequencies in the categories of the independent variable, which is done by totaling those columns to 100%. A column percentage table, then, is most often used in determining existence, meaning that the columns should total 100% but the rows will not.

In Table 5-1, the column percentages are in the second row from the bottom on each cell (68.7, 69.7, 31.3, and 30.3). Notice that the cells are offset, so that the sum of 68.7 and 31.3 equals 100. This will be important later. The example in Table 5-1 shows why column percentages should be used in these analyses. As can be seen in this crosstab, the number of females in the distribution far exceeds the number of males (241 females to 99 males). As a result, the frequency of female victimizations exceeds that of males for all categories. This misrepresents the relationships between the variables, however.

As shown in **Table 5-2**, if column percentages are used for the comparison, thus controlling for the larger number of females in the sample, the cell percentages are much closer. The percentage of persons not victimized is within 1 percentage point between male and female. Additionally, the relationship of males to females victimized is actually reversed when their proportion of the respondents is taken into account (31.3% to 30.3%). A properly percentaged table, then, using the categories of the independent variable, is important for proper comparison of the categories of the dependent variable.

Victimization by Sex				
Sex		**Male**	**Female**	**Total**
Victimization				
No		68.7%	69.7%	69.4%
Yes		31.3%	30.3%	30.6%
	Total	100%	100%	100%

Table 5-2   Column Percentaged Table

Epsilon

Once a table is properly set up, a difference between the variables (denoting the existence of a relationship) can be determined by calculating an *epsilon*. Epsilon is symbolized by the Greek letter ε.

Epsilon (ε) is easily calculated by determining the differences in the column percentages across the rows. Table 5-2 shows an example of a table set up to examine epsilon for the existence of the relationship between victimization and sex. Here, the comparison is by rows, so the table is totaled by columns, as evidenced by both columns totaling to 100% while the rows total to 69.4% and 30.6%, respectively. Comparisons are then made based on the differences in column percentages by row.

In Table 5-2, we want to know how a person's sex may have influenced whether she or he was victimized, so we will look in the Yes row of the table. The difference between male and female victimizations, or ε, is the difference in the first row (31.3% to 30.3% = 1%). Actually, the existence of an epsilon can be found if there is a difference in *any* row of the table; that is, if there is a nonzero ε, there is a relationship. An epsilon of 1% means that there is *some* difference between the variables and that a relationship between the two variables does exist.

The problem with using epsilon as a measure of the existence of a relationship between two variables is that epsilon cannot determine if the difference is by chance or if there is a real difference (is a 1% difference between the variables meaningful?). In social science research, there will always be some differences; however, this difference may be seen in the way the data is collected, bad luck, or some other factors. What is needed is to be able to tell if those differences are meaningful or if the way the data is arranged is due to chance.

Delta

A more precise method of examining the relationship is to determine if it is *statistically significant*. This is important because if the arrangement of the numbers is by chance—if they are not statistically different enough to be considered a true difference—then it may not be of any importance.

It is generally accepted that it is worth the effort to conduct other bivariate analyses only if a relationship is significant. A bivariate table can be tested to see if the relationship is significant by computing a chi-square test of independence. This is a test based on the delta statistic, which tests the hypothesis that there is *no* relationship between the two variables. Let us begin the discussion of chi-square by looking at how to calculate delta. *Delta* (Δ) is calculated by determining what the values (expected frequencies, as discussed below) in the cells would be if there were no association between the variables and then comparing those values with the observed frequencies in the table.

The first step in this process is to determine the *expected frequency* of each of the cells, which is symbolized by f_e. This expected frequency is what we would expect if there were absolutely no association between the variables. The two variables are said to be independent or have no association if the probability that a case falls into a given cell is simply the product of the marginal values (row total and column total) of the two categories that make up the cell. If the expected frequency is not given in a crosstab printout, it can be calculated by multiplying the row total for that row by the column total for that column and then dividing by the N of the distribution. This process is completed for each cell in the crosstab.

This is accomplished for the data in Table 5-1 with the calculations shown in **Table 5-3**. The calculations produce a value that can be compared to the observed frequency for that category. If the observed frequency is something other than the expected value, the variables are said to be associated at least in some way.

Victimization by Sex				
Sex		**Male**	**Female**	**Row Total**
Victimization				
No		$f_e = \dfrac{236 \times 99}{340}$ $= 68.71$	$f_e = \dfrac{236 \times 241}{340}$ $= 167.29$	236
Yes		$f_e = \dfrac{104 \times 99}{340}$ $= 30.28$	$f_e = \dfrac{104 \times 241}{340}$ $= 70.72$	104
	Column Total	99	241	340

Table 5-3   Expected Frequency Table

The distribution of expected frequencies is called a *model of no association*. These values (68.71, 167.29, 30.28, and 70.72) represent what would be expected for observed frequencies if there were no association between the two variables. Deviation from this model of no association represents some degree of relationship between the two variables.

The next step in calculating data is to determine the *observed frequency* of each cell in the distribution, which is symbolized by f_o. These are simply the cell frequencies as calculated in Chapter 4. The cell frequencies for Table 5-1 are 68, 168, 31, and 73. Notice here the switch from percentages to frequencies. This is an important change. For epsilon or other crude comparisons, percentages are the base of analysis because they control for the unequal sample sizes. More powerful statistical procedures, however, benefit from the more precise measure of frequency.

Delta is calculated by taking the difference between the observed (f_o) and the expected (f_e) frequencies for each of the cells. This statistic will determine if there is any association between the variables. If there is a nonzero value of Δ in one of the categories, then there is some association between the variables. In the crosstab in Table 5-1, delta would be calculated as shown in **Figure 5-1**. The nonzero delta values indicate there is an association between the variables. Although all of the deltas calculated here are nonzero, it is not mandatory that all deltas show a difference; if one has a nonzero value, we can conclude that a relationship exists.

$$\Delta = (68 - 68.7)\ (168 - 167.3)\ (31 - 30.3)\ (73 - 73.7)$$
$$= \quad (-0.7) \qquad (0.7) \qquad (-0.7) \qquad (0.7)$$

Figure 5-1   Calculation of Delta

There are two problems concerning the delta statistic, however. First, delta can only determine whether there is a difference between the expected and observed frequencies one cell at a time. A better procedure would check *all* of the differences and provide a single indicator of association. In our example, if all of the delta values were added, they would equal 0 ($-0.7 + 0.7 + -0.7 + 0.7$). Since delta is based on the model of no association, summing deltas always produces a 0 value. This does not aid in determining the total relationship of the two variables. This problem can be overcome, however, by summing the squared ($f_o - f_e$) values—the same procedure as used in calculating the variance of a variable (see Chapter 3). We will obtain a 0 value only if there is a true fit between the two distributions and no difference exists between the observed and expected frequencies. Second, the delta statistic does not account for differences in the magnitude of frequencies in the cells. For example, in measuring the difference between the expected and observed frequencies, delta does not recognize that there are twice as many females as males in the distribution. Overcoming this problem simply requires standardizing the formula above by dividing it by the expected frequencies. The resulting formula is the formula for a statistical procedure called chi-square.

5-2   Chi-square

The *chi-square* test, symbolized by χ^2, is the primary method of establishing the significant existence of a relationship between two nominal or, sometimes, higher-level variables. Chi-square allows researchers to move from simply checking the existence of a relationship to testing the statistical significance of the relationship through the null hypothesis, which we will talk about in a later chapter.

The null hypothesis being tested here is that there is no statistically significant relationship between the variables being studied—specifically that there is no difference between the values in the rows and the values in the columns of the table being examined (that the groups were sampled from the same population). If that null hypothesis can be rejected, it can be said with a particular degree of certainty that there is a relationship between the two variables.

In testing for the existence of a relationship, chi-square examines the difference between the observed and expected frequencies. Differences between these two imply one of two conclusions: either the difference is truly due to chance and the null hypothesis is correct, or the values are so different that it cannot be said that the difference is due to chance and the null hypothesis must be rejected in favor of alternative hypotheses.

To determine chi-square, three pieces of information are needed: (1) the value of chi-square obtained by the chi-square formula (the same as for delta in Table 5-3), (2) the degrees of freedom for the crosstab being examined, and (3) the critical value, which is obtained by using a column in Appendix A that corresponds to how sure you want to be of your results.

Calculating a chi-square essentially sums the values of the delta statistic squared, divided by the expected value for each cell. This calculation measures the extent to which the observed frequencies in the table differ from those that would be expected if the hypothesis of no association were true. The result of the formula is the absolute value of the divergence between the observed and expected values.

When the results of this calculation are interpreted, the larger the differences between the observed and expected frequencies, the larger the chi-square value. chi-square values can run from 0 into the hundreds. Chi-square will be 0 if all observed and expected values are equal. In the example from Table 5-1, chi-square would be calculated as shown in **Figure 5-2**. Here, all we have done is to calculate delta $(f_o - f_e)$ for each cell in the table, square that value, divide by f_e for that cell, and then sum all of those scores.

$$\chi^2 = \sum \frac{(f_o - f_e)^2}{f_e}$$

$$= \frac{(68 - 68.7)^2}{68.7} + \frac{(168 - 167.3)^2}{167.3} + \frac{(31 - 30.3)^2}{30.3} + \frac{(73 - 73.7)^2}{73.7}$$

$$= \frac{(-0.7)^2}{68.7} + \frac{(0.7)^2}{167.3} + \frac{(0.7)^2}{30.3} + \frac{(-0.7)^2}{73.7}$$

$$= \frac{0.49}{68.7} + \frac{0.49}{167.3} + \frac{0.49}{30.3} + \frac{0.49}{73.7}$$

$$= 0.0071 + 0.0029 + 0.0162 + 0.0066$$

$$= 0.0328$$

Figure 5-2   Calculation of a Chi-square

Computing a chi-square in this manner provides a value for the likelihood of the data arrangement occurring by *chance*. But a method of interpreting this value is needed. This is accomplished by determining the degrees of freedom for the variables and making comparisons with a table of chi-square values.

The next step, then, is to determine the degrees of freedom for the bivariate table. Calculating the *degrees of freedom*, denoted by df, is a statistical method of compensating for error that arises when samples are used rather than populations. In descriptive analyses, it is also a compensation for small data sets, where some of the data values may have occurred by chance even if not all of the data values did. Since researchers can rarely be certain of the accuracy of all of the values, they must compensate for differences between the data drawn and the true nature of the distribution, even assuming it is a population. Degrees of freedom are calculated by the number of rows minus 1 times the number of columns minus 1. For a 2×2 table, the degrees of freedom are $(2 - 1)(2 - 1)$, or 1.

The last element of chi-square to be determined before consulting the table is the level of confidence, or statistical significance, desired to make a conclusion about the data. In other words, how sure do we want to be that the relationship does not occur by chance? In statistical analyses, two levels of statistical significance are used most often: 95% and 99%. These mean that there is a 95% or a 99% probability that the relationship between the variables did not occur by chance (and a corresponding 5% or 1% chance that it did).

To use these three pieces of information, look at Appendix A. You select the row that has the degrees of freedom for the table being examined—in this case it is 1. Then select the column that contains the desired level of significance. Where the row and column intersect is the *critical value* of the χ^2 (chi-squared). If we want to be 95% sure, we select the third column, corresponding to 0.95.

If the *obtained value* of χ^2 is greater than the *critical value*, then the null hypothesis can be rejected and it can be concluded that there is a statistically significant relationship. If the *obtained value* is less than the *critical value*, then we fail to reject the null hypothesis, and it can be concluded that the relationship may have occurred by chance.

In Appendix A under the 0.95 probability and at 1 degree of freedom, there is a value of 3.841. This means that, for 1 degree of freedom, distributions that have a chi-square value of 3.841 or more would, over time, occur by chance only about 5 times in 100. We could be confident, then, that a decision based on this value would be correct 95% of the time (and would be wrong 5 times in 100). The *critical value* in this case, 3.841, is definitely larger than the 0.0328 calculated using the chi-square formula (the *obtained value*). We therefore fail to reject the null hypothesis and conclude that the difference between the observed values and expected values occurs by chance.

It is not necessary to calculate a chi-square by hand anymore; statistical packages do that for you. The printout in **Table 5-4** shows only the chi-square portion of an SPSS output for the data in Table 5-1.

	Value	df	Asymp. Sig. (2-sided)	Exact Sig. (2-sided)	Exact Sig. (1-sided)
Pearson chi-square	0.035	1	0.853		
Continuity correction	0.003	1	0.955		
Likelihood ratio	0.034	1	0.853		
Fisher's exact test				0.897	0.475
Linear-by-linear association	0.034	1	0.853		
N of valid cases	340				

Table 5-4   Chi-square Output from SPSS

Box 5-1 How Do You Do That?

Obtaining Chi-Square in SPSS

1. Open a data set such as one provided at go.jblearning.com/Walker.

   a. Start SPSS.

   b. Select File, then Open, then Data.

   c. Select the file you want to open, then select Open.

2. Once the data is visible, select Analyze, then Descriptive Statistics, then Cross-tabs.

3. Select the variable you wish to include as your dependent variable and press the ▶ next to the Row(s) window.

4. Select the variable you wish to include as your independent variable and press the ▶ next to the Column(s) window.

5. Select the Cells button and check any of the boxes for information you may want in your crosstab. For a crosstab with full information, select Observed, Expected, Row, Column, and Total; then press Continue.

6. Select the Format button, and check the box marked Descending.

7. Select the Statistics button at the bottom of the window.

8. Check the box next to Chi-square. You can check the box next to one of the Ordinal measures if you have ordinal level data (see below and Chapter 6).

9. Select Continue, then OK.

10. An output window should appear containing a distribution similar in format to Table 5-4.

In this table, the chi-square value is the same as that obtained in the calculation in Figure 5-2 (0.0328 in Figure 5-2; 0.035 in Table 5-4). However, the obtained value of chi-square is not the important piece of information for evaluating the relationship. With this kind of output, the important piece of information is the significance of the Pearson (SPSS nomenclature for the Pearson chi-square). The goal is essentially the same as above, except in reverse. Whereas we would use 90%, 95%, 99%, and so forth in the table to establish the level of significance, here we want to use 0.05, or 0.01, depending on how sure we want to be. If the number in the Significance column is greater than the desired value, we fail to reject the null hypothesis; if the output value is equal to or less than our desired cutoff value, we reject the null hypothesis. In this case, the output value (0.853) far exceeds any desired value (either 0.05 or 0.01), so we fail to reject the null hypothesis.

Requirements for Using Chi-square

Chi-square is a very powerful procedure for determining the statistical significance of a relationship. There are requirements, however, for its acceptable use.

First, the N for the crosstab should be at least 5 times the number of cells. This ensures that there is ample data from which to draw conclusions concerning the relationship. It would not be desirable to have 30 cells in a table and an N of only 10 because most of the cells would be blank, making it impossible to interpret the data.

In the example in Table 5-1, the sample size should be at least 20 (4 cells $\times$ 5 = 20). Since this data set has an N of 340, this requirement is met. If the N does not exceed 5 times the number of cells, it is possible to analyze the data by using the *Yates correction* (1934) for 2 $\times$ 2 tables or *Fisher's exact test* (1922) for larger tables. These are two statistics that compensate for small N values and essentially make it more difficult to reject the null hypothesis by lowering the obtained χ^2 value. SPSS does this automatically, however, so we will not go into the calculations here.

The second requirement of chi-square is that 80% of the cells have expected frequencies greater than 5. Chi-square operates from the difference between observed and expected frequencies. If there are a large number of cells with expected frequencies less than 5, it makes any calculations less reliable. For example, in research including race, it is sometimes unwise to include some racial categories because there may or may not be any people of that race in the sample chosen. Because there can be such small observed or expected frequencies, the probability of an observed frequency occurring by *chance* is fairly large. If more than 20% of the cells of a table contain this kind of data, it can cause the significance testing to be unstable. Whereas a sample size of at least 5 times the number of cells helps ensure there are an adequate number of data points for the calculations, the 80% rule helps ensure that the frequencies are sufficiently spread out in the table to make it useful for analysis. For example, even with a sample size of 300, it would be no help if all of the values were in two cells of a 4×4 table. Like the requirement above, if this rule is violated in SPSS analyses, Fisher's exact test is automatically used. It is also a common practice to collapse categories if this requirement is violated. This means that if there are five categories in a table and one has a very small expected or observed frequency, two of the categories can be combined to boost the observed and expected frequencies.

The third requirement of chi-square is mutually exclusive and exhaustive categories. This is important because there is the assumption that the variables are independent. If the variables are measuring the same phenomena, then the significance of the relationship is corrupted. Additionally, if there is not exhaustion of categories, then the table will be incomplete or the variable will not be correctly measured, making calculations unreliable. These important properties can be shown using the bivariate table construction outlined in Chapter 4. There, the frequencies of two variables were placed in categories with one variable represented in the rows of the table and another variable in the columns of the table. To properly fill in the cells, each joint frequency must fit into only one cell. If the attributes of one variable were such that they could fit into two of the three columns, then it would be difficult or impossible to determine the proper column for the data. Furthermore, if the variable is not completely exhaustive, even after all of the joint frequencies have been placed in the table, the variable will still not be accurately measured.

Limitations of Chi-square

Although chi-square is a valuable tool for determining the existence of a statistically significant relationship, it is not without its problems. There are at least three limitations that must be considered when using chi-square as a measure of existence.

First, chi-square can determine if two variables are significantly related, but little else. It does not address whether the relationship is meaningful or what the nature of the relationship might be. As a result, it is generally considered more of a starting point than an end unto itself.

Second, chi-square is heavily influenced by sample size. This is a kind of a Catch-22. One of the requirements of chi-square is that it have a fairly large N; otherwise it is not reliable as a test of independence. If the N is much larger than what is required for accurate results, however, it quickly reaches a point where almost any association between the variables will show up as significant.

Third, the final limitation of chi-square is true of all hypothesis tests—that the alternative hypothesis is not supported by rejection of the null hypothesis. The fact that we can reject the null hypothesis (that there is no relationship between the variables) does not support the contention that a relationship definitely exists. Additional statistical analyses are required to further examine the strength of the relationship between the variables, as discussed in Chapter 6.

5-3   Tests of Existence for Ordinal and Interval Level Data

Chi-square is the preferred measure of existence for nominal and ordinal level variables. If an ordinal level variable has enough categories that it can be considered "fully ordered" (typically more than five categories), these *Spearman's rho* (also known as *Spearman's correlation*) can be used to determine the statistical significance of the relationship. It is also possible to determine the existence of interval and ratio level data by using Pearson's *r*. We end this chapter with these two measures.

Using Pearson's *r*, we can make statements of rejecting the null hypothesis of no difference in the values of the two variables. Using Spearman's correlation, however, only allows us to reject the null hypothesis concerning differences in the ranks of the values for the two variables.

We will not calculate the values of Spearman's rho or Pearson's *r* here because the typical method of examining these statistics is with a statistical package. Further, both Spearman's rho and Pearson's *r* are measures of the strength of a relationship and are discussed in much greater detail in Chapter 6. Here we just identify how to determine the statistical significance of fully ordered ordinal or interval and ratio variables from an SPSS printout.

The output from SPSS for ordinal and interval analyses is shown in **Table 5-5** (data drawn from skewed interval variables is not shown). The numbers in the Value column will be explained in Chapter 6. More important for the topic at hand are the values in the Approx. Sig. column. These values show that the relationship between the variables is at the 0.664 or 0.789 level of significance. A nonsignificant finding here supports an argument that the measure of the strength value (0.087 for Pearson's *r* and 0.140 for Spearman's correlation) is a product of chance and that the same relationship may not hold if examined in other groups.

Symmetric Measures				
	Value	**Asymp. Std. Error**	**Approx. *T***	**Approx. Sig.**
Ordinal by ordinal: Spearman correlation	0.140	0.287	0.448	0.664
Interval by interval: Pearson's *r*	0.087	0.251	0.275	0.789
N of valid cases	12			

Table 5-5   SPSS Printout of Ordinal and Interval Significance Output

5-4   Conclusion

In this chapter, we introduced methods of testing the existence of a relationship. The discussion proceeded from methods of determining if any relationship exists to procedures for determining the statistical significance for each level of data. This is generally considered the first step in the process of bivariate analysis. If the relationship between the two variables is significant, it is generally acceptable to continue with other analyses to determine the strength, direction, and nature of the data, which are discussed in Chapters 6 and 7. If the relationship between the two variables is not significant, the researcher must decide whether to proceed with other analyses.

5-5   Equations in This Chapter

Delta:

$$\Delta = (f_{o11} - f_{e11}), (f_{o12} - f_{e12}), \ldots$$

Chi-square:

$$\chi^2 = \sum \frac{(f_o - f_e)^2}{f_e}$$

Degrees of freedom for chi-square:

$$df = (\text{number of rows} - 1) \times (\text{number of columns} - 1)$$

5-6   For Further Reading

Conover, W. J. Some reasons for not using the Yates continuity correction on a 2 × 2 contingency table. *Journal of the American Statistical Association*, June 1967, *69*(346), 374–376.

Fisher, R. A. On the interpretation of χ^2 from contingency tables, and the calculation of *P*. *Journal of the Royal Statistical Society*, 1922, *85*, 87–94.

Goodman, L. A., & Kruskal, W. H. Measures of association for cross classifications III: Approximate sampling theory. *Journal of the American Statistical Association*, 1963, *58*, 302, 310–364.

Grizzle, J. E. Continuity correction in the χ^2 test for 2 × 2 tables. *The American Statistician*, October 1967, *21*(4), 28–32.

Pearson, E. S. The choice of a statistical test illustrated on the interpretation of data classed in a 2 × 2 table. *Biometrika*, January 1947, *37*, 139–167.

Pearson, K. On the criterion that a given system of deviations from the probable in the case of a correlated system of variables is such that it can be reasonably supposed to have arisen from random sampling. *The London, Edinburg, and Dublin Philosophical Magazine and Journal of Science*, 1900, *50*, 157–175.

Plackett, R. L. The continuity correction in 2 × 2 tables. *Biometrika*, December, 1964, *51*, 327–337.

Spearman, C. The proof and measurement of association between two things. *American Journal of Psychology*, 1904, *15*, 72–101.

Starmer, C. F., Grizzle, J. E., & Sen, P. K. Comment. *Journal of the American Statistical Association*, June 1967, *69*(346), 376–378.

Yates, F. Contingency tables involving small numbers and the χ^2 test. *Journal of the Royal Statistical Society*, 1934, Ser. B Supp. *1*:2, 217–235.

5-7   Exercises

1. For the data and tables below:

   a. Calculate epsilon.

   b. Calculate delta.

   c. Calculate chi-square.

   d. Determine the degrees of freedom.

   e. Determine if the relationship is significant by comparing your chi-square value to the appropriate value in Appendix A.

Victim by Sex

Sex	1 Male	2 Female	Total
Victim			
2 Yes	20	37	57
1 No	27	48	75
	47	85	132

Crimes per Month	Income, $
15	18,000
5	21,000
15	23,000
10	22,000
10	25,000
5	14,000

Crimes per Month	Income, $
20	23,000
20	46,000
5	15,000
5	17,000
15	24,000
15	18,000
15	21,000
15	31,000
20	52,000
7	21,000
7	17,000
20	48,000
20	45,000
10	19,000

f. In the spaces below, construct an ordinal bivariate table for *crimes per month* (dependent variable) and *income* (independent variable). For crimes per month, use the categories "10 and less" and "greater than 10." For income level, use the categories "$21,000 and more" and "less than $21,000."

_____   by   _____

_____   _____

_____ _____   _____ _____

_____ _____   _____ _____

_____   _____ _____

2. For the following tables, determine the appropriate measure of existence and interpret what it means for the existence of a relationship between the two variables.

VICT_Y_N Recoded VICTIM to yes and no * RACE Race of Respondent Crosstabulation						
			RACE Race of respondent			**Total**
			1 Black	**2 White**	**3 Other**	
VICT_Y_N Recoded VICTIM to Yes and No	**2 No**	Count	101	128	2	231
		Expected Count	99.2	129.0	2.8	231.0
		% within VIC_T_Y_N	43.7	55.4	0.9	100.0
		% within RACE	70.6	68.8	50.0	69.4
		% of Total	30.3	38.4	0.6	69.4
	1 Yes	Count	42	58	2	102
		Expected Count	43.8	57.0	1.2	102.0
		% within VIC_T_Y_N	41.2	56.9	2.0	100.0
		% within RACE	29.4	31.2	50.0	30.6
		% of Total	12.6	17.4	0.6	30.6
Total		Count	143	186	4	333
		Expected Count	143.0	186.0	4.0	333.0
		% within VIC_T_Y_N	42.9	55.9	1.2	100.0
		% within RACE	100.0	100.0	100.0	100.0
		% of Total	42.9	55.9	1.2	100.0

Table 5-6   Victim/race respondent crosstabulation

	Cases					
	Valid		**Missing**		**Total**	
	N	**Percent**	*N*	**Percent**	*N*	**Percent**
VICT_Y_N Recoded VICTIM to Yes and No * RACE Race of Respondent	333	96.0%	14	4.0%	347	100.0%

Table 5-7   Case Processing Summary

	Value	**df**	**Asymp. Sig. (2-sided)**
Pearson Chi-Square	.840[a]	2	.657
Likelihood Ratio	.785	2	.675
Linear-by-Linear Association	.350	1	.554
N of Valid Cases	333		

[a] 2 cells (33.3%) have expected count less than 5. The minimum expected count is 1.23.

Table 5-8   Chi-Square Tests

			Value	Asymp. Std. Error[a]	Approx. T[b]	Approx. Sig.
Nominal by Nominal	Lambda	Symmetric	.000	.008	.000	1.000
		VICT_Y_N dependent	.000	.020	.000	1.000
		RACE dependent	.000	.000	——[c]	——[c]
	Goodman and Kruskal tau	VICT_Y_N dependent	.003	.006		.658[d]
		RACE dependent	.000	.002		.872[d]
Ordinal by Ordinal	Somers' d	Symmetric	−.029	.054	−.528	.598
		VICT_Y_N dependent	−.027	.050	−.528	.598
		RACE dependent	−.031	.059	−.528	.598

[a] Not assuming the null hypothesis.
[b] Using the asymptotic standard error assuming the null hypothesis.
[c] Cannot be computed because the asymptotic standard error equals zero.
[d] Based on chi-square approximation.

Table 5-9   Directional Measures

		Value	Asymp. Std. Error[a]	Approx. T[b]	Approx. Sig.
Ordinal by Ordinal	Kendall's tau-b	−.029	.055	−.528	.598
	Kendall's tau-c	−.027	.051	−.528	.598
	Gamma	−.062	.118	−.528	.598
	Spearman Correlation	−.029	.055	−.528	.598[c]
Interval by Interval	Pearson's R	−.032	.055	−.591	.555[c]
N of Valid Cases		333			

[a] Not assuming the null hypothesis.
[b] Using the asymptotic standard error assuming the null hypothesis.
[c] Based on normal approximation.

Table 5-10   Symmetric Measures

NEIGH_SF Is your neighborhood safety changing? * COP_OK In your neighborhood, how well do you think the police perform their duties? Crosstabulation

| | | | COP_OK In your neighborhood, how well do you think the police perform their duties? | | | | |
			1 Very Well	2 Average	3 Below Average	4 Not At All	Total
NEIGH_SF Is your neighborhood safety changing?	3 Becoming Less Safe	Count	21	88	45	8	162
		Expected Count	29.2	87.2	39.6	5.9	162.0
		% within NEIGH_SF	13.0	54.3	27.8	4.9	100.0
		% within COP_OK	35.6	50.0	56.3	66.7	49.5
		% of Total	6.4	26.9	13.8	2.4	49.5
	2 Not Changing	Count	21	58	33	2	114
		Expected Count	20.6	16.4	27.9	4.2	114.0
		% within NEIGH_SF	18.4	50.9	28.9	1.8	100.0
		% within COP_OK	35.6	33.0	41.3	16.7	34.9
		% of Total	6.4	17.7	10.1	0.6	34.9
	1 Becoming Safer	Count	17	30	2	2	51
		Expected Count	9.2	27.4	12.5	1.9	51.0
		% within NEIGH_SF	33.3	58.8	3.9	3.9	100.0
		% within COP_OK	28.8	17.0	2.5	16.7	15.6
		% of Total	5.2	9.2	0.6	0.6	15.6
Total		Count	59	176	80	12	327
		Expected Count	59.0	176.0	80.0	12.0	327.0
		% within NEIGH_SF	18.0	53.8	24.5	3.7	100.0
		% within COP_OK	100.0	100.0	100.0	100.0	100.0
		% of Total	18.0	53.8	24.5	3.7	100.0

Table 5-11   Is your neighborhood safety changing?

| | Cases | | | | | |
| | Valid | | Missing | | Total | |
	N	Percent	N	Percent	N	Percent
NEIGH_SF Is your neighborhood safety changing? * COP_OK In your neighborhood, how well do you think the police perform their duties?	327	94.2%	20	5.8%	347	100.0%

Table 5-12   Case Processing Summary

			Value	Asymp. Std. Error[a]	Approx. T[b]	Approx. Sig.
Nominal by Nominal	Lambda	Symmetric	.000	.021	.000	1.000
		NEIGH_SF dependent	.000	.039	.000	1.000
		COP_OK dependent	.000	.000	——[c]	——[c]
	Goodman and Kruskal tau	NEIGH_SF dependent	.026	.010		.010[d]
		COP_OK dependent	.022	.007		.001[d]
Ordinal by Ordinal	Somers' d	Symmetric	.172	.048	3.565	.000
		NEIGH_SF dependent	.171	.048	3.565	.000
		COP_OK dependent	.173	.048	3.565	.000

[a] Not assuming the null hypothesis.
[b] Using the asymptotic standard error assuming the null hypothesis.
[c] Cannot be computed because the asymptotic standard error equals zero.
[d] Based on chi-square approximation.

Table 5-13   Directional Measures

		Value	Asymp. Std. Error[a]	Approx. T[b]	Approx. Sig.
Ordinal by Ordinal	Kendall's tau-b	.172	.048	3.565	.000
	Kendall's tau-c	.158	.044	3.565	.000
	Gamma	.279	.076	3.565	.000
	Spearman Correlation	.192	.053	3.518	.000[c]
Interval by Interval	Pearson's R	.201	.053	3.692	.000[c]
N of Valid Cases		327			

[a] Not assuming the null hypothesis.
[b] Using the asymptotic standard error assuming the null hypothesis.
[c] Based on normal approximation.

Table 5-14   Symmetric Measures

		DELINQ Delinquent Incidents for the Census Tract	**BOARDED** Boarded Up Housing Units	**OWNOCCUP** Owner Occupied Housing Units	**JUVENILE** Proportion of Juveniles	**POPCHANG** Population Change, 1980–1990
DELINQ Delinquent Incidents for the Census Tract	Pearson Correlation Sig. (2-tailed) N	1 . 45	−.482** .001 45	−.004 .981 45	.339* .023 45	−.011 .941 45
BOARDED Boarded Up Housing Units	Pearson Correlation Sig. (2-tailed) N	−.482** .001 45	1 . 45	−.234 .122 45	.029 .848 45	−.222 .143 45
OWNOCCUP Owner Occupied Housing Units	Pearson Correlation Sig. (2-tailed) N	−.004 .981 45	−.234 .122 45	1 . 45	.752** .000 45	.323* .030 45
JUVENILE Proportion of Juveniles	Pearson Correlation Sig. (2-tailed) N	.339* .023 45	.029 .848 45	.752** .000 45	1 . 45	.436** .003 45
POPCHANG Population Change, 1980–1990	Pearson Correlation Sig. (2-tailed) N	−.011 .941 45	−.222 .143 45	.323* .030 45	.436** .003 45	1 . 45

**Correlation is significant at the 0.01 level (2-tailed).
*Correlation is significant at the 0.05 level (2-tailed).

Table 5-15   Correlations

3. For the tables above, examine the significance values for Pearson's r and Spearman's correlation and discuss what that would mean for the existence of a relationship if these two variables were fully ordered, ordinal, or interval and ratio level.

Chapter 6
Measures of the Strength of a Relationship

Learning Objectives

- Understand the strength of association between two variables.
- Explain an association from a table of joint frequencies.
- Understand a proportional reduction of errors.
- Understand the difference between symmetric and asymmetric measures.
- Calculate the strength of association for nominal, ordinal, interval, and ratio level data.
- Interpret the strength of association for using lambda, Somers' d, Spearman's rho, and Pearson's r.
- Explain and interpret a correlation matrix.
- Understand the coefficient of determination.

Key Terms

asymmetric
causation
degree of association
lambda
measure of association
Pearson's r

proportional reduction of error
Somers' d
Spearman's rho
strength of association
symmetric

In addition to determining the existence of a relationship, it is important to know the *strength of the association*. This is sometimes called the *degree of association*. This dimension, along with the direction and nature of the association, is often termed a *measure of association*. It warrants repeating at this point that the measure of the strength of an association between two variables is based on the assumption that we are dealing with the entire population of the object of study and not a sample taken from the population. These remain, then, *descriptive* statistical procedures rather than inferential ones.

6-1   What Is an Association?

For nominal and ordinal level data, the goal of a measure of the strength of an association is a process called *proportional reduction of errors*. This is a process of calculating how much better your prediction would be of the value of a dependent variable with knowledge of some independent variable over knowledge of the dependent variable alone.

Table 6-1 shows the joint frequencies and probability of occurrence for the data in Table 6-2. Here, the joint probability of occurrence (total percent) is shown in parentheses. If you were asked to predict the category of D (the dependent variable) for a case drawn at random, knowing nothing about I (the independent variable), which category would you pick? You might pick D_1 because its marginal total is 177 (the modal category) whereas D_2 is only 161. In this case, you have a 52.3% chance of being right with D_1 versus a 47.7% chance of being right with D_2. Alternatively, the probability of getting an error in predicting D_1 is 47.7%, which is calculated by subtracting the probability of being right from 1.

	I_1	I_2	Total
D_1	44	133	177
	(0.13)	(0.399)	(0.523)
D_2	60	101	161
	(0.178)	(0.299)	(.477)
Total	104	234	338
	(0.308)	(0.692)	(1.00)

Table 6-1   Table of Joint Frequencies and Probability of Occurrence

What if you are asked to predict the category of D and are told the category of I from which the case will be drawn? If it will be drawn from I_1, then you would probably choose D_2. Why? The reason is that under the I_1 condition, the case has a higher probability of being drawn from D_2 (60/104, or 57.7%) than from D_1 (44/104, or 42.3%).

With a simple formula of dividing this value (60) by the column total (104), we can determine the chances of error in choosing a category of D with knowledge of I. It is 57.7%. In this example, cell D_2 / I_1 contains 60 of a possible 104 responses for the category of I_1. This means that cell D_2 / I_1 contains 57.7% of the cases in I_1 and cell D_1 / I_1 contains 42.3% of those cases. The probability of getting a correct answer, then, is 57.7%; and the probability of making an error is 42.3%. Notice that, in the first example, when you knew nothing about I and were attempting to correctly predict the category of D, the probability of being wrong was 47.7%. Knowing the category of I, however, reduced the chance of error to 42.3%. We can say, then, that there was a 5.5% reduction of errors associated with knowing information about I. This is the proportional reduction of errors.

6-2   Nominal Level Data

At the nominal level, the function of a measure of association is to predict the mode or category of the dependent variable with knowledge gained from the independent variable. If you were asked to determine whether a person chosen at random was criminal and no other information was available, you would simply have to guess. If given information about the characteristics of that person, however, you could certainly improve the guess. For example, it is well supported in research that more men than women commit crimes. If you knew whether the person was a man or a woman, it would improve the prediction over simply guessing.

A measure of association allows improvement even beyond that. For example, if you knew the criminal history of the person, you would probably want to predict that any person chosen with a prior record of criminal behavior was criminal and any person without a record was not since research has shown that more people are recidivists than commit new crimes. What you have done here is to predict the category of criminal or noncriminal (dependent variable) with knowledge of the criminal history of the person (independent variable). That is the goal of most measures of association, especially at the nominal level.

Lambda

The most popular measure of association at the nominal level is *lambda* (symbolized by λ). Lambda can be defined as follows:

> An *asymmetric* measure of association which measures the proportional reduction in errors made in predicting modal values or categories of a dependent variable Y when information about an independent variable X is used.

This definition has several important parts.

First, it is *asymmetric*. This means that it predicts the dependent variable based on information from the independent variable. In other words, instead of simply determining that there is some relationship between the variables, an asymmetric measure indicates how knowledge of a particular variable (generally the independent variable) would aid in reducing errors in predicting categories of the dependent variable. This is different from a *symmetric* measure, which indicates the strength of an association but does not determine which variable is better able to predict the other. For lambda, it is possible to be able to predict one variable (Y) with information about the other (X), but not be able to predict anything about the second variable (X) with information about the first (Y).

Lambda is also a *proportional reduction of error* (PRE) measure. In the example above, it is possible to calculate from several tries how many times a person would be right and wrong in predicting the criminality of a person with no additional knowledge. We could then calculate how many times a person would be right and wrong in predicting the criminality of a person with the additional knowledge of the criminal history of the person. These two values could then be placed in the formula discussed above to determine the probability of getting a correct answer. For example, with no knowledge at all about the person, all you could do is to guess about the criminality of the person. On average, you might be correct 50% of the time. Knowledge about the criminal history of the person, however, significantly increases the probability of being correct. For example, if you knew that 75% of the people in the study who had criminal histories were currently under arrest for a crime, you could use the following formula to determine the improvement in prediction.

$$\frac{50}{75} = 0.666$$

This means that you would improve your probability of a correct prediction by almost 67% with the additional knowledge of the criminal history of the person. This ratio shows what proportion of error has been reduced by knowing the criminal history of the person. Since lambda is asymmetric and a PRE, it can be said to measure how much error is reduced when a value of X is used to predict a value of Y as opposed to not using X in the prediction.

There are several ways to calculate lambda. We will use a computation model that essentially examines how much error would result from the crosstab data with no information minus the amount of error that would result with information about the independent variable and those two values divided by the amount of error resulting from no information. An SPSS printout showing measures of the strength of association is seen in **Table 6-2**. This formula for lambda can be used with this data to show how lambda would be calculated. This calculation is shown in **Figure 6-1** and results in a computational formula for lambda where $E_1 = [N - $ largest row total $(R_l)]$ and $E_2 = \Sigma($each column total $C_t - $ largest cell frequency $f_i)$. This is then divided by E_1

Is crime a serious enough problem that you have considered moving in the past 12 months? * Recoded VICTIM to yes and no Crosstabulation			Recoded VICTIM to Yes and No		
			Yes	No	Total
CRIM_SER Is crime a serious enough problem that you have considered moving in the past 12 months?	**No**	Count	60	101	161
		Expected Count	49.5	111.5	161.0
		% within CRIM_SER	37.3	62.7	100.0
		% within Recoded VICTIM	57.7	43.2	47.6
		% of Total	17.8	29.9	47.6
	Yes	Count	44	133	177
		Expected Count	54.5	122.5	177.0
		% within CRIM_SER	24.9	75.1	100.0
		% within Recoded VICTIM	42.3	56.8	52.4
		% of Total	13.0	39.3	52.4
Total		Count	104	234	338
		Expected Count	104.0	234.0	338.0
		% within CRIM_SER	30.8	69.2	100.0
		% within Recoded VICTIM	100.0	100.0	100.0
		% of Total	30.8	69.2	100.0

Chi-Square Tests

	Value	df	Asymp. Sig. (2-sided)	Exact Sig. (2-sided)	Exact Sig. (1-sided)
Pearson Chi-Square	6.094[b]	1	.014		
Continuity Correction[a]	5.525	1	.019		
Likelihood Ratio	6.103	1	.013		
Fisher's Exact Test				.018	.009
Linear-by-Linear Association	6.076	1	.014		
N of Valid Cases	338				

[a] Computed only for a 2 × 2 table

[b] 0 cells (0.0%) have expected count less than 5. The minimum expected count is 49.54.

Directional Measures

			Value	Asymp. Std. Error[a]	Approx. T[b]	Approx. Sig.
Nominal by Nominal	Lambda	Symmetric	.060	.037	1.575	.115
		CRIM_SER dependent	.099	.060	1.575	.115
		VICTIM dependent	.000	.000	—[c]	—[c]
	Goodman and Kruskal tau	CRIM_SER dependent	.018	.014		.014[d]
		VICTIM dependent	.018	.014		.014[d]

[a] Not assuming the null hypothesis.

[b] Using the asymptotic standard error assuming the null hypothesis.

[c] Cannot be computed because the asymptotic standard error equals zero.

[d] Based on chi-square approximation.

Table 6-2   SPSS Output for Lambda

again. In this example, N is 338, so the first set of numbers in the formula would be 338 minus the largest row total for the table (which is 177 from Yes). The second set of calculations takes the column total and subtracts the largest cell frequency. The first column has a total of 104, and the largest cell frequency is 60. The second column has a column total of 234, and the largest cell frequency is 133. When all of these calculations are completed, as shown here, the result is 0.09938. This means that we would be able to reduce the number of errors in predicting whether a person considered moving in the past 12 months by about 10% with knowledge of whether he or she had been a victim. Notice also that this is the same value in the lambda portion of the printout in Table 6-2 where whether the person considered moving is the dependent variable.

$$\lambda = \frac{(N - R_l) - \Sigma(C_t - f_l)}{N - R_l}$$

$$= \frac{(338 - 177) - \Sigma(44 + 101)}{338 - 177}$$

$$= \frac{(338 - 177) - \Sigma 44 + 101}{338 - 177}$$

$$= \frac{161 - 145}{161}$$

$$= 0.09938$$

Figure 6-1   Formula and Calculation for Lambda

But is this a good number or not? Lambda has a range of values from 0 to 1. A value of 0 means no strength—the independent variable has no ability to reduce the number of errors in predicting the categories of the dependent variable. A lambda of 1 means a perfect association—the additional knowledge of the independent variable allows correct prediction of the dependent variable every time. In the example above, lambda was 0.099. This is certainly closer to 0 than to 1, indicating this is not a very strong association.

You probably noticed in Table 6-2 that there are three values of lambda for the bivariate relationship of whether a person had been victimized in the previous year and his or her decision to move. The symmetric value is a combination of the two asymmetric values that follow and is little more than the average of the two. The next two values are the asymmetric measures of the two possible lambdas: one with moving dependent and one with victim dependent. To facilitate the greatest degree of flexibility and interpretation, SPSS provides asymmetric lambda values for both variables as dependent. In this case, the person's consideration of moving is the dependent variable; its categories are in the rows of the table. The lambda value here is 0.09938, the same as in the calculations above. This means that there is almost a 10% reduction in errors in predicting whether a person considered moving with knowledge of whether the person had been a victim of crime in the previous year. Notice also that lambda, when attempting to predict victimization with knowledge of consideration of moving, is 0. This means that in trying to predict victimization, knowing whether a person had considered moving is no better than not knowing that information. This makes intuitive sense; there is no reason why information on whether a person had considered moving should have any bearing on whether he or she was victimized. Being victimized might influence a person's decision to move, but moving does not influence whether a person is victimized. Also note that the symmetric measure is less than the asymmetric with a decision to move dependent but more than with a victim dependent. This is so because this calculation takes both asymmetric measures into account.

Box 6-1   How Do You Do That?

Measures of Strength of an Association with Crosstabs

Note: The procedures outlined below are for use with a crosstab. If you are analyzing interval or ratio level data without a crosstab, see the box in the section of this chapter on Pearson's *r*.

1. Open a data set such as one provided at go.jblearning.com/Walker.
    a. Start SPSS.
    b. Select File, then Open, then Data.
    c. Select the file you want to open, then select Open.
2. Once the data is visible, select Analyze, then Descriptive Statistics, then Crosstabs.
3. Select the variable you wish to include as your dependent variable, and press the *triars* next to the Row(s) window.
4. Select the variable you wish to include as your independent variable and press the *triars* next to the Column(s) window.
5. Select the Cells button and check any of the boxes for information you may want in your crosstab. For a crosstab with full information, select Observed, Expected, Row, Column, and Total; then press Continue.
6. Select the Format button, and check the box marked Descending.
7. Select the Statistics button at the bottom of the window.
8. Check the box next to the appropriate measure of strength, as outlined in this chapter (Lambda for nominal level data, Somers' *d* for partially ordered ordinal level data, or Correlations for fully ordered ordinal level data.
9. Select Continue, then select OK.
10. An output window should appear containing output similar in format to Tables 6-2 and 6-3, and Figures 6-2 and 6-3.

6-3   Ordinal Level Data

Ordinal level measures of association are somewhat more powerful than nominal measures because they can indicate both the strength of the association and the direction. For full use of the ordinal level measures of association, both variables should be ordinal, dichotomized nominal, or categorized interval.

With ordinal level data, the goal is to predict the *rank order of pairs of scores* instead of the modal value. The "pairs of scores" are where categories of a dependent variable such as high, medium, or low potential to succeed in school are compared to categories of an independent variable such as upper-, middle-, or lower-class socioeconomic status. Specifically, the function is to determine whether the rank order of cases of one variable is useful in predicting the rank order of cases of the other variable.

If the knowledge of the rank of cases of one variable perfectly predicts the rank of cases of the other variable, the association is said to be perfect and the measure of association will equal 1. If the knowledge of the rank of cases of one variable is of no use in predicting the rank of cases on the other variable, then the measure of association will equal 0, showing that nothing is gained by adding information from the independent variable.

There are five possible situations for the ranks of variables. Concordant pairs, called N_s, are pairs that are ranked in the same order on both variables. Using the example above, a person might be in the low category on socioeconomic status and in the low category in potential to succeed in school. Discordant pairs, called N_d, are pairs that are ranked one way on one variable and the opposite way on the other variable. Using the example above, a person might be in the low category on socioeconomic status and in the high category in potential to succeed in school. Pairs can be tied (have the same rank) on the dependent variable but not on the independent variable, called T_y. Pairs can also be tied on the independent variable but not on the dependent variable, called T_x. Finally, pairs can be tied on both variables, called T_{xy}.

These types of pairs are important for ordinal measures of the strength of association. The difference between the N_s and N_d pairs determines whether the relationship is positive or negative. If there are more N_s than N_d pairs, the relationship is positive. If there are more N_d than N_s pairs, the relationship is negative.

Measures of association for ordinal level variables range from −1 to 0 to +1. Positive values indicate a positive relationship; negative values indicate an inverse, or negative, relationship. The more N_s (or N_d) pairs there are, the closer to 1 (or −1) the value will be. If there is the same number of N_s and N_d pairs, the measure of association is 0. Also, depending upon which measure of the strength of association is used, ties may heavily influence the outcome.

There are several options available for analyzing ordinal level data. It is most common to use tau b and c, gamma, or Somers' *d* with partially ordered, ordinal level variables; and Spearman's rho with fully ordered variables. Each of the partially ordered, ordinal level measures of association has the same numerator (top value), which measures the difference between the N_s and N_d pairs. The difference between various measures lies in the denominators. Some of the measures exclude more of the possible ties while other measures do not exclude any. For this chapter, we will focus on Somers' d and Spearman's rho. An example of the different types of measures is shown in **Table 6-3**.

WALK_NIT How often do you walk in your neighborhood at night? *
CRIM_PRB How big a problem is crime? Crosstabulation

			CRIM_PRB How big a problem is crime?			
			1 No Problem	2 Small Problem	3 Big Problem	Total
WALK_NIT How often do you walk in your neighborhood at night?	1 Often	Count	2	2	0	4
		Expected Count	2.7	1.2	0.2	4.0
		% within WALK_NIT	50.0	50.0	0.0	100.0
		% within CRIM_PRB	1.2	2.8	0.0	1.6
		% of Total	0.8	0.8	0.0	1.6
	2 Occasionally	Count	20	13	3	36
		Expected Count	23.9	10.4	1.7	36.0
		% within WALK_NIT	55.6	36.1	8.3	100.0
		% within CRIM_PRB	12.1	18.1	25.0	14.5
		% of Total	8.0	5.2	1.2	14.5
	3 Never	Count	143	57	9	209
		Expected Count	138.5	60.4	10.1	209.0
		% within WALK_NIT	68.4	27.3	4.3	100.0
		% within CRIM_PRB	86.7	79.2	75.0	83.9
		% of Total	57.4	22.9	3.6	83.9
Total		Count	165	72	12	249
		Expected Count	165.0	72.0	12.0	249.0
		% within WALK_NIT	66.3	28.9	4.8	100.0
		% within CRIM_PRB	100.0	100.0	100.0	100.0
		% of Total	66.3	28.9	4.8	100.0

Chi-Square Tests

	Value	df	Asymp. Sig. (2-sided)
Pearson Chi-Square	3.613[a]	4	.461
Likelihood Ratio	3.539	4	.472
Linear-by-Linear Association	2.462	1	.117
N of Valid Cases	249		

[a] 4 cells (44.4%) have expected count less than 5. The minimum expected count is .19.

Table 6-3   SPSS Output for Ordinal Level Measures of Association

Directional Measures

			Value	Asymp. Std. Error[a]	Approx. T[b]	Approx. Sig.
Nominal by Nominal	Lambda	Symmetric	.000	.000	____[c]	____[c]
		WALK_NIT dependent	.000	.000	____[c]	____[c]
		CRIM_PRB dependent	.000	.000	____[c]	____[c]
	Goodman and Kruskal tau	WALK_NIT dependent	.010	.013		.268[d]
		CRIM_PRB dependent	.009	.012		.331[d]
Ordinal by Ordinal	Somers' d	Symmetric	.100	.062	1.578	.115
		WALK_NIT dependent	.079	.050	1.578	.115
		CRIM_PRB dependent	.136	.085	1.578	.115

[a] Not assuming the null hypothesis.
[b] Using the asymptotic standard error assuming the null hypothesis.
[c] Cannot be computed because the asymptotic standard error equals zero.
[d] Based on chi-square approximation.

Symmetric Measures

		Value	Asymp. Std. Error[a]	Approx. T[b]	Approx. Sig.
Ordinal by Ordinal	Kendall's tau-b	.104	.065	1.578	.115
	Kendall's tau-c	.056	.036	1.578	.115
	Gamma	.263	.149	1.578	.115
	Spearman Correlation	.107	.067	1.686	.093[c]
Interval by Interval	Pearson's R	.100	.065	1.574	.117[c]
N of Valid Cases		249			

[a] Not assuming the null hypothesis.
[b] Using the asymptotic standard error assuming the null hypothesis.
[c] Based on normal approximation.

Table 6-3   SPSS Output for Ordinal Level Measures of Association, *continued*

Somers' d

Somers' d is an asymmetric ordinal level measure of association. To be asymmetric, ties on the dependent variable must be taken into account and ties on the independent variable must be excluded. This allows responses on the dependent variable (Y) to remain as long as the independent variable (X) is ranked differently. The formula for Somers' *d* is shown in **Figure 6-2**.

To obtain the number of concordant pairs (N_s) for the data in Table 6-3, we begin in the lower left cell of a table and multiply that value by the sum of all cells above and to the right of it. This process will be repeated for any columns that have values above and to the right (see Figure 6-2). Next, we calculate the number of discordant

$$d_{yx} = \frac{N_s - N_d}{N_s + N_d + T_y}$$

$N_s = [143 \times (13 + 3 + 2 + 0)] + [57 \times (3 + 0)] + [20 \times (2 + 0)] + [13 \times (0)]$

$= (143 \times 18) + (57 \times 3) + (20 \times 2) + (13 \times 0)$

$= 2{,}574 + 171 + 40 + 0$

$= 2{,}785$

$N_d = (9 \times [13 + 20 + 2 + 2)] + [57 \times (20 + 2)] + [3 \times (2 + 2)] + [13 \times (2)]$

$= (9 \times 37) + (57 \times 22) + (3 \times 4) + (13 \times 2)$

$= 333 + 1{,}254 + 12 + 26$

$= 1{,}625$

$T_y = [2 \times (2+0)] + [2 \times (0)] + [20 \times (13 + 3)] + [13 \times (3)] + [143 \times (57 + 9)] + [57 \times (9)]$

$= (2 \times 2) + (2 \times 0) + (20 \times 16) + (13 \times 3) + (143 \times 66) + (57 \times 9)$

$= 4 + 0 + 320 + 39 + 9{,}438 + 513$

$= 10{,}314$

$$d_{yx} = \frac{N_s - N_d}{N_s + N_d + T_y}$$

$$= \frac{2{,}785 - 1{,}625}{2{,}785 + 1{,}625 + 10{,}314}$$

$$= \frac{1{,}160}{14{,}724}$$

$$= 0.07878$$

Figure 6-2   Calculation of Somers' d

pairs (N_d) with the same process; but this time, we begin with the value in the lower right cell of the table and multiply that value by the sum of all cells above and to the left of it. Repeat the process for any columns that have values above and to the left (see Figure 6-2). The final piece of information (T_y) is calculated by multiplying the frequencies in each row by the sum of the frequencies to the right of it and then adding those. Plugging all three values into the formula (see Figure 6-2), we get a d_{yx} value of 0.07878.

Somers' *d* is interpreted in essentially the same way as lambda. Values range from −1 through 0 to +1. In cases where all pairs are concordant, Somers' *d* will be +1; in cases where all pairs are discordant, Somers' *d* will be −1. If there are an equal number of concordant and discordant pairs, Somers' *d* will be 0. For square tables, Somers' *d* will only reach +1 or −1 when all of the values fall on the diagonal. For a rectangular table, Somers' *d* only requires that the values be monotonic. A monotonic relationship exists when the frequencies of the dependent variable move across the table in a stepwise manner, where a single value of the dependent variable does not take more than one value of the independent variable. There can be more than one frequency in a given column, but there cannot be more than one frequency in a given row. In the example above, a Somers' d_{yx} value of 0.07878 indicates there are more concordant pairs than discordant pairs, and the PRE is about 8%. Again, we can conclude this is a very weak relationship.

Spearman's Rho

Ordinal level data that is fully ordered and interval level data that is not normally distributed—a skewed distribution—is generally analyzed using Spearman's rho (often called Spearman's correlation), which is symbolized by r_s. This symmetric statistic measures significance, strength (as in Chapter 5), and direction (in Chapter 7) of the differences in rankings of individuals' scores of the two variables. Spearman's rho is not a PRE measure; however, r_s^2 is a PRE measure. Spearman's rho is simply Pearson's *r* (discussed in the next section) applied to the ranks of data points rather than to the points themselves.

SPSS calculates Spearman's rho differently in different procedures. In the crosstabs procedure, the formula for Pearson's *r* is applied to the ranks of the scores. In others, a specialized Spearman formula is used. Since SPSS uses different formulas, the hand calculations of this statistic will not be shown and the SPSS printout will be used for interpretation.

Like Somer's *d*, Spearman's rho will be +1 if the ranks of the variables match perfectly (positive association) and −1 if they are ranked inversely (negative association). If there is no association between the variables (no pattern in the ranking), then Spearman's rho is 0. Anything other than a 0 means there is an association.

The value of Spearman's rho in Table 6-3 is 0.107. This shows a very weak association between the two variables. Squaring this value to achieve a PRE measure accentuates how weak the relationship between the two variables is. We can reduce the errors in predicting the rank of the dependent variable 1%. This is supported by a significance value of 0.093, far above the 0.05 or 0.01 cutoff for statistical significance.

As with any statistical procedure, Spearman's rho has a particular limitation. It is influenced by a large number of ties of the ranks. An integral assumption of this statistic is that there are few or no ties in the data. If there are a large number of ties, Spearman's rho will be reduced.

One last note about ordinal level measures of the strength of an association. Because you are moving into data that can be ordered and has the possibility of being relatively continuous, the nature of the data (which we talk about in Chapter 7) becomes more important. A curvilinear relationship (skewed data) can greatly reduce the value of the measure of association and make the interpretation difficult or erroneous. If the measure of association produces a value lower than expected, it should signal the need to examine the nature of the relationship.

6-4 Interval and Ratio Level Data

If both of the variables are interval or ratio level, it is possible to use the more advanced, interval level statistical analyses to work with them. The real difference between Spearman's rho and Pearson's r is that Spearman's rho measures the monotonicity of a relationship between two variables whereas Pearson's r requires linearity. A relationship may be monotonic, but not necessarily linear.

Although it is often used incorrectly with nominal and ordinal level data, the move to interval level data facilitates advancement to co-relation (correlation) between the variables under examination. PRE measures, up to and including Spearman's rho, cannot provide the level of interpretation about the proportion of variation in one variable explained by change in another variable; they are capable only of addressing the proportional reduction of errors in making predictions of categories or ranks of the variables. Correlation methods, such as those described here, move beyond predicting categories to describing the linear relationship between the variables.

More importantly, analyses at this level support the conclusion that an independent variable might be producing the variations in the dependent variable. The goal of interval level bivariate analysis is to make a better prediction of the exact score of a dependent variable than is possible from the mean of the dependent variable. This is accomplished by using information from the independent variable.

As discussed in Chapter 2, the mean is a good measure of the most typical value of a distribution, given no information other than the fact that a data set is interval level, to predict a score in a set of data. If we can improve the prediction of the mean with information about the independent variable, then the requirements for a proportional reduction in error have been met.

Suppose we made a prediction about where a certain point will fall in a distribution, or on a graph. These we will call Y. By going back and plotting the actual values, we could calculate how well the predictions served as a PRE measure. This is under-taken through the formula for a straight line, which is $Y = a + b(X)$, where Y is the value we want to predict, a is the constant starting point for the line (where it crosses the Y axis), b is the slope of the line (the angle of the line in a graph), and X is the value of the independent variable that corresponds to the dependent variable. With a num-ber of scores, it would be possible to use these calculations to show how well or how poorly the predicted scores matched the actual scores. The goal of this process is to get the best-fitting straight line that summarizes the linear relationship between the values of the two variables. One method of achieving this goal is to use the least-squares method—this is the variance. This method establishes a line in a position where the sum of the squares of distances from each (X, Y) data point to the line is minimized. This straight line summarizes the relationship between the dependent variable Y and the independent variable X. It will not improve every prediction, but it will improve the average prediction. This process can be shown in **Figure 6-3**.

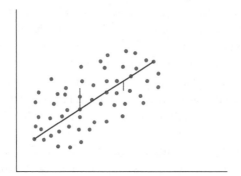

Figure 6-3   Scattergram of Data with Best-Fitting Line Overlay

Here, the data points are clustered in a relatively uniform pattern. A line can be drawn through these data points such that the variance (the sum of the squared dis-tance between each point and the line) is minimized. For example, in Figure 6-3, two of the data points have lines drawn from them to the best-fitting line. If this were completed for each point and the distances summed, it would represent the smallest of the summed distances for any line drawn through the values. This is also a graphical description of the variance. We stress here that this must be a straight line. Curvilinear relationships will always produce lower Pearson's r values, even when a strong rela-tionship exists (as will be further explained in Chapter 7). For this reason, the nature of the relationship must be carefully monitored, and curvilinear relationships trans-formed or otherwise taken into account.

Pearson's r

The way a best-fitting line is used in bivariate analysis is through the Pearson's product moment correlation (or Pearson's r). Pearson's r represents the extent to which the same cases or observations occupy the same relative position on two variables. It can measure the strength of a relationship, examine the existence of the relationship, and determine the direction. Pearson's r is the most widely used measure of association. It requires normally distributed, interval level data. Pearson's r can also be used to examine the relationship between a continuous, interval level variable and a dichotomized variable. Pearson's r can also be used for two dichotomized variables and is called a *phi coefficient* in this instance. Pearson's r typically precludes the use of bivariate tables because there are usually too many values to put in a table format.

The way Pearson's r works is through the least-squares line we just talked about. Pearson's r measures the amount of spread around the least-squares line and the slope of the line. The amount of spread determines the strength of the association. If all of the values are on the line, then there will be a perfect association between the variables—a 1-unit increase in one variable will result in a consistent 1-unit increase in the other variable. If the values are spread such that the best line that can be drawn runs parallel to the X axis, however, it will indicate a 0 correlation.

The formula to calculate Pearson's r is shown in **Figure 6-4**. Although it appears imposing, this is actually not a difficult formula. It is simply summing the values of XY, $X \times Y$, X^2, and Y^2. The top part of Figure 6-4 shows the data for education level and number of crimes for which a person was convicted. Here we have an independent variable (X) that is the education level and a dependent variable (Y) that is crime. The table was developed in Excel and makes the calculations of Pearson's r easy. These values sum to 91 (for X) and 49 (for Y). Multiplying each X and Y together and then adding them produces a value of 499. Squaring each value of X and adding them produces a value of 1,435. Squaring each value of Y and adding them produces a value of 455. Then you just plug these numbers into the formula above. These calculations produce a Pearson r of -0.8214, which indicates a strong relationship.

Interpreting Pearson's r is the same as interpreting other measures of strength. It also has values that fall between ± 1, with $+1$ being a perfect positive relationship and -1 a perfect negative relationship. A Pearson r of 0 generally means there is no relationship, but caution must be exercised to ensure that the relationship is not curvilinear. Low Pearson r values may mean that there is a weak association; it may mean, however, that the relationship is strong, but because it is curvilinear. In this case, the Pearson's r is not a true representation of the relationship.

It is not common for Pearson's r (or Spearman's rho) to be displayed in a crosstab format in SPSS. More typically, they are displayed in what is termed a *correlation matrix*. A correlation matrix is shown in **Table 6-4**.

X Education	Y Crimes	XY	X²	Y²
7	13	91	49	169
4	11	44	16	121
13	9	117	169	81
16	7	112	256	49
10	5	50	100	25
22	3	66	484	9
19	1	19	361	1
ΣX 91	ΣY 49	ΣXY 499	ΣX² 1435	ΣY² 455

$$r = \frac{N\Sigma(XY) - (\Sigma X)(\Sigma Y)}{\sqrt{[N\Sigma(X^2) - (\Sigma X)^2][N\Sigma(Y^2) - (\Sigma Y)^2]}}$$

$$= \frac{7(499) - (91)(49)}{\sqrt{[7(1,435) - (91)^2][7(455) - (49)^2]}}$$

$$= \frac{3,493 - 4,459}{\sqrt{(10,045 - 8,281)(3,185 - 2,401)}}$$

$$= \frac{-966}{\sqrt{(1,764)(784)}}$$

$$= \frac{-966}{\sqrt{1,382,976}}$$

$$= \frac{-966}{1,176}$$

$$= -0.8214$$

Figure 6-4   Calculating Pearson's r

There is nothing different in these numbers, or in their interpretation—only in the way they are presented. The nature of interval level analyses is that they are often a part of an analysis of many variables. In these cases, it is generally not possible to include separate tables because, as discussed above, the data is often too extensive to include in a table. Furthermore, it would be a waste of space to report all combinations of correlation separately in a display such as a crosstab where each value is reported

		DELINQ Delinquent Incidents for the Census Tract	BOARDED Boarded Up Housing Units	OWNOCCUP Owner Occupied Housing Units	JUVENILE Proportion of Juveniles	POPCHANG Population Change, 1980–1990
DELINQ **Delinquent Incidents** **for the Census Tract**	Pearson Correlation Sig. (2-tailed) N	1 . 45	−.482** .001 45	−.004 .981 45	.339* .023 45	−.011 .941 45
BOARDED **Boarded Up** **Housing Units**	Pearson Correlation Sig. (2-tailed) N	−.482** .001 45	1 . 45	−.234 .122 45	.029 .848 45	−.222 .143 45
OWNOCCUP **Owner Occupied** **Housing Units**	Pearson Correlation Sig. (2-tailed) N	−.004 .981 45	−.234 .122 45	1 . 45	.752** .000 45	.323* .030 45
JUVENILE **Proportion of** **Juveniles**	Pearson Correlation Sig. (2-tailed) N	.339* .023 45	.029 .848 45	.752** .000 45	1 . 45	.436** .003 45
POPCHANG **Population Change,** **1980–1990**	Pearson Correlation Sig. (2-tailed) N	−.011 .941 45	−.222 .143 45	.323* .030 45	.436** .003 45	1 . 45

**Correlation is significant at the 0.01 level (2-tailed).
*Correlation is significant at the 0.05 level (2-tailed).

Table 6-4   Correlation Matrix

on a different line or different output. What Table 6-4 shows is the correlation among five variables. Notice that each of these variables is listed across the top of the table and along the side. This allows each variable to be correlated with all other variables. Since each variable is listed twice, if all correlations were included, each correlation would occur twice in the table. For example, the correlation between Delinquency and Boarded up Housing Units (0.01) would show up in the column under Delinquency and the row of Boarded up Housing Units (not shown) and in the column under Boarded up Housing Units and the row of Delinquency (where it does appear). Since there is no need for the correlations to be listed twice, a correlation matrix generally takes the form of one-half of a table, with the scores falling either below the diagonal or above the diagonal. Along the line of the diagonal is a series of values of 1.00. This represents the dividing line between the two sets of correlations. Each of these correlations is 1.00 because it is reporting the correlation between each variable and itself (for example the correlation between population change in the Popchange column and population change in the Popchange row).

Pearson's *r* has another advantage to its analysis that deserves further discussion. Pearson's *r* squared (r^2) is known as the *coefficient of determination*. This tells us about the proportion of the variation in the dependent variable that is accounted for by variation in the independent variable. In Table 6-4, Pearson's *r* was -0.82. Squaring this value makes the coefficient of determination 0.67. This means that 67% of the variation in criminal activity can be explained by the variation in years of school completed. This is actually a very strong relationship for social science data.

This value, and interpretation of correlation and a coefficient of variation, should be undertaken with caution. An often heard phrase in statistics courses is that "correlation does not equal *causation*." This is so because many people conclude, incorrectly, that if two variables are correlated, one must be the *cause* of the other. This is not necessarily true. Research may bring us *closer* to determining the cause, but it is not close enough to be able to draw a causal nexus. A strong and significant correlation definitely supports an argument of causality and should certainly lead to further exploration of the possibility of causation. Other methodological tools such as temporal ordering or eliminating rival causal factors must be used, however, before any notions of causality can be established.

Like other measures of association, Pearson's *r* has limitations. The most serious limitation of Pearson's *r* is that it is highly susceptible to nonnormal data. Curvilinear relationships may show a low strength (and perhaps nonsignificance), even though there may be definite patterns in the data. This will be further addressed in Chapter 7. The significance of Pearson's *r* is also seriously affected by sample size. Weak correlations may be found to be statistically significant when the sample size is large. Additionally, small sample sizes may produce unstable correlations.

6-5 Conclusion

This chapter has introduced methods of testing the strength of a relationship. The discussion builds on Chapter 5 to determine if the relationship found to be statistically significant has any ability to predict values of the dependent variable. This is generally considered the second step in the process of bivariate analysis. This step is necessary because tests of significance do not provide all the needed information. If we obtain a statistically significant χ^2, we can say the two variables are not independent of each other. It does not, however, provide information about the strength of that relationship. We know that statistical relationships that are almost nonexistent can show up as highly statistically significant χ^2 results if the sample size is large. This can delude a researcher into a false sense of accomplishment. Measures of the strength of the association, however, determine the ability to predict (the mode, median, or mean) and add validity to findings. This chapter provided discussions of measures of the strength of an association for nominal, partially ordered ordinal, fully ordered ordinal, and interval and ratio level data. The final parts of measures of association (direction and nature) are discussed next in Chapter 7.

6-6 Equations in This Chapter

Lambda:

$$\lambda = \frac{(N - R_l) - \Sigma(C_t - f_l)}{N - R_l}$$

Pearson's r (Product Moment Correlation):

$$r = \frac{N\Sigma(XY) - (\Sigma X)(\Sigma Y)}{\sqrt{[N\Sigma(X^2) - (\Sigma X)^2][N\Sigma(Y^2) - (\Sigma Y)^2]}}$$

Somers' d:

$$d_{yx} = \frac{N_s - N_d}{N_s + N_d + T_y}$$

6-7 Exercises

For the following tables (the same as used in the exercises in Chapter 5):

1. Determine the level of measurement for each variable.
2. Determine the appropriate measures of the strength of the association and discuss why they were chosen.
3. Make the appropriate calculations for each of the measures of association.
4. Discuss the strength of the relationship and which variable is causing the variation.

VICT_Y_N Recoded VICTIM to Yes and No * RACE Race of Respondent Crosstabulation			RACE Race of respondent			
			1 Black	2 White	3 Other	Total
VICT_Y_N Recoded VICTIM to Yes and No	**2 No**	Count	101	128	2	231
		Expected Count	99.2	129.0	2.8	231.0
		% within VIC_T_Y_N	43.7	55.4	0.9	100.0
		% within RACE	70.6	68.8	50.0	69.4
		% of Total	30.3	38.4	0.6	69.4
	1 Yes	Count	42	58	2	102
		Expected Count	43.8	57.0	1.2	102.0
		% within VIC_T_Y_N	41.2	56.9	2.0	100.0
		% within RACE	29.4	31.2	50.0	30.6
		% of Total	12.6	17.4	0.6	30.6
Total		Count	143	186	4	333
		Expected Count	143.0	186.0	4.0	333.0
		% within VIC_T_Y_N	42.9	55.9	1.2	100.0
		% within RACE	100.0	100.0	100.0	100.0
		% of Total	42.9	55.9	1.2	100.0

Table 6-5   Victim/race respondent crosstabulation

	Cases					
	Valid		Missing		Total	
	N	Percent	N	Percent	N	Percent
VICT_Y_N Recoded VICTIM to yes and no * **RACE** Race of respondent	333	96.0	14	4.0	347	100.0

Table 6-6   Case Processing Summary

	Value	df	Asymp. Sig. (2-sided)
Pearson Chi-Square	.840[a]	2	.657
Likelihood Ratio	.785	2	.675
Linear-by-Linear Association	.350	1	.554
N of Valid Cases	333		

[a] 2 cells (33.3%) have expected count less than 5. The minimum expected count is 1.23.

Table 6-7   Chi Square Summary

			Value	Asymp. Std. Error[a]	Approx. T[b]	Approx. Sig.
Nominal by Nominal	Lambda	Symmetric	.000	.008	.000	1.000
		VICT_Y_N dependent	.000	.020	.000	1.000
		RACE dependent	.000	.000	——[c]	——[c]
	Goodman and Kruskal tau	VICT_Y_N dependent	.003	.006		.658[d]
		RACE dependent	.000	.002		.872[d]
Ordinal by Ordinal	Somers' d	Symmetric	−.029	.054	−.528	.598
		VICT_Y_N dependent	−.027	.050	−.528	.598
		RACE dependent	−.031	.059	−.528	.598

[a] Not assuming the null hypothesis.
[b] Using the asymptotic standard error assuming the null hypothesis.
[c] Cannot be computed because the asymptotic standard error equals zero.
[d] Based on chi-square approximation.

Table 6-8   Directional Measures

		Value	Asymp. Std. Error[a]	Approx. T[b]	Approx. Sig.
Ordinal by Ordinal	Kendall's tau-b	−.029	.055	−.528	.598
	Kendall's tau-c	−.027	.051	−.528	.598
	Gamma	−.062	.118	−.528	.598
	Spearman Correlation	−.029	.055	−.528	.598[c]
Interval by Interval	Pearson's R	−.032	.055	−.591	.555[c]
N of Valid Cases		333			

[a] Not assuming the null hypothesis.
[b] Using the asymptotic standard error assuming the null hypothesis.
[c] Based on normal approximation.

Table 6-9   Symmetric Measures

NEIGH_SF Is your neighborhood safety changing? * COP_OK In your neighborhood, how well do you think the police perform their duties? Crosstabulation

| | | | COP_OK In your neighborhood, how well do you think the police perform their duties? | | | | |
			1 Very Well	2 Average	3 Below Average	4 Not At All	Total
NEIGH_SF Is your neighborhood safety changing?	3 Becoming Less Safe	Count	21	88	45	8	162
		Expected Count	29.2	87.2	39.6	5.9	162.0
		% within NEIGH_SF	13.0	54.3	27.8	4.9	100.0
		% within COP_OK	35.6	50.0	56.3	66.7	49.5
		% of Total	6.4	26.9	13.8	2.4	49.5
	2 Not Changing	Count	21	58	33	2	114
		Expected Count	20.6	16.4	27.9	4.2	114.0
		% within NEIGH_SF	18.4	50.9	28.9	1.8	100.0
		% within COP_OK	35.6	33.0	41.3	16.7	34.9
		% of Total	6.4	17.7	10.1	0.6	34.9
	1 Becoming Safer	Count	17	30	2	2	51
		Expected Count	9.2	27.4	12.5	1.9	51.0
		% within NEIGH_SF	33.3	58.8	3.9	3.9	100.0
		% within COP_OK	28.8	17.0	2.5	16.7	15.6
		% of Total	5.2	9.2	0.6	0.6	15.6
Total		Count	59	176	80	12	327
		Expected Count	59.0	176.0	80.0	12.0	327.0
		% within NEIGH_SF	18.0	53.8	24.5	3.7	100.0
		% within COP_OK	100.0	100.0	100.0	100.0	100.0
		% of Total	18.0	53.8	24.5	3.7	100.0

Table 6-10   Is your neighborhood safety changing?

| | Cases | | | | | |
| | Valid | | Missing | | Total | |
	N	Percent	N	Percent	N	Percent
NEIGH_SF Is your neighborhood safety changing? * **COP_OK** In your neighborhood, how well do you think the police perform their duties?	327	94.2	20	5.8	347	100.0

Table 6-11   Case Processing Summary

			Value	**Asymp. Std. Error**[a]	**Approx. T**[b]	**Approx. Sig.**
Nominal by Nominal	Lambda	Symmetric	.000	.021	.000	1.000
		NEIGH_SF dependent	.000	.039	.000	1.000
		COP_OK dependent	.000	.000	____[c]	____[c]
	Goodman and Kruskal tau	NEIGH_SF dependent	.026	.010		.010[d]
		COP_OK dependent	.022	.007		.001[d]
Ordinal by Ordinal	Somers' d	Symmetric	.172	.048	3.565	.000
		NEIGH_SF dependent	.171	.048	3.565	.000
		COP_OK dependent	.173	.048	3.565	.000

[a] Not assuming the null hypothesis.
[b] Using the asymptotic standard error assuming the null hypothesis.
[c] Cannot be computed because the asymptotic standard error equals zero.
[d] Based on chi-square approximation.

Table 6-12   Directional Measures

		Value	**Asymp. Std. Error**[a]	**Approx. T**[b]	**Approx. Sig.**
Ordinal by Ordinal	Kendall's tau-b	.172	.048	3.565	.000
	Kendall's tau-c	.158	.044	3.565	.000
	Gamma	.279	.076	3.565	.000
	Spearman Correlation	.192	.053	3.518	.000[c]
Interval by Interval	Pearson's R	.201	.053	3.692	.000[c]
N of Valid Cases		327			

[a] Not assuming the null hypothesis.
[b] Using the asymptotic standard error assuming the null hypothesis.
[c] Based on normal approximation.

Table 6-13   Symmetric Measures

5. For each of the combinations of variables in the correlation matrix of Table 6-14, discuss the value of Pearson's r in terms of the strength of the relationship.

		DELINQ Delinquent Incidents for the Census Tract	BOARDED Boarded Up Housing Units	OWNOCCUP Owner Occupied Housing Units	JUVENILE Proportion of Juveniles	POPCHANG Population Change, 1980–1990
DELINQ **Delinquent Incidents** **for the Census Tract**	Pearson Correlation	1	−.482**	−.004	.339*	−.011
	Sig. (2-tailed)	.	.001	.981	.023	.941
	N	45	45	45	45	45
BOARDED **Boarded Up** **Housing Units**	Pearson Correlation	−.482**	1	−.234	.029	−.222
	Sig. (2-tailed)	.001	.	.122	.848	.143
	N	45	45	45	45	45
OWNOCCUP **Owner Occupied** **Housing Units**	Pearson Correlation	−.004	−.234	1	.752**	.323*
	Sig. (2-tailed)	.981	.122	.	.000	.030
	N	45	45	45	45	45
JUVENILE **Proportion of** **Juveniles**	Pearson Correlation	.339*	.029	.752**	1	.436**
	Sig. (2-tailed)	.023	.848	.000	.	.003
	N	45	45	45	45	45
POPCHANG **Population Change,** **1980–1990**	Pearson Correlation	−.011	−.222	.323*	.436**	1
	Sig. (2-tailed)	.941	.143	.030	.003	.
	N	45	45	45	45	45

**Correlation is significant at the 0.01 level (2-tailed).
*Correlation is significant at the 0.05 level (2-tailed).

Table 6-14   Correlations

Chapter 7
Measures of the Direction and Nature of a Relationship

Learning Objectives

- Understand the direction and the nature of association between two variables.
- Explain a positive relationship and a negative relationship.
- Determine the direction of association between two variables using a crosstab and using measures of the strength of an association.
- Explain linearity and monotonicity.
- Determine the nature of association between two variables using a crosstab and using measures of the strength of an association.

Key Terms

best-fitting line
direction
linearity
monotone decreasing
monotone increasing

monotonicity
nature
negative relationship
positive relationship

Obviously, knowing the existence (significance) and strength of an association is important. Two additional pieces of information are also important to a full understanding of a bivariate relationship of ordinal, interval, and ratio level data.

First, it is important to know the *direction* of the relationship. The discussion of concordant and discordant pairs that introduced this concept can be found in

Chapter 6. Here, you will learn how to recognize when high scores on one variable are associated with high scores on the other variable or when high scores are associated with low scores.

The other piece of information concerns the *nature* of the relationship. This builds on the concepts learned in an earlier chapter concerning the form, and it can indicate when the data is arranged in such a manner as to make the bivariate analyses erroneous.

Before we get to the measures of direction and nature, some terminology needs to be discussed. For nominal and ordinal level data, it is generally more accepted to speak of the nature in terms of *monotonicity* than linearity. Monotonicity addresses the general nature (and direction) of the relationship. It shows whether a variable remained the same or shifted in a certain direction with change in a second variable. A *monotone-increasing* relationship is represented by a positive direction and a generally straight line in the table. A *monotone-decreasing* relationship is represented by a negative direction and a generally straight line in the table (a stair step in the table in a negative direction). A relationship with multiple modes or one displaying serious departures from a straight line in a table is generally considered nonmonotonic. Monotonicity is especially important when we examine rectangular tables. It is not possible to establish perfect linearity in these tables because of the way the cells are arranged. In these cases, it is impossible for there to be a straight line of values. It is possible to have a stair step that indicates monotonicity.

7-1   Direction of an Association

Where both of the variables are at least ordinal, the *direction* of the association can be determined. It is not possible to directly measure the direction of nominal level data because the ordering of the categories is arbitrary. Male and female could be coded as 1 and 2 or 2 and 1. That makes direction irrelevant. It is possible to make statements about the general direction of the values in a nominal bivariate table, but conclusions about the direction of the relationship between the two variables exceed what the data can produce.

Direction is established by the ratio of N_s to N_d pairs in ordinal level data and the way the scores are arranged in interval and ratio level data. If high values or ranks on one variable are associated with high values or ranks on the other variable, the relationship is said to be a *positive relationship*. If high values of one variable are associated with low values on the other variable, the relationship is said to be a *negative relationship*.

Direction of a relationship can be established in one of two ways. A less precise method is to examine the distribution of values in a table or scatterplot. A more common and more accurate method is to use one of the ordinal or interval level measures of association discussed in Chapter 6, which also indicate the direction of the relationship.

Generally, examining the distribution of scores in a table is useful only for ordinal level variables. Establishing direction in this manner for nominal level data is problematic at best, and interval and ratio level data typically is not placed in tables because of the complexity and number of categories. So, when you consider the use of a table to examine direction, make sure the data is at least ordinal level and that there are not too many interval and ratio level categories.

The procedure for determining the direction of the relationship in a table larger than 2×2 begins by underlining the highest column percentage values in each row. In **Table 7-1**, this means underlining 48.5% in column 1, 38.5% in column 2, and 58.9% in column 3. This is essentially the same as calculating an epsilon and is an indicator of where the bulk of cross-tabulated values are in the distribution.

Once those values are underlined, it is a simple matter of determining how those highest values are arranged in the table. This procedure requires that the table be set up with the variables and categories arranged properly, as discussed in the chapter on constructing tables.

To determine the direction of the value arrangement, draw a line through each of the highest values. If the line drawn through the underlined values generally moves from lower left to upper right, it is a positive association. This is the case in Table 7-1. If the line drawn through the underlined values generally moves from upper left to lower right, it is a negative association. If the line drawn through the values runs directly across the table, there is no association or the association is nonlinear/nonmonotonic (as would probably be supported by chi-square and the measures of strength). The reason for this is in the ability of the independent variable to predict values of the dependent variable. Using the example of a PRE measure, if all of the highest values are in the same row, then nothing has been gained with the additional information. In predicting criminality, as we discussed earlier, if you were to guess whether the 10 people were criminals and they were all criminal, you would be correct only on those times that you predicted them to be criminal. If additional information was added, such as income, it would not make any difference and you would not reduce your errors in prediction with the additional variable and information.

As discussed in Chapter 6, the stronger the association between the two variables, the higher the percentage of the values that will lie directly on the diagonal. It was also discussed, however, that there are almost never perfect associations between variables. Herein lies a problem for determining direction by examining the table. Most of the time, the highest values in each column will not lie on the diagonal. These values will probably vary above and below the diagonal, often alternating between lying above and below it. It is a judgment call, then, concerning the general direction. If most of the values are in a positive direction, the relationship is most likely positive; alternatively if most of the values are in a negative direction, it is probably a negative relationship. If the association is weak, the values may be spread in a seemly random pattern. If

How much has fear of crime affected your decision to walk during the daytime? * How much has fear of crime affected supervision of your children? Crosstabulation

How much has fear of crime affected your decision to walk during the daytime?			How much has fear of crime affected supervision of your children?			Total
			1 Great Effect	2 Small Effect	3 No Effect	
	3 No Effect	Count	20	17	43	80
		Expected Count	39.4	19.1	21.5	80.0
		% within How much has fear of crime affected your decision to walk during the daytime?	25.0	21.3	35.8	100.0
		% within How much has fear of crime affected supervision of your children?	14.9	26.2	58.9	29.4
		% of Total	7.4	6.3	15.8	29.4
	2 Small Effect	Count	49	25	18	92
		Expected Count	45.3	22.0	24.7	92.0
		% within How much has fear of crime affected your decision to walk during the daytime?	53.3	27.2	19.6	100.0
		% within How much has fear of crime affected supervision of your children?	36.6	38.5	24.7	33.8
		% of Total	18.0	9.2	6.6	33.8
	1 Great Effect	Count	65	23	12	100
		Expected Count	49.3	23.9	26.8	100.0
		% within How much has fear of crime affected your decision to walk during the daytime?	65.0	23.0	12.0	100.0
		% within How much has fear of crime affected supervision of your children?	48.5	35.4	16.4	36.8
		% of Total	23.9	8.5	4.4	36.8
Total		Count	134	65	73	272
		Expected Count	134.0	65.0	73.0	272.0
		% within How much has fear of crime affected your decision to walk during the daytime?	49.3	23.9	26.8	100.0
		% within How much has fear of crime affected supervision of your children?	100.0	100.0	100.0	100.0
		% of Total	49.3	23.9	26.8	100.0

Table 7-1   Example of Direction

the relationship is curvilinear, as discussed below, the direction may change radically within the table. When this occurs, the only way to accurately predict the direction is with one of the measures of association that provides an indication of direction.

During the limited times that there is a need to determine direction using a 2 × 2 table, the direction can be determined by the placement of the variables. First, determine the location of the largest frequency in the table (the mode). If the largest frequency is in the lower left-hand corner, the relationship is positive, indicating high values of the dependent variable and high values of the independent variable. If the largest frequency is in the upper right-hand corner, the relationship is still positive; low values of the dependent variable associated with low values of the independent variable. If the largest frequency is in the lower right-hand corner, the relationship is negative, indicating high values on the dependent variable and low values on the independent variable. If the largest frequency is in the upper left-hand corner, the relationship is still negative; low values of the dependent variable associated with high values of the independent variable.

Regardless of whether the data is ordinal, interval, or ratio, perhaps the best way to examine direction is through one of the measures of association discussed in Chapter 6. All of the ordinal and higher measures of association are able to examine direction as a part of their interpretation.

To determine direction from the measures of strength, just look at one of those values. If the measure has a positive value, the relationship is positive. If the measure has a negative value, the relationship is considered negative. This method has the additional advantage of allowing determination of the direction of the data as a part of the other bivariate analyses rather than having to underline portions of the table.

A final note concerning direction. It is often easy to confuse the concepts of direction, asymmetry, and one-tailed versus two-tailed tests (talked about in inferential statistics). This is understandable since these concepts show similar characteristics of data or represent similar statistical procedures. They are quantitatively different, however.

The direction of a relationship concerns the data itself. One cannot alter the direction of the data without altering the data itself. It is, simply, how the scores of one variable are arranged in terms of the scores of another variable for the same case.

Symmetric or asymmetric measures of association examine the strength of the relationship between two variables in a certain manner. Asymmetric measures examine, typically, the proportional reduction of errors that can be made when the categories and values of the independent variable are used to predict the category and values of the dependent variable. This is a decision made by the researcher in terms of which variable will be dependent and whether an asymmetric procedure will be used. For each pair of variables, two asymmetric measures (one for each variable as dependent) and one symmetric measure can be calculated. Which one of these to choose is up to the researcher.

Finally, there is the issue of one-tailed versus two-tailed *t*-tests. Again, this has little to do with the data and more to do with what the researcher wants to examine. One-tailed tests look for specific change or a specific association between two (or more) variables, while a two-tailed test looks for statistical significance but does not specify the change desired. For example, in research concerning weight change, a one-tailed test would examine only weight loss, while a two-tailed test would not care whether subjects gained or lost weight, only that they did not stay the same. In this way, one-tailed tests are similar to asymmetric measures except that they are examining the significance of a relationship rather than the strength.

7-2   Nature of the Association

The final characteristic of a bivariate analysis is the *nature* of the association. Essentially, the nature of an association is an examination of the degree of *linearity* or *monotonicity* of the relationship. This characteristic does not necessarily add to information concerning the bivariate relationship, but it does provide a great deal of information about how the measures of association can be influenced by the relationship between the variables.

The nature of the association for nominal and ordinal level variables can build upon the steps taken to determine the direction of an association using a bivariate table. While column percentages were used to determine direction, to determine the nature of an association, the highest row percentage values in each row of the table should be underlined, as shown in **Table 7-2**. Here, we would underline 53.8% in the top row, 53.3% in the middle row, and 65.0% in the bottom row. Also differing from the method of determining direction, it is generally helpful to underline any row percentage values in a row that are close to the highest value. Although not a bright-line rule, generally, any value within 1% of the highest value should also be underlined. In Table 7-2, this was not necessary because there were no values within 1%. The pattern of the underlined values will indicate the nature of the association. If the underlined values are arranged generally along the diagonal, the association probably approaches linearity or monotonicity. This is the case in Table 7-2.

If the values curve, form an arc or a U, or seem randomly distributed, then the nature of the relationship is nonlinear or nonmonotonic.

Establishing the nature of an association for interval and ratio level data is probably more crucial to the analysis and interpretation than with nominal and ordinal level data. The reason is that the primary bivariate measure of association for interval and ratio level data is Pearson's *r*, which explicitly assumes a linear relationship between the two variables.

At the most basic level, the nature of an interval level association can be examined using a scattergram of the data and overlaying a *best-fitting line*, as discussed in

How much has fear of crime affected your decision to walk during the daytime? * How much has fear of crime affected supervision of your children? Crosstabulation

How much has fear of crime affected your decision to walk during the daytime?			How much has fear of crime affected supervision of your children?			Total
			1 Great Effect	2 Small Effect	3 No Effect	
	3 No Effect	Count	20	17	43	80
		Expected Count	39.4	19.1	21.5	80.0
		% within How much has fear of crime affected your decision to walk during the daytime?	25.0	21.3	53.8	100.0
		% within How much has fear of crime affected supervision of your children?	14.9	26.2	58.9	29.4
		% of Total	7.4	6.3	15.8	29.4
	2 Small Effect	Count	49	25	18	92
		Expected Count	45.3	22.0	24.7	92.0
		% within How much has fear of crime affected your decision to walk during the daytime?	53.3	27.2	19.6	100.0
		% within How much has fear of crime affected supervision of your children?	36.6	38.5	24.7	33.8
		% of Total	18.0	9.2	6.6	33.8
	1 Great Effect	Count	65	23	12	100
		Expected Count	49.3	23.9	26.8	100.0
		% within How much has fear of crime affected your decision to walk during the daytime?	65.0	23.0	12.0	100.0
		% within How much has fear of crime affected supervision of your children?	48.5	35.4	16.4	36.8
		% of Total	23.9	8.5	4.4	36.8
Total		Count	134	65	73	272
		Expected Count	134.0	65.0	73.0	272.0
		% within How much has fear of crime affected your decision to walk during the daytime?	49.3	23.9	26.8	100.0
		% within How much has fear of crime affected supervision of your children?	100.0	100.0	100.0	100.0
		% of Total	49.3	23.9	26.8	100.0

Table 7-2   Example of Nature

Chapter 6. This becomes important for examining the nature of an association in terms of what the line looks like and where it is on the scattergram. A best-fitting line might have to take a number of curves and bends to be the best fitting for a distribution. As shown in the middle graph of **Figure 7-1**, a best-fitting line might even have to make

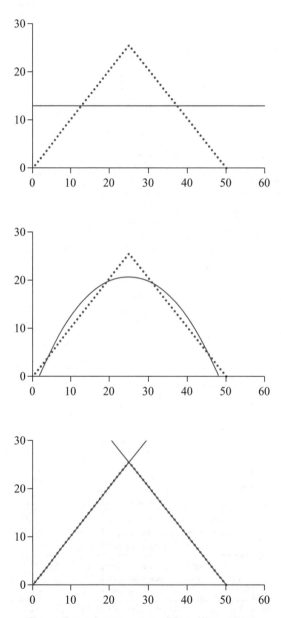

Figure 7-1   Scattergram of Curvilinear Data

an arc to fit the data. In reality, the best-fitting line would not bend or curve, it would simply shift to horizontal to create the best fit. This would result in a correlation (measure of strength) of 0. A best-fitting line made to fit the scattergram shown in Figure 7-1 would show no association, as seen in the top graph. The correlation and regression would probably also show no association between the two variables. This is so because the straight line to best fit the data would have to be horizontal. As shown in the bottom graph of Figure 7-1, though, this data set could actually be represented by two lines indicating an association of 1.00 and −1.00: one positive and one negative. These offset to produce a 0 association, but the two variables are actually highly correlated, just in a curvilinear nature. These scattergrams demonstrate why it is important to know the nature of interval and ratio level data. Simply relying on Pearson's r in this case would produce an erroneous interpretation. Pearson's r would no doubt be 0, and the interpretation would be no association. Understanding the nature of the data, however, allows an interpretation that more accurately represents the true association of the data. Knowing that the data was curvilinear would also facilitate more accurate analyses because it would alert the researcher that the data should be transformed. A simple exponential transformation of the data shown in Figure 7-1 would likely produce a positive linear association that would approach a Pearson's r of 1.00.

7-3   Conclusion

This chapter completes the analysis of two variables (bivariate analysis). It introduces methods of testing the direction and nature of a relationship. This chapter addressed whether a relationship is positive or negative and whether it is linear, monotonic, or curvilinear. This information is important because it may influence the findings of the strength of the association, and it provides an additional piece of information about the two variables. Knowing the existence, strength, direction, and nature of the relationship between two variables provides a fairly full understanding of their interaction.

7-4   Exercises

For the data and tables below (the same ones from the exercises of Chapter 6):

1. Determine the direction of the association from the table.
2. Determine the direction of the association from the univariate measures for each pair of variables.
3. Determine the nature of the association from the table.
4. Determine the nature of the association from the univariate measures for each pair of variables.
5. Examine and discuss the nature of the association for each data set.

VICT_Y_N Recoded VICTIM to Yes and No * RACE Race of Respondent Crosstabulation						
			RACE Race of respondent			
			1 Black	**2 White**	**3 Other**	**Total**
VICT_Y_N Recoded VICTIM to Yes and No	**2 No**	Count	101	128	2	231
		Expected Count	99.2	129.0	2.8	231.0
		% within VIC_T_Y_N	43.7	55.4	0.9	100.0
		% within RACE	70.6	68.8	50.0	69.4
		% of Total	30.3	38.4	0.6	69.4
	1 Yes	Count	42	58	2	102
		Expected Count	43.8	57.0	1.2	102.0
		% within VIC_T_Y_N	41.2	56.9	2.0	100.0
		% within RACE	29.4	31.2	50.0	30.6
		% of Total	12.6	17.4	0.6	30.6
Total		Count	143	186	4	333
		Expected Count	143.0	186.0	4.0	333.0
		% within VIC_T_Y_N	42.9	55.9	1.2	100.0
		% within RACE	100.0	100.0	100.0	100.0
		% of Total	42.9	55.9	1.2	100.0

Table 7-3   Victim/race respondent crosstabulation

NEIGH_SF Is your neighborhood safety changing? * COP_OK In your neighborhood, how well do you think the police perform their duties? Crosstabulation

			COP_OK In your neighborhood, how well do you think the police perform their duties?				
			1 Very Well	2 Average	3 Below Average	4 Not At All	Total
NEIGH_SF Is your neighborhood safety changing?	3 Becoming Less Safe	Count	21	88	45	8	162
		Expected Count	29.2	87.2	39.6	5.9	162.0
		% within NEIGH_SF	13.0	54.3	27.8	4.9	100.0
		% within COP_OK	35.6	50.0	56.3	66.7	49.5
		% of Total	6.4	26.9	13.8	2.4	49.5
	2 Not Changing	Count	21	58	33	2	114
		Expected Count	20.6	16.4	27.9	4.2	114.0
		% within NEIGH_SF	18.4	50.9	28.9	1.8	100.0
		% within COP_OK	35.6	33.0	41.3	16.7	34.9
		% of Total	6.4	17.7	10.1	0.6	34.9
	1 Becoming Safer	Count	17	30	2	2	51
		Expected Count	9.2	27.4	12.5	1.9	51.0
		% within NEIGH_SF	33.3	58.8	3.9	3.9	100.0
		% within COP_OK	28.8	17.0	2.5	16.7	15.6
		% of Total	5.2	9.2	0.6	0.6	15.6
Total		Count	59	176	80	12	327
		Expected Count	59.0	176.0	80.0	12.0	327.0
		% within NEIGH_SF	18.0	53.8	24.5	3.7	100.0
		% within COP_OK	100.0	100.0	100.0	100.0	100.0
		% of Total	18.0	53.8	24.5	3.7	100.0

Table 7-4   Is your neighborhood safety changing?

Statistics		Is your neigh-borhood safety changing?	In your neighborhood, how well do you think the po-lice perform their duites?	Race of respondent	Recoded VICTIM to yes and no
N	Valid	336	335	333	347
	Missing	11	12	14	0
Mean		2.34	2.13	1.58	1.69
Median		2.00	2.00	2.00	2.00
Mode		3	2	2	2
Std. Deviation		0.731	0.756	0.518	0.461
Variance		0.534	0.571	0.268	0.213
Skewness		−0.618	0.332	−0.073	−0.848
Std. Error of Skewness		0.133	0.133	0.134	0.131
Kurtosis		−0.905	−0.129	−1.393	−1.288
Std. Error of Kurtosis		0.265	0.266	0.266	0.261
Range		2	3	2	1

		DELINQ Delinquent Incidents for the Census Tract	BOARDED Boarded Up Housing Units	OWNOCCUP Owner Occupied Housing Units	JUVENILE Proportion of Juveniles	POPCHANG Population Change, 1980–1990
DELINQ **Delinquent Incidents** **for the Census Tract**	Pearson Correlation Sig. (2-tailed) N	1 . 45	.482** .001 45	−.004 .981 45	.339* .023 45	−.011 .941 45
BOARDED **Boarded Up** **Housing Units**	Pearson Correlation Sig. (2-tailed) N	.482** .001 45	1 . 45	−.234 .122 45	.029 .848 45	−.222 .143 45
OWNOCCUP **Owner Occupied** **Housing Units**	Pearson Correlation Sig. (2-tailed) N	−.004 .981 45	−.234 .122 45	1 . 45	.752** .000 45	.323* .030 45
JUVENILE **Proportion of** **Juveniles**	Pearson Correlation Sig. (2-tailed) N	.339* .023 45	.029 .848 45	.752** .000 45	1 . 45	.436** .003 45
POPCHANG **Population Change,** **1980–1990**	Pearson Correlation Sig. (2-tailed) N	−.011 .941 45	−.222 .143 45	.323* .030 45	.436** .003 45	1 . 45

**Correlation is significant at the 0.01 level (2-tailed).

*Correlation is significant at the 0.05 level (2-tailed).

Table 7-5   Correlations

Statistics						
		Delinquent Incidents for the Census Tract	Boarded Up Housing Units	Owner-Occupied Housing Units	Proportion of Juveniles	Population Change, 1980–1990
N	Valid	45	45	45	45	45
	Missing	0	0	0	0	0
Mean		39.02	17.31	792.16	688.29	5.3563
Median		28.00	3.00	727.00	643.00	−5.7374
Mode		9	0	1046	476	−60.00
Std. Deviation		40.194	29.602	752.134	506.344	51.27772
Variance		1,615.568	876.265	565705.453	256383.846	2629.40449
Skewness		1.465	2.874	1.868	1.321	2.084
Std. Error of Skewness		0.354	0.354	0.354	0.354	0.354
Kurtosis		1.814	10.104	5.010	3.625	4.380
Std. Error of Kurtosis		0.695	0.695	0.695	0.695	0.695
Range		162	154	3,810	2,613	250.37
Multiple modes exist. The smallest value is shown.						

Chapter 8
Introduction to Inferential Statistics

Learning Objectives

- Understand inferential statistics.
- Explain the difference between a population and a sample.
- Explain the difference between a parameter and a statistic.
- Understand the expected value and standard error.
- Calculate and interpret a Z score.
- Understand the normal curve and the central limit theorem.
- Examine probability.
- Determine confidence intervals.

Key Terms

central limit theorem
confidence interval
expected value
inference
inferential analysis
interval estimation
parameter

point estimation
population
probability
sample
standard error
statistic

When discussing the process of research in Chapter 1, you decided whether you wanted to describe a data set (for example, telling something about the general characteristics of college students) or make inferences from a sample to a population (for example, using those characteristics about students at one university to draw conclusions about

135

all students in the United States). The chapters to this point have focused on describing the characteristics of a known population. This chapter deals with those techniques that allow researchers to examine the characteristics of a sample (a small group drawn from the population) and make inferences about the population. These procedures are called *inferential analyses.*

Inferential analyses are useful because, in many cases, collecting data on an entire population is too costly, too time-consuming, or perhaps even impossible. For example, even with the smallest portion of the criminal population (those in prison) there are over 1 million people in the United States for whom data would have to be collected to study with descriptive statistics. This would take a great deal of money. Additionally, researchers could spend the rest of their professional lives attempting to study all of the people in the United States who are on probation and parole; and since this number changes continually, they would still not have an accurate portrait of this population. Finally, we have no idea who are all the people in the United States who have committed a crime (even a felony), so there would be no way to examine this population.

Inferential analysis takes advantage of specific sampling techniques that permit researchers to make inferences from a sample to a population. The information gleaned from the sample is generalized to the larger population from which it was selected. Inferential analyses permit a decision to be made with a known probability of error about whether a sample characteristic is different from a population characteristic and whether these differences are large enough to allow the conclusion that the population represented by the sample is different on a certain characteristic. We talk about inferential analyses, specifically in terms of hypothesis tests, in Chapter 9. This chapter is designed to give you the terminology and concepts you need to understand how to do hypothesis testing.

8-1 Terminology and Assumptions

Although the concepts of descriptive and inferential analyses are essentially the same, inferential statistics have some unique terminology that needs to be discussed before you can understand what is going on. The terminology is changed in inferential analyses to reflect the need to determine whether one is speaking of the sample (statistic) or the population (parameter).

A *population* is an entire group of study. A population may be small, such as all prisoners in the North Dakota Department of Corrections, or the population can be very large, such as all criminals in the United States.

A *sample* is a subset of the population drawn to allow statistical analysis. The basis of inferential analyses is determining whether a sample draw can reasonably be concluded to belong to the population or is different from it.

A *parameter* is a characteristic of the population. For example, a parameter might be the average income of all auto mechanics in the United States. Parameters are linked to statistics as populations are linked to samples.

A *statistic* is a characteristic of the sample for which researchers may make inferences to the population parameter. For example, a statistic might be the average income of all auto mechanics in Indiana.

Results of analysis of a sample are considered estimates of the population parameters. For example, we know it is unlikely that the average income of a sample of auto mechanics will be the exact average income of all auto mechanics in the United States. We may argue, however, that it is an accurate estimate of that parameter.

An *expected value* is the estimated population parameter. Most of the time, the estimated value will be the mean of the population. Similar to the mean, the expected value does not relate how closely a particular statistic is to the parameter. It simply assures us that *on the average* the statistic will be an accurate estimate of the parameter.

Finally, the *standard error* is a measure the variation of the statistic around the parameter it is estimating. For example, the standard error of the mean measures the variability of sample means around the population mean. The standard error may be interpreted in the same way as the standard deviation. It is influenced by sample size such that as the sample size increases, the standard error decreases.

The foundation of inferential statistical procedures is making inferences. An *inference* involves performing an analysis of the sample, and then concluding that the findings apply to the population.

As with any statistical procedure, inferential analyses have a number of assumptions that must be met before they can be considered reliable. The assumptions for inferential analyses are perhaps more important because we do not know the population parameter. Since we cannot confirm conclusions made concerning the data, as is possible with descriptive analyses, it is imperative that the assumptions of the inferences be met so that we can rely on the mathematical proofs of the analyses to support the conclusions.

The first assumption of inferential analyses is that the sample must be taken from the same population for which inferences are to be made. This is actually the watermark of inferential analyses. The bottom line of any inferential analysis is rejecting or failing to reject the null hypothesis that there is no difference between the sample and a population.

The second assumption is that the population and sample must be normally distributed. There are methods of dealing with data that may not be normally distributed, but the foundation of inferential analyses is that a normal distribution is assumed. This assumption is necessary because the components of inferential analyses—the normal curve, central limit theorem, and sampling distribution—all require normality. The robustness of these measures, however, often allows researchers to assume that the data is normally distributed.

The third assumption is that inferential analyses require that a random sample of the data be taken. As discussed below, researchers must assume that there is no systematic error in the sample drawn. We know that error will be present in any sample—that it will not be a true measure of the population parameter. We must assume, however, that the error is random (some errors may be above the mean and other errors below the mean), such that the errors will essentially cancel one another out. If there is error in the sample that is not random, then we cannot assume that sample statistics will be proper estimates of the population.

These assumptions are put into practice through components of inferential analysis that are essential to their use as a statistical tool. These are the normal curve, sampling distributions, and the central limit theorem. These important concepts are discussed below.

8-2   *Z* Scores: A Return to the Normal Curve

Before addressing these concepts, we need to discuss *Z* scores. The *Z* scores were introduced in Chapter 3. There we talked about the area under the normal curve and that there was a constant area between any standard deviation and the mean. We stated that between the mean and 1 standard deviation was 34.1% of all the values in a data set; that between the mean and 2 standard deviations, there was 47.72% of the data; and between the mean and 3 standard deviations there was 49.87% of the data. Doubling these figures gave us some pretty important numbers—that 95.44% of the data fell within 2 standard deviations either side of the mean and 99.74% of the data fell within 3 standard deviations either side of the mean. But what if we wanted exactly 95% or 99% of the data? This is easily calculated using *Z* scores.

The *Z* scores are nothing more than standard deviations put into a standard distance from the mean of a normal curve. The *Z* scores convert any value in the distribution to standard deviation units. These are critical to inferential analysis, as discussed below.

The process of converting values to *Z* scores is simply a method of deriving standard scores. To be able to make comparisons between things, it is necessary to set some standard upon which both items may be measured. If measuring distance, we could use feet or meters; weight could be in pounds or kilograms. But what about social data such as crime? Crime is generally discussed in terms of crime rates. Calculating crime rates is simply a process of standardizing crime in terms of the population of a city. The same can be done with the mean, standard deviation, and the normal curve through *Z* scores. This standardizes scores are based on the normal curve. Thus if a researcher knows the mean (μ) and standard deviation (σ) of a population, *Z* scores can be used to calculate the distance between any value and the mean. Using the area under the normal curve allows inferential analyses to be used to determine the chances that any number in a distribution will be in a sample drawn from that population, which is discussed below.

The process of calculating a Z score, determining the area under the normal curve between that value and the mean, and then examining how that score relates to the mean is rather simple. First, subtract the raw score from the mean. This determines whether the number is above the mean or below the mean: Negative numbers are below the mean, and positive numbers are above the mean. Then divide the number by the standard deviation to determine how many standard deviation units the number is above or below the mean. This is shown in the formula for a Z score:

$$z = \frac{X - \mu}{\sigma}$$

The answer obtained from this calculation is the score's deviation from the mean in standard units (the Z score in standard deviation units). Note that you may get a negative number; all this means is that the Z score is to the left of the mean. It does not affect the calculations at all and can be dropped in the rest of the procedure.

The next step is to take this number and turn to Appendix B. The row to use is taken from your Z score that you calculated. The columns to use within this row depend on what area under the normal curve is being examined. If you are looking for the area between the score and the mean, look to column b in the table; if examining the area beyond that score, which is farther in the tail of the distribution, use column c. Let us look at an example.

Suppose the number of complaints against a police department averaged 12 per month with a standard deviation of 1.5. Then suppose the chief wants you to determine what percentage of the scores fell between the mean and the current month's score of 14. This would require determining the area between the mean and 14. To do this, first calculate a Z score, as shown in **Figure 8-1**. Then look at column a in Appendix B

$$z = \frac{X - \mu}{\sigma}$$

$$= \frac{14 - 12}{1.5}$$

$$= \frac{2}{1.5}$$

$$= 1.33$$

Figure 8-1   Calculating a Z score

under the row for 1.33 (bottom of second set of columns). Since you are looking for the area between the score and the mean, you use column *b* to get the percentage of the area under the normal curve that falls between the mean and 14. This value is 0.4082, so the area in this distribution between 12 and 14 is 40.82%. What does this mean? It means that almost 41% of the months in this year had fewer complaints than the current month.

But what if the chief wanted to know how many months had more complaints than the current month? To determine the percentage of scores greater than 14, you calculate the *Z* score exactly as before. That number, 1.33, is then found in column *a* of Appendix B. Since you are trying to determine the number of scores greater than 14, column *c* in the table would be used. The value in column *c* that corresponds to a *Z* score of 1.33 is 0.0918, so 9.18% of the scores in the distribution are greater than 14, which means that almost 10% of the months had more complaints than the current month. This procedure could also be done in finding, for example, the number of months in which complaints were higher than 14 and less than 9. This is not used all that much in inferential analyses, though, so we will skip this calculation.

8-3   The Normal Curve in Inferential Analyses

Now we can use our knowledge of *Z* scores to talk more about the normal curve. The concept of the normal curve was also introduced in Chapter 3. Here, the normal curve is discussed in terms of its utility for inferential analysis.

Now that you know how to calculate the mean, standard deviation, and *Z* scores, you can begin to look at how data distributions are arranged and to make inferences (conclusions) about the data. One way to make these conclusions is through the use of the normal curve. With this knowledge, *Z* scores can be used as standard deviations from the mean to examine where a particular sample value may fall in the normal distribution of a population. The difference between calculating a *Z* score here and the calculations performed above is that we are now attempting to work with data in a sample and use it to estimate population parameters. The obvious question here is, If we know the population mean and standard deviation, why do we not just use them for the study? That brings up an interesting point for social science research. There are times when researchers know the population parameters, or they believe they have valid estimates of it. In these instances, it is useful to compare samples to the population. For example, it has been established that IQs are normally distributed, with a mean of 100 and a standard deviation of 15. Research can be conducted on prisoners, then, to compare this sample to the population as a whole. It is much more difficult, if not impossible, however, to determine the population parameters in other areas. In these cases, the use of *Z* scores is limited at best. Let us look at an example of how the normal curve and *Z* scores could be used in inferential analysis.

If research on Colorado state employees ($N = 30$) found they have an average IQ of 80, would this mean that they were substantially (significantly) different from the "normal" population with an average IQ of 100? The Z score formula above can be used to examine this hypothesis. Using the information on IQs discussed above and the knowledge of the average IQ of prisoners produces the calculations shown in **Figure 8-2**. Here, the mean IQ score of the state employees (80) is subtracted from the "normal" population's average IQ score (100). This value is divided by the standard error of the mean [calculated by the standard deviation of population IQ (15) divided by the square root of sample size]. The result of the calculation is a Z score of -7.30. If we want to be 95% sure we are getting accurate results, we could use the Z score of 1.96 standard deviations from the mean as the critical value. This can be found in Appendix B. What we are looking for, then, is whether our obtained score falls outside the $+1.96$ value or inside the range (between -1.96 and 1.96). If it falls outside the ± 1.96 score, we reject the null hypothesis that there is no statistically significant difference between the IQ of state employees and that of "normal people." If it falls inside the range, we fail to reject the null hypothesis and have to assume the differences in IQs are not that dramatic. Since our obtained Z score was smaller than -1.96, we would reject the null hypothesis. In this case, we conclude that this sample was not from the "normal" population.

$$z = \frac{\overline{X} - \mu}{\dfrac{\sigma}{\sqrt{N}}}$$

$$= \frac{80 - 100}{\dfrac{15}{\sqrt{30}}}$$

$$= \frac{-20}{2.74}$$

$$= -7.30$$

Figure 8-2   Normal Curve and Z score Example

In the sterile confines of the classroom, the example used here works well; but not all populations or samples taken from them are normal. Populations that are not normal in distribution could present a potential problem to the researcher, particularly regarding any inferences made from a sample of that nonnormal population. Most of the populations studied in the social sciences are not normal. This could cause great problems in the ability to use the normal curve and inferential analyses. Fortunately, there are other statistical techniques that allow researchers to use the principles of the normal curve with nonnormal populations. These are sampling distributions of the mean and the central limit theorem. We discuss these below, but first we need to lay the foundation by discussing probability.

8-4 Probability

Probability is a concept that is central to research in the social sciences. In fact, most social science theories can be reduced to a measure of probability. For example, when researchers attempt to explain criminal behavior, they are essentially trying to establish the probability that a person will commit a crime because of the conditions, abnormalities, or other characteristics that are the subjects of the research. Probability is also used in other places in the criminal justice system. The concept of probable cause is central to police work; judges decide on the probability of a person's committing more crimes or fleeing from justice when they set bail, and juries base their decisions on the probability that a person has committed a crime. All of these rely on probability in making decisions.

Probability does the same thing for inferential analysis and interpretation. Even with all the advantages of statistical theory, the end result is that researchers do not know the true answer. We do not know the true outcome, so we work to make the best estimate of what the actual outcome will be. Using the principle of the normal curve, researchers can estimate the probability of an event's occurring and the probability that a certain sample statistic will match a population parameter. *Probability* refers to the relative likelihood of the occurrence of an event or the number of times *an* event can occur relative to the number of times *any* event can occur.

Probability values range from 0 to 1 and are expressed as either a decimal or a percentage. A probability of 0 means something is impossible, while a probability of 1 means that it is certain. Probability is important for inferential analysis because it represents the possibility of being wrong on a decision to reject or fail to reject a null hypothesis. In Chapter 5, chi-square was used to examine the existence and significance of a relationship. There, 0.05 was used as a general cutoff. This means that you would be correct in rejecting the null hypothesis 95% of the time. It also means, however, that you would be wrong 5% of the time. The probability of being wrong, then, is 5%. It is this probability that is the foundation of decisions made in inferential analysis.

The proportion of the area under the normal curve can also be used to establish probability. The probability that a Z score will be less than or equal to -1.96 is 0.025 $(0.05 \div 2)$; likewise for greater than or equal to 1.96. The probability that a Z score will be less than or equal to -1.96 *or* greater than or equal to 1.96 is 0.05, as discussed above. What we could do, then, is to figure out the probability that we would get, say,

60 heads in 100 tosses of a coin, and whether that would mean we had a nonnormal game or it was just a part of the chance of tossing a coin. This is inferential statistics.

When examining the probabilities above, we could have developed a *probability distribution* of the coin tosses. When probability distributions are used specifically for inferential analysis, they are often called *sampling distributions*. A sampling distribution would be created in this case if a coin were flipped 100 times and the number of heads and tails recorded, and then this process were repeated 100 times. Each of these 100 samples might have some aberrations from the expected 50/50 ratio, but we would expect the overall result of these samples to be very close to 50% heads and 50% tails. The usefulness of a sampling distribution is that if a sufficiently large number of samples are drawn (between 30 and 120, depending on what source is consulted), and a characteristic such as the mean is calculated for each of the samples, then the sampling distribution approximates a normal curve. If these samples are taken from a normal population, the sampling distribution is also normal. Even if the samples are taken from a nonnormal population, the sampling distribution still approximates normality. Since we know that the sampling distribution of a statistic from a smaller number of samples approximates the normal curve, we do not have to use the entire population to get an estimate of the population parameters.

The real value of a sampling distribution is that a researcher does not have to draw a large number of samples to examine their characteristics. One sample can be drawn, and the principles of the central limit theorem (which are addressed below) can be used to make inferences about the sample to the population. All parameters of a population, and their associated sample statistics, have sampling distributions. For example, there are sampling distributions of the variance of a distribution (actually this is the χ^2 distribution used in Chapter 5). More importantly for inferential analysis, there are sampling distributions of the measures of central tendency. A sampling distribution of the means is often displayed as a *t*-table, as will be addressed in Chapter 9. It can be shown that the expected value of the sample mean approximates the population mean regardless of the form of the population distribution or the sample size.

8-5 Central Limit Theorem

The final piece of the process of inferential analyses is what brings together the other parts and allows us to use inferential analyses even if we do not know the population. As discussed earlier, we typically do not know the population mean and standard deviation. Also, we typically do not have populations, and certainly not samples, that are normally distributed. Finally, we do not have the time to draw a sampling distribution of the means to be able to estimate the population parameters. There is another statistical concept, though, that allows us to overcome these problems. This is the central limit theorem.

The *central limit theorem* provides the researcher with an empirically proven concept that allows estimates and generalizations based on a sample to be inferred to the population from which the sample was drawn. The central limit theorem states that, given any population (regardless of whether it is a normal distribution), as the sample size increases, the sampling distribution of the means approaches a normal distribution. This is so because the standard error of the sampling distribution of the means decreases as the sample size increases (the clustering of the sample means around the population mean grows smaller as the sample size grows larger). This allows the use of a normal probability distribution for testing hypotheses about populations with any form of distribution.

The central limit theorem is based on the foundations of the sampling distribution of the mean and the normal curve that repeated random samples taken from normal or nonnormal populations have sample means that approximate a normal distribution. Extending the theory of sampling distributions, the central limit theorem allows researchers to conclude that even when they take only one sample, the sample mean will approximate the population mean, and will become a closer estimate of the population mean as the sample size increases. For almost all populations, virtually without regard to the shape of the original population, the sampling distribution of the means derived from the population will be approximately normally distributed provided that the associated sample size is sufficiently large.

The key to the central limit theorem is sample size. Sampling distributions of less than 30 are generally considered insufficient to approximate a normal curve. The sampling distribution will only approximate a normal distribution with a sample size of 30. As the sample size increases to 120 and beyond, the sampling distribution becomes more normal in form and thus more accurate. So, for our research purposes, we like to have sample sizes larger than 120.

8-6   Confidence Intervals

Before moving to testing hypotheses, we need to discuss *confidence intervals*. The analyses discussed to this point are commonly referred to as *point estimations*. This is a process of attempting to identify the expected value (typically the mean) of a population based on sample data. Hypothesis testing can also take the form of *interval estimation*. This is the use of confidence intervals to address the sampling error of an analysis and to establish a range of values that, if enough samples are drawn in the sampling distribution, will have a high probability of estimating the true population parameter. Even for smaller sample sizes, researchers can establish, with a certain degree of confidence, where the population parameter might fall. Researchers cannot always, or sometimes do not want to, know exactly where a population mean value is. Sometimes it is enough simply to know the range within which it falls. Confidence intervals are used to estimate the range of mean values drawn from a sampling distribution within which the true population parameter is likely to fall. They are also used to estimate the probability that the population mean actually falls within that range of mean values. You have seen this form of statistical analysis before in election polls. The polls will say that a certain candidate has a particular percentage of the vote, plus or minus a certain percentage. This predicted percentage of the vote is the point estimate in this case—the expected value of the mean of the population. The plus and minus signs are the range of values within which they think the true population mean will fall. These are the confidence intervals.

Confidence intervals are calculated using a Z score for the particular range we are attempting to predict. Researchers typically use 95% or 99% confidence when working with confidence intervals in social sciences. Remember that the Z score corresponding to 95% of the area under the normal curve is 1.96, and the Z score corresponding to 99% of the area under the normal curve is 2.58. These numbers correspond to the 0.05 and 0.01 critical values. The formula for calculating a confidence interval (CI) is shown in **Figure 8-3**, where $\overline{X}$ is the mean of the sample that has been drawn, z_{CI} is the Z score of the desired confidence interval, and the standard deviation of the population (σ) divided by the square root of the sample size (N) is the *standard error of the mean*.

$$\overline{X} \pm z_{CI} \times \left(\frac{\sigma}{\sqrt{N}} \right)$$

$$95\%(CI) = 5.2 \pm 1.96\left(\frac{0.75}{\sqrt{157}} \right)$$

$$= 5.2 \pm 1.96\left(\frac{0.75}{12.53} \right)$$

$$= 5.2 \pm 1.96(0.06)$$

$$= 5.2 \pm 0.12$$

Figure 8-3   Calculating Confidence Intervals

For a sample with a mean ($\overline{X}$) of 5.2, a sample size (N) of 157, and the standard deviation of the population of 0.75, and for a test at the 95% confidence interval, the calculation is as shown in Figure 8-3. Here, a 95% confidence interval is used. This means that the z in the formula will be 1.96. Since the mean is 5.2, it will be the base from which the other values are subtracted. The values in parentheses are the standard deviation (0.75) and N (157). The product of these calculations puts the confidence interval running from 5.08 to 5.32. The two extreme values of this range are called the *confidence limits*. What this calculation means is that we are 95% confident that the mean in the population falls between 5.08 and 5.32. It is common to interpret confidence intervals by saying, "There is a 95% chance that the parameter (population mean) is between these two values."

In all cases of confidence intervals, as in this case, the range of the interval is a function of the level of confidence desired and the sample size. For example, higher confidence requires a wider interval; if a researcher wants to be 99% accurate, she or he must allow for a greater range of scores to estimate the parameter value. Small samples also beget wider intervals. If the sample size is small, we must allow for a wider confidence interval because the standard error of the mean is larger and we are less sure of our results. If the sample size is large, however, we can be more certain of our results because we know the standard error is smaller—and smaller than the population standard deviation.

8-7   Conclusion

This chapter sets the stage for inferential analyses that are discussed in Chapter 9. The concepts of the normal curve, probability, and sampling distributions are applied to hypothesis testing. Without the knowledge of sampling distributions, hypothesis testing would not be possible because researchers could not have confidence that the expected value of a sample drawn from a population would closely approximate the population parameter. The normal curve facilitates the use of sampling distributions through probabilities and the understanding of the area under the normal curve and Z scores. Confidence intervals expand the ability to estimate the population parameter by moving from a point estimate to an interval estimate, allowing researchers to estimate a population parameter with some allowance for error. All of these concepts will become important in the discussion of hypothesis testing as it applies to inferential analysis. That is the topic of Chapter 9.

8-8   Equations in This Chapter

Z score (sample):

$$Z = \frac{X - \overline{X}}{s}$$

Z score (population):

$$Z = \frac{\overline{X} - \mu}{\sigma}$$

Confidence intervals:

$$\bar{X} \pm z_{CI}\left(\frac{\sigma}{\sqrt{N}}\right)$$

8-9   For Further Reading

DeMoivre, A. *The doctrine of chances.* New York: Chelsea Publishing Company, 1967. Reprint of the original 1718 work.

Dudycha, A. L., & Dudycha, L. W. Behavioral statistics: An historical perspective. In R. E. Kirk (Ed.), *Statistical issues: A reader for the behavioral sciences.* Monterey, CA: Brooks/Cole Publishing Company, 1972.

Gauss, C. F. *Theoria motus corporum celestium.* Translated. Boston: Little, Brown, 1963.

Kachigan, S. K. *Statistical analysis: An interdisciplinary introduction to univariate and multivariate methods.* New York: Radius Press, 1986.

Laplace, P. S. *Oeuvres complètes de Laplace.* Paris: Gauthier-Villars, 1878-1912.

Pate, A. M., Wycoff, M. A., Skogan, W. G., & Sherman, L. *Reducing fear of crime in Houston and Newark: A summary report.* Washington, D.C.: The Police Foundation, 1986.

Sutherland, E. H. *The professional thief.* Chicago: University of Chicago Press, 1937.

8-10   Exercises

1. Test the concepts of probability.
    a. Flip a coin 10 times and see what percentage of heads you get.
    b. Flip a coin for 9 more sets of 10, and calculate the mean number of heads that you get (create a sampling distribution of your coin flips).
    c. What are the expected value and standard error of this distribution?
    d. For the largest run of heads or tails in a row, calculate the probability of that circumstance occurring.
    e. Using the mean number of heads from your first set of 10 coin flips, construct confidence intervals of what you expect the population mean to be.
        (i) How do your results compare to the known population parameter of 50% heads?
        (ii) How do your results compare to your sampling distribution?

2. For a distribution with a mean of 50 and a standard deviation of 10:
   a. Calculate the Z score for a score of 40.
   b. Determine the area under the normal curve between the mean and this value.
   c. Determine the area under normal curve beyond this value.
   d. Calculate a Z score for a score of 65.
   e. Determine the area under the normal curve between the mean and this value.
   f. Determine the area under normal curve beyond this value.

3. Say a parole board has a policy that it will only release prisoners who meet a minimum amount of time served, have a minimum number of good-time points, and have made an acceptable score on the test in their drug awareness class. Given: the mean of this distribution is 90, the minimum acceptable score on these criteria is 70, and the standard deviation of scores is 15.
   a. Calculate the Z score for a score of 90.
   b. Calculate the Z score for a score of 50.
   c. Determine the area under normal curve beyond these values.
   d. Calculate a Z score for a score of 70.
   e. Determine the area under the normal curve between the mean and this value.
   f. Determine the area under normal curve beyond this value.

Chapter 9
Hypothesis Testing

Learning Objectives

- Examine the process of hypothesis testing.
- Evaluate research and null hypotheses.
- Determine one- or two-tailed tests.
- Understand obtained values, significance and critical regions.
- Distinguish between Type I and Type II error.

Key Terms

alpha	one-tailed test
beta	two-tailed test
critical probability	type I error
critical value	type II error
hypothesis testing	

Often in research, we want to compare groups. We might want to answer a question such as, Are students who study more for tests different from those who do not? More specifically, when comparing two groups, usually you have an idea about the characteristics of the groups, and you are trying to find out if that idea is true. You formulate a statement, or hypothesis, based on the idea—students who study more for tests should make higher grades than those who do not—and try to find out if the idea is true. This is the process of *hypothesis testing*.

Through inferential analyses and the characteristics discussed in Chapter 8, decisions can be made with a known probability of error about whether a sample is different from the population (are homeless people different from the rest of the population on educational background?) or two samples are different from each other (are unemployment patterns in one jurisdiction different from those in another jurisdiction?). This process of hypothesis testing begins with carefully thought-out research and null hypotheses, and is put into practice through the steps in hypothesis testing.

9-1   Steps in Hypothesis Testing

We can now begin to look at the process of hypothesis testing. Hypothesis testing can be thought of as a specialized decision-making process. First, assumptions are established through the research and null hypotheses. Then a sample or samples are drawn from groups with characteristics that the researchers are interested in studying. Sample characteristics are then compared to the assumptions made about the unknown population parameters to see if the data drawn supports the assumptions. The results of that comparison allow a decision to be made concerning the rejection of, or failure to reject, the null hypothesis.

Although the particular strategy and steps in hypothesis testing, by and large, depend on the type of analyses being conducted, certain standard procedures should be followed. These steps are identified and discussed in the rest of this chapter.

Step 1: The Research Hypothesis

The first step involves putting the idea into the form of a research hypothesis. The research hypotheses typically are very similar to the research questions of a project or the propositions of a theory. Research hypotheses are derived from theory or primary questions and research questions, and the hypotheses place conceptual language in a format that can be empirically examined. For example, a research hypothesis might read as follows:

> Probation officers who have prior criminal justice experience (police officers, corrections officers) are less supportive of rehabilitation than probation officers who have no prior criminal justice experience.

Using the example research hypothesis above, the argument can be made that, statistically, the samples drawn from probation officers with prior criminal justice experience and from those without prior experience have different sample means. Additionally, there is the assumption that the difference is *so large* that it cannot be attributed to chance.

Step 2: The Null Hypothesis

The next step in the process is to develop the null hypothesis. Because it is difficult to prove that there is a difference between these two groups in the population, the null hypothesis is used to facilitate hypothesis testing. The null hypothesis places the research hypothesis in a form that can be tested empirically. This is the reverse of the research hypothesis. It states that the means of the two samples are equal, or that the difference is so small that it could have occurred by chance or because of sampling error.

Hypothesis testing is set up so that, if possible, we can reject the null hypothesis. By rejecting the null hypothesis, we have reason to support the research hypothesis, keeping in mind the guidelines established above for accepting the research hypothesis. The null hypothesis is important to inferential analyses because we do not know the true parameters of the population, so conclusions or hypotheses cannot be confirmed. Also, samples vary from one to the next, and there is error present in each sample drawn. The chances of proving a research hypothesis, then, are uncertain. It is even more important, therefore, to examine the data in terms of rejecting a null hypothesis. The null hypothesis associated with the research hypothesis above might read as follows:

> There is no statistically significant difference in the attitude toward rehabilitation between probation officers with prior criminal justice experience and probation officers without this experience.

Step 3: Drawing Samples

The third step in the hypothesis testing process is to take samples from the populations to be studied. It is imperative that the samples drawn be representative of the target population; otherwise, the ability to generalize from the sample to the population is limited. This is more of an issue for a research methods class than a statistics discussion, so we do not go into that here.

Step 4: Selecting the Test

The fourth step involves selecting the appropriate statistical test to properly analyze the data drawn. Two decisions must be made at this point. First, which hypothesis test is most appropriate for the data? These are discussed further below. Second, should a one- or two-tailed test, which is discussed here, be conducted?

In hypothesis testing, the results of tests are discussed in terms of where they fall under the normal curve. At times, researchers want the obtained values of the research to fall toward the middle of the normal curve (confidence intervals) and within the boundaries of ± 1.96 (or 2.58, or whatever level is set). At other times, the goal is to reject the null hypothesis by stating that one variable is so different from another that it is outside the boundaries of ±1.96. In these cases, scientists refer to the variable of interest as being "in the tails of the distribution." For example, if a researcher is conducting research on teaching children about weight loss, there are three possible outcomes:

- The program could result in a reduction in weight among the children.
- The program could produce no significant change in the children.
- The program could provide the children with information that may make them more likely to gain weight.

Although all of these are possible outcomes, the researcher may not want to test them all. If the goal of the project is to examine the success of the program, the researcher may want to test only the first outcome; or he or she may want to know if there is change, but does not care whether the change is positive or negative. These examples represent the two types of hypotheses or tests: one-tailed tests and two-tailed tests.

A *two-tailed test* states that there is a difference between the groups being tested without specifying the direction of the difference. For this type of analysis, the normal curve is divided, essentially, into three sections. The focus of the analysis, then, is to examine whether the program produced children who lost significantly more weight than normal (more than −1.96 standard deviations from the mean), whether there was no significant difference between children who go through the program and those who did not (between ±1.96 standard deviations from the mean), or whether the program produced children who had weight increases significantly higher than normal (more than +1.96 standard deviations from the mean). Specifically, the researcher would be looking to see if the sample of children in the program was significantly different from other children in weight change. If there was a difference, that would be sufficient. It would not be important in this analysis if the children in the program gained or lost weight—only that there was a difference. To say that a researcher would not care if the children in the program gained more weight than those not in the program is a little absurd, however. More likely, the success of the program would be based only on a finding that children in the program lost more weight than children not in the program. This determination could be made using a one-tailed test.

A *one-tailed test* looks for a directional difference between the two groups; in this case, children in the program lost more weight than children not in the program. The hypothesis for a one-tailed test would predict one variable to be greater than or less than the other, but not both.

The next logical question, then, is which one to use. This can be decided on three criteria. The first criterion for use of a one-tailed test is ". . . when a difference in the unpredicted direction, while possible, would be . . . meaningless." An example here might be an anger training program for violent offenders in prison. The goal of the research would be to show that the anger training program makes the prisoners less violent. A finding in an unpredicted direction is certainly possible, but it would be meaningless (and detrimental) to the research. The second criterion is that results in the unpredicted direction are no different than finding no difference at all. You might think of this as analogous to predicting that the scores of a basketball game will have no difference at the end of the game. The research hypothesis in this case might be that the home team wins. Since the prediction is in a specific direction (home team wins) and it is not possible to tie, a finding in the unpredicted direction would be the same as no difference (either way, the home team did not win). The third criterion for using a one-tailed test over a two-tailed test is ". . . when a directional hypothesis is deducible from . . . theory but results in the opposite direction are not deducible from coexisting . . . theory." An example here might be that a certain antisocial behavior would result in children committing violent crimes. If the assumption is true, then this theory would explain that behavior. If the children in the research were no different from normal children, then the theory would have no response for that behavior or finding. We address only one-tailed tests in this chapter. Two-tailed tests are only slightly different in practice, and they can be calculated quickly if you know how to calculate a one-tailed test.

Step 5: Calculating the Obtained Value

The fifth step involves using the analysis procedure chosen to calculate the obtained value. This is the process of using chi-square as in Chapter 5, Z tests and t-tests that will be addressed below, or a multivariate test such as ANOVA that is discussed in Chapter 11.

Practically, this step in the process is often skipped because statistical packages calculate the obtained value for you. Obtained values are printed in the output of most statistical programs; but, as with chi-square in Chapter 3, the significance value of the analysis is also printed. So this measure can be used to make a decision (step 7) rather than calculating the obtained value and comparing it to the critical value.

Step 6: Significance and Critical Regions

The sixth step involves determining the *critical value* of the test statistic (significance level). The critical value is determined by the type of test used in the research, the level of certainty desired, the degrees of freedom, and whether the research is a one-tailed or a two-tailed test. This critical value will also represent the probability of making a Type I error (alpha) as discussed below. As discussed over the previous several chapters, this critical value is typically either 95% (0.05) or 99% (0.01).

Step 7: Making a Decision

The final step in the hypothesis-testing process is to make a decision. This is a very straightforward process in which the value obtained from the statistical test is compared to the critical value as determined above. Using the output from a statistical analysis program, this step involves comparing the significance value obtained in the output to the acceptance level set prior to testing. As discussed in previous chapters, if the obtained value of the statistical test is greater than the critical value (or if the significance value is less than the level set in step 6), the null hypothesis may be rejected at that significance level. This means that the differences between the two groups are so large that we are confident (95% or 99% confident) that they could not have occurred by chance or through sampling error. If the obtained value of the statistical test is less than the critical value (that is, if the significance value is greater than the acceptance level set in step 6) we fail to reject the null hypothesis at that significance level.

In completing this process of hypothesis testing, some issues need to be addressed. This includes the decisions about Type I and Type II errors and selecting the proper test. The decisions about Type I and Type II errors are addressed below. Selection of the appropriate test is discussed in Chapter 10.

9-2   Type I and Type II Errors

In inferential analysis, there are several possible outcomes to the hypothesis testing—some correct and others incorrect. This can be demonstrated by the process of a criminal trial, where we essentially test the null hypothesis that a person is not guilty of the crime; or in inferential analysis terms, there is no difference between the person on trial and other "innocent" people. The first outcome is to reject a null hypothesis where there truly are differences between the variables; a jury could find a person guilty who truly is guilty. The second outcome is to fail to reject a null hypothesis where there truly is no statistically significant difference between the variables; a jury could find a person not guilty who truly is not guilty. The null hypothesis can also be rejected by mistake—when there actually is no difference between the variables; the jury could find a person guilty who is not guilty. Finally, we can fail to reject a null hypothesis by mistake—when there actually are differences between the variables; a jury could find a person not guilty who is guilty. These last two situations are where errors are committed in hypothesis testing.

A *Type I error* refers to the rejection of a null hypothesis that is actually true. This occurs when a null hypothesis is rejected when in reality there is no difference between the two variables. There are situations (1% or 5% of the time, for example) in which it appears that the difference between the variables is so great that it could not be caused by chance, but in fact it was chance or random variation between the two variables and there actually was no difference.

The probability associated with committing a Type I error is the significance value or critical value of the test. For example, a hypothesis test at the 0.05 level would be correct 95% of the time; but 5% of the time a Type I error would be committed. This is referred to as the *critical probability*, and is designated by the Greek letter alpha (α). Any time a null hypothesis is rejected at a given significance value, there is the risk of committing a Type I error, the probability of which is equal to alpha. The probability of committing a Type I error can be reduced by making the alpha region small (for example, using a significance level of 0.00001); however, this increases the risk of committing a Type II error.

A *Type II error* is failure to reject a false null hypothesis when there actually is a difference between the variables. The probability of committing a Type II error is designated as the Greek letter beta (β). Beta is calculated by subtracting the sample mean from the population mean and dividing by the standard deviation. This is shown in the formula

$$\beta = \frac{\mu_{H_o} - \mu_{true}}{\sigma}$$

where μH_o is the calculated mean of the sample chosen to represent the null hypothesis, μ_{true} is the actual mean if the null hypothesis is true, and σ is the standard deviation of the population.

To illustrate this calculation, take the example used in Chapter 8 concerning the IQ of state employees. The null hypothesis was that there was no difference between state employees and normal people in the population. When the state employees were tested, they had an average IQ of 80. The null hypothesis, then, would have been that both state employees and normal people have an IQ of 80. We know from the population, however, that the average IQ is 100 and that the standard deviation is 15. If we plug these into the formula, we get -1.33.

$$\beta = \frac{80 - 100}{15}$$

$$= \frac{-20}{15}$$

$$= -1.333$$

If the research design was a two-tailed test of significance at the 0.05 level, $\pm$ 1.96 would be used as the values. These would then be adjusted based on the findings of the formula above. Adding the value above to the lower limit would produce a Z score of -3.29 ($-1.96 - 1.33$). Adding the value to the upper limit would produce a Z score of 0.63 ($1.96 - 1.33$). If the area under the normal curve was calculated for each of these values, they would equal 0.4995 for the lower limit and 0.2357 for the upper limit. Adding these two would result in a probability of 0.7352 of making a Type II error in this case.

An often asked question at this point in the discussion is, Which type of error is better? It is obvious that, for any given research, lessening the probability of committing one type of error leads to an increase in the probability of committing the other type of error. Given this balancing act, which should a researcher attempt to lessen? The answer lies in what the researcher is attempting to do.

Researchers can guard against making a Type I error by setting the significance level (the alpha level) high. If conducting research that had the potential to change the entire education system in the state, a researcher would want to be very certain of his or her results. In this case, the researcher might set the significance level for rejecting the null hypothesis at 0.001 or even 0.0001. This would set strict standards, and it would be difficult to reject the null hypothesis. The chances of committing a Type I error, however, and changing the entire system based on a false assumption are substantially less.

At other times, it may be more important to guard against making Type II errors. Researchers working on the leading edge of research may want to guard more against Type II errors because Type I errors will be brought out in future research, whereas a Type II error might kill the research forever. For example, if conducting research on a new fuel that could reduce U.S. dependency on oil, the researcher might want to set the rejection level at 0.90, 0.80, or even 0.60. It is true that there would be up to a 40% chance of committing a Type I error, but that may be acceptable. In this case, if the fuel provides *some* benefits, the program may be considered a success and should be continued. Future research could use stricter alpha levels and a more rigorous evaluation of the fuel. It may be more important at this stage, though, to create the fuel and give it time to see if it can be refined. Setting a high significance level may not give the fuel that opportunity.

9-3   Conclusion

This chapter concluded the discussion of concepts of inferential analyses. This chapter discussed the difference between descriptive and inferential analyses and the importance of each type in conducting research. Inferential analysis is built upon the foundations of the central limit theorem, the normal curve, and sampling distributions. In this chapter, inferential analysis was further clarified and brought to practice with the differences between one-tailed and two-tailed tests and Type I and Type II errors. All of these feed into the process of hypothesis testing and give researchers the ability to conduct research on samples of all types and sizes, to make inferences between the samples, or to compare a sample to a population. The Z test and t-test provides hypothesis-testing tools that enable analysis of nominal level to ratio level data and facilitate comparison of one sample to a population or comparison of two samples. These tests are covered in Chapter 10.

9-4   Equations in This Chapter

Beta:

$$\beta = \frac{\mu_{H_o} - \mu_{\text{true}}}{\sigma}$$

9-5   For Further Reading

Burke, C. J. A brief note on one-tailed tests. *Psychological Bulletin*, 1953, *50*, 384–387.

Hick, W. E. A note on one-tailed and two-tailed tests. *Psychological Review*, 1952, *59*, 316–318.

Jones, L. V. Tests of hypotheses: One-sided vs. two-sided alternatives. *Psychological Bulletin*, 1949, *46*, 43–46.

—— A rejoinder on one-tailed tests. *Psychological Bulletin*, 1954, *51*, 585–586.

Kimmel, H. D. Three criteria for the use of one-tailed tests. *Psychological Bulletin*, 1957, *54*, 351–353.

Marks, M. R. One- and two-tailed tests. *Psychological Review.* 1953, *60*, 207–208.

Marsh, H. W. Hau, K. T., Balla, J. R., & Grayson, D. Is more ever too much? The number of indicators per factor in confirmatory factor analysis. Unpublished manuscript, 1997.

Neyman, J., & Pearson, E. S. On the use and interpretation of certain test criteria for purposes of statistical inference. *Biometrika*, 1928, *20A*, 175–240.

—— & ——. On the problem of the most efficient test of statistical hypotheses. *Philosophical Transactions of the Royal Society of London*, 1933, *231(A)*, 289–337.

Zetterberg, H. L. *On theory and verification in sociology*. Totowa, NJ: Bedminster Press, 1963.

9-6   Exercises

1. Find one or more journal articles that deal with hypothesis testing.

   a. Determine the research and null hypotheses of the research.

   b. Determine if the researchers are using a one-tailed or two-tailed analysis. What led you to this conclusion?

   c. Attempt to determine what method of sampling the researchers used.

   d. Attempt to determine what statistical test the researchers used. If you need help, refer to Chapter 10 for a discussion of the different types of tests.

   e. If provided, discuss the obtained and critical values of the analysis. A review of chi-square or the tests in Chapter 10 may be beneficial.

   f. Discuss the decision of the researchers. Was this decision reasonable given the analyses? Why or why not?

2. Type I and Type II errors are not often discussed in research articles, so it would be counterproductive to require a number of articles explaining these concepts. There is one article, however, that does address this issue: L. W. Sherman, & D. Weisburd, General deterrent effects of police patrol in crime "hot spots": A randomized study. *Justice Quarterly*, 1995, *12*(4), 625–648. Get this article and prepare to discuss the advantages and disadvantages of their arguments in class.

3. Find one or more journal articles in which a power analysis is performed or a discussion of statistical power is provided. What general conclusions about the research can you draw from this analysis or discussion?

Chapter 10
Hypothesis Tests

Learning Objectives

- Discuss the assumption for a Z test.
- Calculate and interpret the Z test analysis.
- Discuss the assumption for a t-test.
- Calculate and interpret the t-test analysis.
- Evaluate SPSS output for Z and t-tests.

Key Terms

chi-square	t-test
one-sample t-test	two-sample t-test
Student's t distribution	Z test

Now we get down to the business of hypothesis testing. Several tests can be used to examine the null hypotheses associated with inferential analysis. The test used depends on the data available. There are four types of inferential hypothesis tests: chi-square, Z test, t-test, and ANOVA. We discussed chi-square essentially as a test of a hypothesis in Chapter 5, so we do not get into that here. ANOVA is addressed in Chapter 11. In this chapter we address the Z test and t-test.

10-1   *Z* Test

The foundation of inferential hypothesis testing is the Z test. The Z test examines whether a sample could have come from a known population or whether two samples come from the same population. The Z test is only suitable for large samples. This is typically taken to mean it should only be used with samples larger than 120.

The Z test draws directly from the normal curve, central limit theorem, and sampling distributions to test whether it is likely that two distributions are similar enough that they could be considered as being from the same population. Essentially, if the means of two distributions are close together and toward the middle of a normal curve, probability theory can be used to state that the means are likely from the same population. If the mean of one distribution is in the extreme tail of another distribution, however, it is unlikely that those means share the same population. The Z test is used to determine the relative location of these means.

Certain requirements must be met to use a Z test. First, the dependent variable must be interval level. Second, the population must be normal in distribution. Third, the means of the two samples drawn are equal. This is not an assumption; however, that is the goal of the research. Researchers actually want to violate this assumption in most hypothesis testing because if the null hypothesis is rejected, it is assumed that this requirement is violated.

As shown in **Figure 10-1**, the formula for a Z test is a combination of the formula for a Z score and confidence intervals. In essence, the formula for a Z test takes

$$z = \frac{\overline{X} - \mu}{\dfrac{\sigma}{\sqrt{N}}}$$

$$= \frac{78 - 84}{\dfrac{16}{\sqrt{125}}}$$

$$= \frac{78 - 84}{\dfrac{16}{11.8}}$$

$$= \frac{78 - 84}{1.43}$$

$$= \frac{-6}{1.43}$$

$$= -4.19$$

Figure 10-1   Calculation of a Z Test

the formula for the calculation of a Z score and applies it to hypothesis testing. This requires the inclusion of more information about the population and its relationship to the sample—information supplied by the formula for confidence intervals. In this formula, $\overline{X}$ is the mean of the sample, μ is the population mean or the mean of the sampling distribution, and the standard deviation of population (σ) divided by the square root of sample size (N) is the standard error of the mean.

Calculation and Example

Let us look at an example of a Z test using the steps outlined in Chapter 9. These steps are outlined below as they apply to conducting hypothesis tests using a Z test.

Step 1 is to determine the research hypothesis (H_r). For example, a research project seeks to determine if juvenile delinquents have a shorter attention span than other juveniles their age.

Step 2 is to develop the null hypothesis (H_0). In this case, the null hypothesis would be that the average attention span of juvenile delinquents is shorter than or equal to that of other juveniles.

Step 3 is to draw the sample. For this research, we might administer an attention-span survey instrument to 150 students in a particular high school and then to 125 juvenile delinquents from that same school, chosen at random from those passing through juvenile court in one year. We are thus examining the difference between the population of juveniles in this school and a sample selected from them (the juvenile delinquents).

Step 4 is to select the test. The test in this case would probably be a one-tailed Z test because, while it is possible that "normal" juveniles have a shorter attention span than juvenile delinquents, it would be meaningless and it would not add to the interpretation of the findings. Also, the level of significance will be set at 0.05 for this test.

Step 5 is to calculate the obtained value. When the instrument was administered to measure attention span in the high school, a mean attention span level of 84 was obtained. The same test was then given to a sample of juvenile delinquents, and a mean score of 78 was obtained with a standard deviation of 16. This information can be used to calculate the obtained value of the Z test. Using the formula for a Z test would produce the calculations in Figure 10-1. These calculations resulted in an obtained value of -4.19.

Step 6 is to obtain the critical value. Since this is a one-tailed test at the 0.05 level, we know the critical value will be 1.65.

The final step, step 7, is to make a decision. Here, the obtained value is -4.19 and the critical value is 1.65. An obtained value that is less than 1.65 would be considered nonsignificant. In other words, we cannot reject the null hypothesis (that is, $\mu \mathrel{<=} 84$) to favor the alternative hypothesis (that is, $\mu > 84$). A conclusion can be made that juvenile delinquents have shorter attention spans than the population as defined in this study. This does not necessarily mean, however, that all juvenile delinquents have a shorter attention span than all "normal" juveniles. That conclusion would go beyond the population to which we can generalize. We can generalize, however, to the population within the school and area examined.

The example above was treated as if a sample of juvenile delinquents were being drawn and compared to a population. You can see, however, that actually two samples were drawn and compared: one sample representing "normal juveniles"—the high school; and one sample representing the research (experimental) group—the juvenile delinquents. The Z tests (and t-tests) can also be used when the goal is specifically to compare two samples. A two-sample Z test has the same assumptions as a one-sample test, but there are two other assumptions for the two-sample test. First, for the central limit theorem and other concepts essential to inferential analysis to be fully applicable, both samples must meet the sample size requirements of a Z test. If only one of the samples is sufficiently large, then a t-test is more appropriate. Second, the two samples should be independent and random. This ensures that sampling units in each sample have an equal probability of being selected for the sample. This assumption can also be met if one sample is drawn and then divided into two groups, such as selecting one sample from the population and then dividing between male and female to examine the differences between these two samples.

10-2   *t*-Test

The Z test is the basic test of hypotheses. The problem is that sometimes researchers cannot obtain samples of more than 120. In these cases, a Z test should not be used. When the population standard deviation is known, or when the sample size is large enough to give confidence that the sample standard deviation is an accurate estimate of the population standard deviation, a Z test can be used with some confidence. When the sample size is small, however, the sample standard deviation is a more biased estimate of the population standard deviation than allowable for use with the central limit theorem. For this reason, a t-test is preferred under these circumstances. The only differences between a t-test and a Z test are that in a t-test

- s is used instead of σ (which was actually the case in the operational formula for a Z test as shown above).
- $N - 1$ is used instead of N in the denominator (which some texts use in the formula for a Z test).
- The critical value is adjusted for the sample size.

Assumptions of a *t*-Test

A *t*-test has the same assumptions and goals as a *Z* test, but in a somewhat modified fashion. First, it assumes that the data is at interval level, although the *t*-test can somewhat overcome this assumption, which is another reason why you would use a *t*-test over a *Z* test. A *t*-test also assumes a normal distribution; although the actual shape of the *t* distribution is not exactly normal, especially when sample sizes are smaller. Second, a *t*-test assumes that a probability sample has been used to select the sample elements. Finally, a *t*-test assumes that the observations are independent, as with a *Z* test.

There are also differences between a *t* distribution and a *Z* distribution. When sample sizes are small, the *t* distribution is much more platykurtic than a *Z* distribution. This is so because the data is likely to be more spread out around the mean of the distribution (where one data point can offset a point near the mean) rather than having lots of points (especially around the mean) that can compensate for data points farther in the tails. This is a good thing for *t*-tests, however, because it means that the critical value of *t* at a given significance level will be greater than the comparable value of *Z* at that significance level, making it more difficult to reject the null hypothesis. As the sample size increases, the shape of the *t* distribution gets taller, approximating the *Z* distribution. The critical values of *t* and *Z* also get closer together as *t* moves toward 120. At 120, the critical value of *t* is 1.98 (when at 0.05 significance level)—not very far from the 1.96 used with a *Z* test.

Calculation and Example

Let us look at an example of a *t*-test. Suppose the sample of juveniles taken above was only 20. A *Z* test could not be used reliably with that data, although a *t*-test could be used.

The same steps in the hypothesis-testing process up to determining the obtained value could also be used, so we will not go through those again.

In step 5, for the sake of comparison, assume that the same results were obtained as with the *Z* test: a mean attention span level of 84 for the population and a mean score of 78 with a standard deviation of 16 for the sample of juvenile delinquents. This would be comparing a small sample to the population of the high school. This information can then be used to calculate the obtained value of the *t*-test. The calculations for a *t*-test are shown in **Figure 10-2**. Since, in this case, a sample mean score of 78 was obtained from the juvenile delinquents, the null hypothesis would be that $H_0: \mu \leq 84$ and the alternative hypothesis would be $H_1: \mu > 84$.

Notice in this formula that the denominator has changed. This is so because we can no longer have as much confidence that we are obtaining an accurate estimate of the value of the population standard error. With large samples, there was confidence that even a sample standard deviation would be a sound estimate of the population standard error. With smaller samples, however, that assumption cannot be made. As such, the

$$t = \frac{\bar{X} - \mu}{\dfrac{s}{\sqrt{N-1}}}$$

$$= \frac{78 - 84}{\dfrac{16}{\sqrt{20-1}}}$$

$$= \frac{78 - 84}{\dfrac{16}{4.36}}$$

$$= \frac{78 - 84}{3.67}$$

$$= \frac{-6}{3.67}$$

$$= -1.63$$

Figure 10-2   Calculating a t-test

denominator of the formula must be changed to show that we are estimating the standard error and to make an adjustment for larger error in the calculations. Including the value of $N - 1$ in the denominator of this formula has the same effect as having larger critical values. Since we are making more-biased estimates of the mean and standard deviation of the population, we are less sure of our results, especially as the sample size decreases. As a result, precautions are taken by making it harder to reject the null hypothesis (harder to commit a Type I error). This is done by making the critical value larger than for z (and increasingly larger as the sample size decreases). This is accomplished by reducing the value of the denominator by 1. This makes the ratio obtained by the calculations smaller, thus making it more difficult to reject the null hypothesis. The value of $N - 1$ is also the degrees of freedom for this test. This will be important in determining the critical value. Using this formula, we get a value of -1.63.

Step 6 is to obtain the critical value. Since this is a one-tailed test at the 0.05 level using 19 degrees of freedom ($N - 1$), the table in Appendix C would be used to determine the critical level. Using this table, the critical value will be 1.729. As you can tell from the calculations, we did not attain as large an absolute value for the obtained value of t as when calculating z, and the absolute critical value for this sample size is larger than for the Z test. Both of these work to make it harder to reject the null hypothesis in this case.

Step 7 is to invoke the decision criteria. Here, the obtained value is -1.63 and a critical value is 1.729. An obtained value that is less than 1.729 would be considered nonsignificant. Using the decision criteria, we would fail to reject the null hypothesis at the 0.05 level and conclude that there is no statistically significant difference between the attention spans of "normal" juveniles and delinquents.

10-3   SPSS Analysis for *Z* Tests and *t*-Tests

SPSS includes only *t*-tests in its analysis. This is probably for several reasons. First, it is possible to calculate a Z score for a given variable or distribution. Since the cutoff values for a Z test are well known (1.65, 1.96, 2.58, for example), it would be a simple matter to compare the obtained Z score with a desired critical value. Also, as discussed above, as sample sizes associated with *t*-tests increase, the *t* distribution becomes a closer approximation of a *z* distribution. There is also very little practical difference between the calculations for a *t*-test and those for a Z test. Furthermore, as discussed above, the critical values for a Z test and a *t*-test become closer at sample sizes above 120. Since one requirement of the Z test is a sample size above 120, the critical values will be very close or the same for these two tests. For large sample sizes (of at least 120), therefore, the SPSS *t*-test could be used as a Z test.

One-Sample *t*-Test

Table 10-1 is a sample output from SPSS showing a one-sample *t*-test comparing the sample mean to the population parameter (0 in this case). Notice that this output contains two sections. The first section displays descriptive values for the variable that is

One-Sample Statistics				
	N	Mean	Std. Deviation	Std. Error Mean
Delinquent Incidents for the Census Tract	45	39.02	40.194	5.992

One-Sample Test						
	Test Value = 0					
	t	df	Sig. (2-tailed)	Mean Difference	95% Confidence Interval of the Difference	
					Lower	Upper
Delinquent Incidents for the Census Tract	6.513	44	0.000	39.02	26.95	51.10

Table 10-1   SPSS Output for One-Sample *t*-test

chosen to be compared to the population. The second set of values shows the results of the *t*-test.

The first section of this output contains the same values that could be displayed with a frequency distribution of this variable or with any other descriptive analysis. This underscores the importance of conducting thorough univariate and other descriptive analyses even when conducting inferential tests. This output shows the sample size (45), from which it can be determined that a *t*-test is appropriate. It also shows the mean of the sample (the expected value of the population), which is the value that we would use in a null or research hypothesis to compare to the theoretical population parameter. Also included is the standard deviation of the sample. This shows a large standard deviation within the sample. The final piece of information is the estimated standard error of the mean, which could be used in hand calculations of the *t*-value if something other than the standard SPSS output was desired.

Box 10-1   How Do You Do That?

1. Open a data set such as one provided at go.jblearning.com/Walker.
   a. Start SPSS.
   b. Select File, then Open, then Data.
   c. Select the file you want to open, then select Open.
2. Once the data is visible, select Analyze, Compare Means, One-Sample *t*-Test
   . . .
3. Select the variable you wish to examine and press the ▶ next to the Test Variable(s) window.
4. Click OK.
5. An output window should appear containing tables similar to the One-Sample *t*-Tests results displayed in Table 10-1.

The second section of the output in Table 10-1 is the results of the *t*-test, which include several pieces of important information. The first value is the obtained value of the *t*-test (*t*). This is the value that is compared to the critical value in the *t* table if this test is done by hand. The next value in the table is the degrees of freedom. This is calculated as $N - 1$. The next value is the significance of the *t*-test. Instead of using the cutoff values in a table, this output provides the exact significance value for the obtained *t*-value. Incidentally, notice that the significance value is for a two-tailed test. To obtain results for a one-tailed test, simply compare the *t*-value to the critical value in a one-tailed *t* table at 44 degrees of freedom, as was done above. Here, the significance value is 0.000. This means that there is a statistically significant difference between the sample mean and the population parameter (0 in this example), and the null hypothesis could be rejected. This is the same procedure as used with other measures of the statistical significance or hypothesis testing. The next value in this output is called the *mean difference*. This is the mean as stated in the descriptive analysis in the first section of the output. The final portion of the output is the confidence intervals around the mean. These are the boundaries around which we are 95% sure the population parameter (mean) lies. It can be stated with confidence that the population parameter should lie between 26.95 and 51.10, with the expected value being 39.02.

To return again to the issue of one-tailed versus two-tailed tests, there is an additional caution for the *t*-test. Remember that one of the reasons for using a *t*-test is that there is less assurance of a normal population distribution.

Two-Sample *t*-Tests

As discussed above, although *Z* tests and *t*-tests are established and based on calculations of one sample compared to a population, it is rare that researchers actually know (or can even approximate) population parameters. It is more likely that a researcher will draw two samples—one sample that is the subject of the research (usually an experimental group) and one sample to "represent" the population (usually a control group). In this case, the experimental group is usually examined in an attempt to determine if it is different in some ways from the control group. If that is the case, the researcher usually concludes that the difference is the result of the treatment or whatever research is being conducted. The difference between the groups is interpreted as a difference between two population means. Examining the differences between these two samples is accomplished with a two-sample *t*-test (or *Z* test).

The procedures for conducting a two-sample *t*-test are the same as those for a *t*-test comparing a sample to a population, with the exception of a change in calculating the obtained value. The formula for a two-sample *t*-test is

$$t = \frac{\overline{X}_1 - \overline{X}_2}{\sqrt{\dfrac{s_1^2}{N_1 - 1} + \dfrac{s_2^2}{N_2 - 1}}}$$

Essentially, the only difference here is that this formula takes into account the means and standard deviations of the two samples rather than the mean of one sample and the mean and standard deviation of the population. Also, since the main difference between a *Z* test and a *t*-test is the denominator, this formula can be used for a two-sample *Z* test simply by replacing the value in the denominator (*N* instead of *N* − 1).

Box 10-2   How Do You Do That?

1. Open a data set such as one provided on the CD in the back of this book.

   a. Start SPSS.

   b. Select File, then Open, then Data.

   c. Select the file you want to open, then select Open.

2. Once the data is visible, select Analyze, Compare Means, Independent-Samples *t*-Test . . .

3. Select the variable you wish to examine and press the ▶ next to the Test Variable(s) window.

4. Select the two category variable you want to group by and press the ▶ next to the Grouping Variable window.

5. Click on Define Groups.

6. Insert the two-pronged numeric coding associated with that variable in each box.

7. Click Continue.

8. Click OK.

9. An output window should appear containing tables similar to the Two-Sample *t*-Tests results displayed in Table 10-2.

An example SPSS output for a two-sample *t*-test is shown in **Table 10-2**. Here, those juveniles who reported being a member of a gang are compared to those reporting that they were not in a gang in relation to whether the juvenile had been arrested.

As with a one-sample *t*-test, the first section of the output contains descriptive values for the two samples. This section provides information on the different sample sizes. More importantly, it provides information on the differences in the means and standard deviations between the two groups. As with the one-sample *t*-test, this output also shows the expected standard error of the mean for both samples.

The requirement for independent samples also applies here, although it is more typical for independence to be maintained in a two-sample *t*-test because researchers are often physically drawing two samples. There is also the requirement of equality of variances with a two-sample test. The equality of variances is examined in SPSS with Levene's test for equality of variances. This is the same test that will be used in ANOVA, and for the same reason. In this case, Levene's test has a significant value for the equality of variances (0.023), so the *t*-test should be reconsidered. If Levene's test is not significant, the *t*-test should be reconsidered.

Group Statistics

Recoded ARREST varible to represent Yes or No	Are there people in your neighborhood or school who say they are in a gang?	N	Mean	Std. Deviation	Std. Error Mean
	Yes	178	1.90	0.295	0.022
	No	104	1.94	.234	0.023

Independent Samples Test

		Levene's Test for Equality of Variances		t-Test for Equality of Means					95% Confidence Interval of the Difference	
		F	Sig.	t	df	Sig. (2-tailed)	Mean Difference	Std. Error Difference	Lower	Upper
Recoded ARREST	Equal variances assumed	5.203	0.023	−1.118	280	0.265	−0.04	0.034	−0.104	0.029
	Equal variances not assumed			−1.186	254.782	0.237	−0.04	0.032	−0.101	0.025

Table 10-2　Two-Sample Test

The output for a two-sample t-test is essentially the same as that for a one-sample test. The value of t is the obtained t-value for the two samples. Here, the value is -1.186. This value could be compared to the critical value in a t table for the same degrees of freedom. A difference between a one-sample and a two-sample test is in the calculation of the degrees of freedom. Since there are two samples, degrees of freedom must be calculated for each sample. The expression for calculating degrees of freedom for a two-sample t-test is $N_1 + N_2 - 2$. In this case, it would make the degrees of freedom $178 + 104 - 2 = 254.782$. The value given under Sig. is the significance level for the null hypothesis. With a 0.237 value in this case, we would fail to reject the null hypothesis. Since the null hypothesis could not be rejected, the confidence intervals may be of value. Instead of testing whether the two means are different, the confidence intervals attempt to determine the actual location of the parameter value. This output also contains values for the mean of the difference between the samples and the standard error of the difference.

A final note about t-tests. Although a t-test is used over a Z test because we are less able to invoke the central limit theorem, it is important to remember that the central limit theorem has not been abandoned. Without the central limit theorem, it would be impossible to determine that the values used in a t-test are approximations, however gross, of the population parameters. It is more a degrading of the ability to use the central limit theorem, rather than an abandonment of it.

10-4   Conclusion

This concludes the discussion of bivariate inferential analyses. In this discussion, you should have learned the process of hypothesis testing that gives researchers the ability to conduct research on samples of all types and sizes, to make inferences between the samples, or to compare a sample to a population. You should also have learned the difference between Z tests and t-tests, when to use them, and how to interpret them. Chapter 11 focuses on the last type of inferential statistic, the F-test. A discussion of analysis of variance (ANOVA) will facilitate the F-test, as the F-test is one of the key statistics found in ANOVA output.

10-5   Equations in This Chapter

Z Test (population):

$$Z = \frac{\overline{X} - \mu}{\dfrac{\sigma}{\sqrt{N}}}$$

Z Test (sample):

$$Z = \frac{\overline{X} - \mu}{\dfrac{s}{\sqrt{N}}}$$

t-Test (obtained value):

$$t = \frac{\overline{X} - \mu}{\dfrac{s}{\sqrt{N - 1}}}$$

t-Test (two-sample):

$$t = \frac{\overline{X}_1 - \overline{X}_2}{\sqrt{\dfrac{s_1^2}{N_1 - 1} + \dfrac{s_2^2}{N_2 - 1}}}$$

10-6 For Further Reading

Gosset, W. S. *"Student's" collected papers*, Ed. Pearson, E. S., & Wishart, J. (Eds.). London: Biometrika Office, University College, 1943.
Laplace, P. S. *Celestial mechanics.* New York: Chelsea Publishing Co., 1966.

10-7 Exercises

1. A researcher at a counseling clinic wants to evaluate the effectiveness of the program. To do this, she gathers data on 10 people who have been assigned by the court to counseling. She also gathers a control group of people who have the same characteristics and who are receiving counseling at the clinic but who have never been arrested. The data gathered by the researcher is as follows:

   a. Find the mean number of counseling visits for the criminals and noncriminals.

   b. Find the standard deviation for the criminals and noncriminals.

   c. Using sample 1, find the probability (area under the normal curve) of finding a criminal with between 4 and 6 visits.

   d. Assume that the standard deviation in sample 1 is the *population* standard deviation.

    (i) Find the standard error of the mean.

    (ii) Find the 95% confidence interval.

  e. For sample 2:

    (i) Find the standard error of the mean.

    (ii) Find the 99% confidence interval.

  f. State the null hypothesis to test the difference between the two samples.

  g. State the research hypothesis to test for *any* difference between the two groups.

  h. Test the hypothesis at the 0.01 level of a difference between the criminals as a sample and noncriminals as the population.

| Number of Visits for Professional Counseling ||
Sample 1, Criminals	Sample 2, Noncriminals
7	4
7	2
7	5
8	1
8	1
6	4
5	4
6	3
7	5
7	4

2. A group of social scientists wanted to determine if police officers have a higher IQ than the normal public. To test this theory, they took a sample of 140 police officers and administered an IQ test. The mean score for officers was 110. Knowing that the average IQ in the general public is 100 with a standard deviation of 15, test to see if these researchers were right. Use the steps in the research process to outline your answer.

3. What would the result be if the researchers had taken a sample of only 30 officers?

Chapter 11
Multivariate Statistics, ANOVA, and OLS Regression

Learning Objectives

- Identify the underlying concepts of multivariate analyses.
- Explain how the underlying concepts of multivariate analyses can impact research methodologically.
- Understand analysis of variance (ANOVA).
- Interpret the statistics associated with ANOVA.
- Understand ordinary least-squares (OLS) regression.
- Interpret the statistics associated with OLS regression.

Key Terms

additive effect
ANOVA
beta
causation
coefficients
confounding variables
error
F test
interaction
OLS regression

parsimony
R-square
robustness
specification error
sum of squares between groups
sum of squares within groups
synergy effect
temporal ordering
unstandardized coefficient

The world is not a simplistic place. It is seldom that a single variable will be wholly responsible for changes in another variable. Likewise it is possible that multiple samples will result in different outcomes when we compare samples to each other or compare samples to a population. In the social sciences, many actions and/or characteristics factor into decisions and outcomes, some of which go unnoticed. As such, multivariate statistics are necessary to evaluate the relationship among three or more variables.

This chapter addresses multivariate analyses. The chapter begins with an examination of the building block concepts and theoretical and methodological issues associated with multivariate analyses. While many of these issues are more methodological than statistical, this discussion will facilitate an understanding of multivariate statistics. The chapter focuses on two of the most prevalent multivariate statistical techniques: analysis of variance (ANOVA) and ordinary least squares (OLS) regression. *ANOVA* is commonly used as a multivariate inferential analysis technique, whereas *OLS regression* is used as a multivariate descriptive technique.

11-1 Multivariate Concepts

This section examines the theoretical and methodological underpinnings of multivariate analyses. Although many of the issues addressed in this section are more methodological than statistical, they are important for multivariate analyses because they can influence the analysis or the interpretation of findings.

Interaction

Analyzing the interaction among variables is the specialty of multivariate analysis techniques. In its most general sense, *interaction* can be any change in one variable that produces, or is associated with, change in another variable. When most researchers speak of interaction among variables in research, however, they typically are speaking of the effect that two or more variables have on the dependent variable. This is the combined effect, cause, or association of all of the combined variables on the dependent variable.

If two variables explain some variation in a dependent variable, they can be said to interact with each other and with the dependent variable. These two variables have at least an *additive effect*. That is, they each explain a part of the variation in the dependent variable, much as you would explain the whole of a pie chart by simply explaining each of the parts and how much they contribute to the total. Interactions can explain more of the variation in the dependent variable than the simple sum of their separate effects, however. Variables should come together in a *synergy effect*, in which the sum of their contribution is greater than their individual effects. This is most typically how interaction of variables is discussed in research.

Causation

Causal ordering is the reason many researchers undertake multivariate analysis. Establishing causal ordering requires certain steps, including establishing association among the variables, determining temporal ordering, and eliminating confounding variables.

There must be some relationship between the variables, or nothing is gained from the research. The first step in attempting to establish causality is to determine if an association exists. Although not infallible, a general rule is that if two variables are not associated, one cannot be the cause of the other. The procedures used in previous chapters to examine a bivariate relationship, and the univariate measures upon which those bivariate analyses are based, then, should be the first step in any attempt to establish causality.

There are two components to association that should be stressed. These are the magnitude and the consistency of the association. The magnitude of an association is the existence and strength of the association. Consistency (often addressed as reliability) concerns address whether association remains constant under a variety of conditions. If an association has sufficient magnitude (it has a substantial and statistically significant association) and it is consistent over time, it lends credence to the argument that some causal nexus may exist.

The second major step in establishing causality is to examine the *temporal ordering* of the variables. Temporal ordering is the relationship in time between two variables. Temporal ordering examines the variables at time 1 and any change that has occurred at time 2. The change, difference, or relationship between time 1 and time 2 is the temporal ordering.

Temporal ordering comes into play in causal modeling because the independent, causal variable must either occur first or change prior to the dependent variable's changing. Remember that research typically examines change in the independent variable that is producing or related to change in the dependent variable. If the independent variable does not change and the dependent variable does, it makes it difficult to establish a relationship based on that change. Additionally, if the dependent variable changes before the independent variable changes, it would be difficult to state that the change in the independent variable produced the change in the dependent variable. If the independent variable changes first, however, and then the dependent variable changes, there is at least some probable cause to further examine the relationship to determine whether the variables just happened to change in this order or the change in one produced change in the other.

The final step in dealing with causality is to eliminate confounding variables, often called *rival causal factors* when used in this context. *Confounding variables* are often present in research. Unknown confounding variables can seriously influence the explanation of a causal relationship, both theoretically and in the interpretation of the analysis, because you do not have all of the variables that are important to the model identified for examination. Confounding variables can be dealt with either theoretically or through analysis.

Eliminating rival causal factors is important because the theory, explanation, and interpretation of a causal relationship require not only that the independent variable change first but also that it produce change in the dependent variable. If there is another variable that is producing the change—even if the independent variable is producing change in the confounding variable, which is then producing change in the dependent variable—then the relationship is not adequately explained and the model is not complete.

Robustness

Robustness of a statistical procedure is important when one wishes to use analyses appropriate for interval and ratio level data. Interval level analyses require the data to be interval level and normally distributed. In certain cases, there is the exception that dichotomized nominal data or ordinal data of a sufficiently large scale can be used with interval level analyses. In these cases, the data should be as close to a normal distribution as possible. *Robustness* is the ability of a statistical procedure to provide accurate results in spite of the fact that its assumptions have been violated. Typically, this translates to an interval level statistical procedure that is able to work with less than truly interval level data or with data that is not normally distributed.

Error

Related to the issue of robustness is that of *error*. There are different kinds of error: measurement error, observation error, random error, systematic error, and others. Error is present in all research. Error is such a part of multivariate analysis that it is specifically accounted for in some statistical analyses. For example, the formula used for regression is $Y = a + b(X) + e$. The e in this formula represents random error in the model. This e can simply be thought of as what we do not know. For instance, if we were examining the effects of genetics on the possibility of a child having ADHD, we would want to examine both family behavior and the behavior of the child. In research it is common not to be able to capture variables for both these concepts. Here, e captures the missing information we did not have in the analytic model. Error must be dealt with and accounted for as much as possible in theoretical and methodological planning and in the statistical analysis of any research project.

Parsimony

Attempts to obtain a complete model often lead researchers to include as many variables as possible. While this may result in the highest amount of explained variation in the dependent variable, it may make the model more complex than necessary. Many of the included variables may not add much to the model, may not add anything to the model, or may reduce the variation explained. In these cases, it may be better not to have the variables in the model at all. Balancing the need to include all necessary variables, the need to explain as much of the variation in the dependent variable as possible, and the need to have the most straightforward model is the concept of *parsimony*.

Parsimony is the attempt to identify the smallest number of the most important influences on a dependent variable. Especially in something as complex as studying human behavior, there are almost always more influences on a model than can possibly be measured. Parsimony means that if a variable can be removed from a model without seriously affecting it, the variable should be removed so the model may be as simple as possible. It is important to remember, however, that the principle of parsimony does not mean that the simplest model should always be accepted, only that if two models are equal and competing, the simpler should be chosen or that if a variable can be removed without seriously affecting the model, it should be removed and the model made simpler.

11-2   Analysis of Variance (ANOVA)

Sometimes comparisons must be made among three or more groups in conducting inferential research. This can be accomplished with Z tests or t-tests, but that would require testing each pair of possible groups and then combining the results for hypothesis testing, which is not only time-consuming but also tedious. This would also be a problem because it would greatly increase the possibility of a Type I error (rejecting a null hypothesis that is true) because the different tests would not be completely independent and could double-measure some differences. There would also be the problem of finding some pairs of groups that were statistically significant and others that were not. Then a decision would have to be made concerning which to believe. Multiple z or t-tests are not required to explain more than two groups because the F-test allows researchers to make comparisons among three or more groups accurately.

The F-test is put into place through a statistical procedure called *analysis of variance*, or *ANOVA*. ANOVA is a test of the measure of dispersion between group means.

This test allows the simultaneous comparison of the means of more than two samples. Specifically, ANOVA tests the null hypothesis that several group means are equal (H_0: $\overline{X_1} = \overline{X_2} = \overline{X_3}$. . .). It does this by examining the variability of data within each group and the variability of data between group means.

There are two types of ANOVA procedures for univariate and multivariate analyses. The first is *one-way ANOVA*. This is essentially a bivariate procedure where there is a single dependent variable with different categories. For a multivariate model, a simple factorial ANOVA (often called MANOVA) is used. This section focuses on one-way ANOVA.

Assumptions of ANOVA

There are several assumptions important for ANOVA analyses. These are generally the same as those for Z and t-tests.

The first assumption is that the data should be random samples from normal populations. If the sample is not random or if the population is not normal, then it makes the inferences suspect at best and likely impossible.

The second assumption is that the population variances are equal for all groups. This seems rather severe since we do not know the population parameters (or we could simply examine them with descriptive statistics). It is possible to measure the extent to which the variances are equal in the population; this is accomplished through a Levene test. The *Levene test* addresses the null hypothesis that all variances are equal. If the significance value for the Levene test is significant, then you can reject this null hypothesis and assume that the variances are not equal. If this value is not significant, then you should reconsider using ANOVA. The results of the Levene test for the data to be used in the ANOVA analysis example used in this chapter are shown in **Table 11-1**. The analysis comes from the data set entitled 2010 General Social Survey. Notice here that the Levene test is statistically significant, so we could reject the null hypothesis that all of the variances are not equal and continue with our interpretation of the ANOVA results.

FAVOR SPANKING TO DISCIPLINE CHILD			
Levene Statistic	**df$_1$**	**df$_2$**	**Sig.**
3.723	12	1,394	0.000

Table 11-1   Test of Homogeneity of Variances

Finally, it is important for a one-way ANOVA that the variables be independent. You should not use ANOVA in a time series or similar design where the same variables are observed over time. This is so because it makes the test think it has more degrees of freedom than are actually present in the data, thus negatively influencing the results. Further, it is possible the same person will be observed more than once and ANOVA calculations will assume it is a different person.

Calculation and Interpretation

Although the calculations for an *F*-test are more complicated, and more suited to the use of computers, the procedures for using an *F*-test as an inferential analysis procedure are the same as with a *Z* test or *t*-test.

Box 11-1   How Do You Do That?

1. Open a data set such as one provided at go.jblearning.com/Walker.
   a. Start SPSS.
   b. Select *File*, then *Open*, then *Data*.
   c. Select the file you want to open, then select *Open*.
2. Once the data is visible, select *Analyze, Compare Means, One-Way ANOVA. . . .*
3. Select the dependent variable you wish to examine, and press the ▶ next to the *Dependent List* window.
4. Select the independent variable you want to use, and press the ▶ next to the *Factor* window.
5. Click on *Options*.
6. Place a check by the *Descriptive* box and the *Homogeneity of Variance Test* box.
7. Click *Continue*.
8. Click on *Post Hoc. . . .*
9. Place a check by the *Bonferroni* box and click *Continue*.
10. Click *OK*.
11. An output window should appear containing tables similar to the One-Way ANOVA results displayed in Tables 11-1 through 11-5 in this chapter.

The first three steps in conducting an ANOVA are the same as with other hypothesis tests we examined in Chapter 9. Steps 1 and 2 in conducting an ANOVA are to determine the research and null hypotheses. The procedure for creating a research hypothesis and a null hypothesis for an *F*-test is the same as creating one for a *Z* test or *t*-test. The only difference is that the research hypothesis may be more complex because there are more samples to deal with. The null hypothesis is stated in such a way that the assumption is that the samples were drawn from the same population. Step 3 is to draw the samples for analysis.

Step 4 is to select the test. The *F*-test is the choice when there are more than two samples to be examined. The *F*-test is different from other hypothesis tests in that there is no issue of one-tailed versus two-tailed tests. Since there are more than two samples used, it is only possible to examine a hypothesis of whether there is a difference between some or all of the groups. As such, there is only one type of *F*-test associated with this kind of hypothesis test, a two-tailed test examining the differences among the groups.

Step 5 in the procedure is to examine the univariate statistics for each of the variables. This is important for ANOVA because it allows an examination of the central tendency and dispersion of the variables. Since ANOVA uses the means and variances to make comparisons, knowing these measures for the variables can provide a preliminary understanding of what is expected in the analysis.

In example below, we will explore the variance between samples of individuals who feel good about using corporal punishment on children with the type of religion an individual prefers. The variables used in this example are Relig (What is your religious preference/denomination?) and Spanking [Do you agree with spanking children as a primary form of discipline? (measured on a fully ordered ordinal scale)]. The univariate statistics for these variables are shown in **Table 11-2**.

Descriptive Statistics						
	N	Mean	Std. Dev.	Variance	Skewness	Kurtosis
Religious Preference	2,031	2.57	2.574	6.624	2.420	5.622
Favor Spanking to Discipline Child	1,417	2.15	0.869	0.755	0.423	−0.457
Valid *N* (listwise)	1,407					

Table 11-2   Univariate Measures for Religious Preference and Favoring
Spanking as Discipline

It is also important here to examine the combined descriptive statistics. This is essentially the univariate measures for the combined categories of the two variables under observation. This is necessary because there may be nothing unusual about each of the variables, but their joint measures may be nonnormal. The combined descriptive statistics for the variables above, as well as in a typical ANOVA, are shown in **Table 11-3**.

FAVOR SPANKING TO DISCIPLINE CHILD

	N	Mean	Std. Dev.	Std. Error	95% Confidence Interval for Mean		Minimum	Maximum
					Lower Bound	Upper Bound		
Protestant	666	2.01	0.822	0.032	1.95	2.07	1	4
Catholic	340	2.23	0.894	0.048	2.14	2.33	1	4
Jewish	19	2.47	1.073	0.246	1.96	2.99	1	4
None	261	2.37	0.883	0.055	2.26	2.48	1	4
Other (Specify)	10	1.90	1.101	0.348	1.11	2.69	1	4
Buddhism	15	2.27	0.799	0.206	1.82	2.71	1	3
Hinduism	3	2.33	0.577	0.333	0.90	3.77	2	3
Other Eastern	2	3.50	0.707	0.500	−2.85	9.85	3	4
Moslem/Islam	7	2.43	0.787	0.297	1.70	3.16	1	3
Orthodox–Christian	4	1.25	0.500	0.250	0.45	2.05	1	2
Christian	64	2.08	0.841	0.105	1.87	2.29	1	4
Native American	2	1.00	0.000	0.000	1.00	1.00	1	1
Inter-Nondenominational	14	2.21	0.802	0.214	1.75	2.68	1	4
Total	1,407	2.14	0.869	0.023	2.10	2.19	1	4

Table 11-3   Combined Descriptives Religious Preference and Favoring Spanking as Discipline

Step 6 is to examine the variability of the groups. This is a two-part procedure. The first part examines variability of data around the mean in each group. This is the *sum of squares within groups (SS$_w$)*, which is the sum of the squared deviations between each score and the group mean. This measures the variability within each of the categories. The second part of the procedure examines the variability between the group means. This analysis produces the *sum of squares between groups (SS$_b$)*, which is the sum of the squared deviations between each sample mean and the total mean for all observed values.

Each of these analyses has its own formula and analysis procedure. The formula for SS$_w$ is

$$SS_w = \Sigma(n_i - 1)s_i^2$$

where n_i is the sample size for each of the categories and s_i^2 is the variance for each of the categories. This totals (sums) the variance of each of the categories.

For the data in Table 11-3, SS$_w$ is calculated using the *N* and Std. Dev. columns. This results in the following calculations:

$$
\begin{aligned}
SS_w &= (666 - 1)(0.8222)^2 + (340 - 1)(0.8942)^2 + (19 - 1)(1.0732)^2 \\
&\quad + (261 - 1)(0.8832)^2 + (10 - 1)(1.1012)^2 + (15 - 1)(0.7992)^2 \\
&\quad + (3 - 1)(0.5772)^2 + (2 - 1)(0.7072)^2 + (7 - 1)(0.7872)^2 \\
&\quad + (4 - 1)(0.5002)^2 + (64 - 1)(0.8412)^2 + (2 - 1)(0)^2 + (14 - 1)(0.8022)^2 \\
&= (665)(0.67) + (339)(0.79) + (18)(10.15) + (260)(0.78) + (9)(1.21) \\
&\quad + (14)(0.64) + (2)(0.33) + (1)(0.49) + (6)(0.61) + (3)(0.25) + (63)(0.71) \\
&\quad + (1)(0) + (13)(0.64) \\
&= 445.6 + 267.81 + 20.7 + 202.8 + 10.89 + 8.96 + 0.66 + 0.49 + 3.66 \\
&\quad + 0.75 + 44.73 + 0 + 8.32 \\
&= 1,015.37
\end{aligned}
$$

Due to rounding issues associated with hand calculations, this number differs slightly from the SS$_w$ value indicated in **Table 11-4**.

FAVOR SPANKING TO DISCIPLINE CHILD					
	Sum of Squares	**df**	**Mean Square**	**F**	**Sig.**
Between groups	40.994	12	3.416	4.662	0.000
Within groups	1,021.428	1,394	0.733		
Total	1,062.422	1,406			

Table 11-4   Output of One-Way ANOVA

The formula for SS_b is

$$SS_b = \Sigma n_i(\overline{X}_i - \overline{X})^2$$

where n is the sample size for each of the categories, $\overline{X}_i$ is the mean of each of the categories, and $\overline{X}$ is the total mean for all categories. This, in effect, subtracts the variance of each sample mean from the total mean, squares it, multiplies it by the number of samples, and then sums this value. For the data in Table 11-3, SS_b is calculated using the N and Mean columns, as shown in the following calculations:

$$
\begin{aligned}
SS_b = {} & 666(2.01 - 2.14)^2 + 340(2.23 - 2.14)^2 + 19(2.47 - 2.14)^2 \\
& + 261(2.37 - 2.14)^2 + 10(1.9 - 2.14)^2 + 15(2.27 - 2.14)^2 \\
& + 3(2.33 - 2.14)^2 + 2(3.5 - 2.14)^2 + 7(2.43 - 2.14)^2 + 4(1.25 - 2.14)^2 \\
& + 64(2.08 - 2.14)^2 + 2(1 - 2.14)^2 + 14(2.21 - 2.14)^2 \\
= {} & 666(0.02) + 340(0.01) + 19(0.11) + 261(0.05) + 10(0.06) + 15(0.02) \\
& + 3(0.04) + 2(1.84) + 7(0.08) + 4(0.79) + 64(0.003) + 2(1.29) + 14(0.07) \\
= {} & 13.32 + 3.4 + 2.09 + 13.05 + 0.6 + 0.3 + 0.12 + 3.68 + 0.56 + 3.16 + 0.19 \\
& + 2.58 + 0.98 \\
= {} & 44.03
\end{aligned}
$$

Again, due to rounding issues associated with hand calculations, the number differs slightly from the SS_b value indicated in Table 11-4.

The calculation for the F-test is somewhat different than other hypothesis tests in that the degrees of freedom must be taken into account in calculating the obtained value as well as in determining the critical value. Step 7 is to calculate the degrees of freedom for the F-test. The degrees of freedom for an F-test must take into account all of the variability within the model. To do this, you must account for variation both between groups and within groups. The formula for calculating the degrees of freedom for an F-test is

$$df_{total} = df_{within} + df_{between} = (N - k) + (k - 1)$$

where N is the number of cases and k is the number of categories. In this example, the degrees of freedom are $(1407 - 13) + (13 - 1) = 1{,}394 + 12 = 1{,}406$. This is also indicated in Table 11-4.

Now that the sums of squares and degrees of freedom have been calculated, we can test to see if the samples are different. Step 8 is to calculate the obtained value. It stands to reason that if different samples are being examined, they should be different from (have more variation around the total mean than) the individual samples themselves. If people are classified into groups based on their environment, history, etc., people in the same groups should be similar (little variation around the mean), but there should be some sharp differences between the groups.

This difference is examined with the F-ratio. The F-ratio is a measure of the size (MS) of the variation between groups relative to the size of the variation within groups. The expression for the F-ratio is

$$\frac{SS_b / df_{between}}{SS_w / df_{within}} \quad \text{or} \quad \frac{MS_b}{MS_w}$$

Only when the MS_b is larger than MS_w can the null hypothesis that there is a true difference between the groups be rejected. If there is no difference at all between the groups, the result of this calculation will be 1. If there is little difference between the groups, the value will be close to 1 or less than 1. As with other tests of the null hypothesis, the larger the value of F, the more likely we are to reject the null hypothesis. For this example, the F-ratio would be calculated as $(44.03/12)/(1,015.37/1,394) = 5.037$ (again slightly off from Table 11-4 due to rounding error).

Step 9 in ANOVA is to obtain the critical value. The use of an F-test requires, like all other hypothesis tests, a determination of the degrees of freedom and the critical value to be used. For an F-test, the degrees of freedom are calculated as described above. Because both types of degrees of freedom are necessary, a separate table is required for each significance level used for an F-test.

As shown in Appendix D, both types of degrees of freedom for an F-test are used in the table to establish the critical value. For an F-test, the degrees of freedom between $(k - 1)$ determines the degrees of freedom across the top of the table, and the degrees of freedom within $N - k$ determines the degrees of freedom down the side of the table. Since the objective is to find more variation between than within, however, all of the values in Appendix D are greater than 1; and the larger the value, the farther into the tail the value is.

With these two values, the critical value of F can be obtained by determining the point at which the degrees of freedom within intersects with the degrees of freedom between. In the example above this would produce a critical value from Appendix D of 1.67.

As with other hypothesis tests, however, determining the critical value in this way is generally not required. The F value is displayed along with its significance value in all computer statistics programs, so a table is not necessary to determine the critical value. The critical value of F and the significance value for the example above are shown in the SPSS printout in Table 11-4. Here you can see the analysis is statistically significant (sig. < 0.05) with an F value of 4.662.

Step 10 is the decision criteria. A decision can be made about whether to reject or fail to reject the null hypothesis that the variances among the groups equal 0. This step is the same as all other hypothesis tests. If the obtained value is greater than the critical value, the null hypothesis is rejected; otherwise, we fail to reject the null hypothesis. Using output from SPSS, if the value of F is significant (less than 0.05), the null hypothesis can be rejected and a conclusion made that the groups were drawn from different populations. If the value is not significant, the null hypothesis cannot be rejected, leading to the conclusion that the groups are equal and the data can be considered as being drawn from the same population. As shown in Table 11-4, the significance value is less than 0.05 (0.000), so the null hypothesis that there is no difference between the means of the groups can be rejected.

Table 11-4 indicates that there is a statistically significant difference across religions as to the acceptability of using corporal punishment to discipline children. The only caution is that the criticisms against hypothesis testing are voiced even more loudly for an F-test. Here, even though the null hypothesis that there is no difference between the groups may be rejected, we cannot say which of the groups are different, only that at least one of them is different from the others.

As with other hypothesis tests, you can determine if there is reason to believe the groups did or did not come from the same population, but little else. It would also be beneficial to know which groups are different in their means. This can be established through additional tests associated with ANOVA, called post hoc or multiple-comparison tests. A number of tests can be used to examine the difference of means between groups. These are somewhat more advanced, multivariate techniques that are not covered in this text.

11-3 Ordinary Least-Squares (OLS) Regression

Ordinary least-squares (OLS) regression is probably the most popular multivariate analysis procedure in criminal justice and criminology research. Often, when researchers say they conducted a regression, they are implying that they conducted an OLS regression. Although the terms *OLS regression* and *regression* are used interchangeably, they are not the same. OLS regression is not necessarily the simplest statistical procedure; but it is often taught first when introducing students to multivariate analysis because it is simply an extension of Pearson's product moment correlation (r) to multivariate analysis. There are other types of regressions (Logit, negative binomial, etc.) beyond OLS, but these are not addressed here.

Like Pearson's r, regression is a measure of association for interval level data (measuring existence, strength, and direction). In practice, it may be bivariate or multivariate (a bivariate regression is the same as Pearson's correlation). Also as for Pearson's r, the goal of regression is to determine the best-fitting straight line that summarizes the linear relationship between values of two or more variables. Regression takes advantage of the least-squares analysis of a line where the sum of the squares of the distance from each point to the line is minimized. This method minimizes the distance to all pairs of X, Y values and summarizes the relationship between the dependent variable (Y) and the independent variable (X). Finally, it should be reinforced that, like Pearson's r, regression will not always improve the prediction; it will only improve the average prediction.

As a means of statistical analysis, regression shows the linear relational effects of an independent variable on a dependent variable, controlling for the effects of other independent variables, plus the combined effects of all the independent variables, that is, predicting scores on a dependent variable using the combined predictive scores of several independent variables. The goal is to produce a combination of independent variables that will correlate as highly as possible with the dependent variable. This combination can then be used to predict values of the dependent variable, and the importance of each independent variable can be assessed.

Assumptions of OLS Regression

The first assumption of OLS regression is that the variables are interval level. Regression uses the mean and variance as the roots of its analysis. Data that is not suitable to be examined using the mean and variance should not be used in a regression analysis. The one exception is dichotomized nominal level data or data that can be dichotomized or dummy coded. A dependent variable with dichotomized data requires a special type of regression (Logit) and/or other specific methodological attention.

The second assumption of regression is that the variables are linearly associated in the coefficients and the error terms. As discussed with Pearson's correlation, a data set that is curvilinear will produce low regression coefficients even if there is a strong association among the variables. As discussed earlier, there are ways to detect nonlinearity. The most common method to detect nonlinearity is to examine bivariate scatterplots.

The next assumption of regression analysis goes back to the idea of parsimony, which is that there is no *specification error* in the model. This means that every independent variable critical to explaining the dependent variable is included in the model, but those that are not critical are excluded. There are four conditions under which this assumption is violated: (1) independent variables are included that should have been excluded; (2) independent variables are excluded that should have been included; (3) the proper variables are included but in the wrong form (for example, a curvilinear relationship that needs to be transformed); and (4) multicollinear variables are included (see below). Each of these misspecifications requires different methods of detecting and dealing with the specification error. The caution here is that misspecification is a theoretical rather than a statistical issue; therefore, misspecification must be dealt with at a theoretical and methodological level rather than a statistical level.

The final assumptions of OLS regression concern the error term. Error is a part of any research. When regression is used, it is important that every effort be made to eliminate measurement error. Two types of measurement error are important for regression analysis. The first is random, or unsystematic, error. This usually arises from coding mistakes and sometimes from using an instrument inappropriate for measurement. This influences the reliability of the findings of the regression analysis. The second type of error is nonrandom, or systematic, error. This is often the result of not eliminating rival causal factors. This source of error heavily influences the validity of the findings.

Analysis and Interpretation

The first step in conducting an OLS regression is similar to that of most statistical analyses covered in this book: developing variables through careful conceptualization and operationalization that will meet the assumption of OLS regression. The second step is to gather and code the data. The third step is to conduct a univariate analysis of all the variables to examine whether the data is appropriate for regression analysis. The fourth step is to conduct bivariate analyses of the data to evaluate potential multicollinearity. The fifth step is to run the regression. This is somewhat more involved than it would seem. Although many people do it, running a regression is not as simple as dumping the variables in a hat and waving the statistical wand over it. The variables should be entered in accordance with the theory, and each step of the regression model should be carefully analyzed to determine the effect that each variable and combination of variables have on the dependent variable. After running the regression, the sixth step is to interpret the output.

The following example uses data from the General Social Survey for 2010. The dependent variable is the number of hours per day an individual watches television. The independent variables include the respondent's age, sex, income, how often the respondent finds work stressful, and if the respondent ever has trouble sleeping. Each of these variables could be argued theoretically to contribute to the amount of television one watches in a single day. These variables were also included to show examples of how different types of variables (for example, dichotomized variables) perform in OLS regression analysis.

Box 11-2   How Do You Do That?

1. Open a data set such as one provided at go.jblearning.com/Walker.

   a. Start SPSS.

   b. Select *File*, then *Open*, then *Data*.

   c. Select the file you want to open, then select *Open*.

2. Once the data is visible, select *Analyze*, *Descriptive*, then *Regression*.

3. A list of different types of regression techniques will appear. Select *Linear*. There are other types of regression, some of which will be discussed in Chapter 12. For OLS regression, simply select *Linear*.

4. Select the dependent variable you wish to include in your analysis, and press the ▶ next to the window marked *Dependent*.

5. Select the independent variables you wish to include in your analysis, and press the ▶ next to the window marked *Independent*.

6. Make sure the word in the box for *Method* reads *Enter*.

7. For now, do not worry about the option boxes at the bottom of the window, and just press *OK*.

8. An output window should appear containing output similar to Table 11-5.

The output for OLS regression is generally more number oriented than anything you have seen to this point. The SPSS output for the OLS regression example is presented in **Table 11-5**. The first two tables in Table 11-5 pertain to the overall model, telling whether the model was significant and how much variance was explained in predicting the dependent variable by knowing all of the independent variables in the model. The third table presents coefficients on the effects of individual independent variables on the dependent variable. Although three tables of output are generated, they are fairly easy to interpret.

Five primary pieces of information should be evaluated in any multiple regression output. These represent the existence of a relationship for the model, the strength of the relationship for the model, the existence of a relationship for individual independent variables, the strength of the relationship for individual independent variables, and the relative importance of the independent variables.

The first piece of information is whether the model is significant (is the combined effect of all of the independent variables on the dependent variable statistically significant?). As with a bivariate analysis, if the relationship is not statistically significant, then there is no real reason to continue with the analyses. You can tell if the model is significant by examining the significance associated with the *F*-test. This is found in the Sig. column immediately to the left of the *F* column in the ANOVA table. As

Model Summary				
Model	R	R^2	Adjusted R^2	Std. Error of Estimate
1	0.225[a]	0.051	0.044	1.830

[a]Predictors: Constant, family income in constant dollars, trouble sleeping last 12 months, respondent's sex, age of respondent, how often does respondent find work stressful.

ANOVA[a]					
Model	Sum of Squares	df	Mean Square	F	Sig.
Regression	129.931	5	25.98	7.758	.000(a)
Residual	2441.803	729	3.35		
Total	2571.733	734			

[a]Dependent variable: hours per day watching TV.

[b]Predictors: Constant, family income in constant dollars, trouble sleeping last 12 months, respondent's sex, age of respondent, how often does respondent find work stressful.

Coefficients[a]	Unstandardized Coefficients		Standardized Coefficients		
Model	B	Std. Error	Beta	T	Sig.
Constant	2.747	0.393		6.985	0.000
Trouble sleeping in the last 12 months	0.085	0.069	0.047	1.228	0.220
How often does respondent find work stressful?	−0.059	0.070	−0.032	−0.850	0.396
Respondent's sex	−0.347	0.137	−0.092	−2.532	0.012
Age of respondent	0.014	0.005	0.103	2.783	0.006
Family income in constant dollars	0.00001	0.000	−0.206	−5.538	0.000

[a]Dependent variable: hours per day watching TV.

Table 11-5   OLS Regression Results with SPSS Output

with other analyses, if the significance is less than 0.05, the model is significant. In the example model above, the probability associated with F is 0.000. This is less than 0.05 and indicates that the model is significant. Since the model is significant, we can proceed to step 2.

The second piece of information addresses the strength of the overall model. This indicates how much the dependent variable can be explained using information from the independent variables. This can be determined by looking at R Square in the SPSS output. If the model is significant, the next logical question concerns how much the model explains in predicting the dependent variable. This can be ascertained by examining the value of the R^2. The value of R^2 is the proportion of variation in the dependent variable associated with variation in the independent variables. For a bivariate regression, this is equal to a squared Pearson's r; for a regression, this is the correlation between the dependent variable and all of the independent variables. In the example, the R^2 is equal to 0.051. When it is multiplied by 100, you get the percentage of variance explained by the model containing all of the variables. In this case, we have explained just over 5% of the variance in predicting how many hours of television the average respondent watches in a day. The model is weak in its ability to predict the number of hours of television viewing.

The third examination for OLS regression is whether the variables in the model are significant. If you know the model is significant and how much variance it explains, then you will want to know more about each individual variable. The first step in determining the importance of an individual variable is to explore the significance associated with T. This can be found on the table labeled *Coefficients* in the SPSS output. Look in the column labeled *Sig.* As always, you want to determine if the variable is statistically significant. Evaluating the significance associated with T in Table 11-5, we see that three of the variables in the model are statistically significant and two of the variables are not statistically significant. For the three significant variables, we can go on to the next steps; for the two that are not statistically significant, a decision should be made about whether they are theoretically needed for the model. If they are, they should be left in; if not, they may be dropped from the model.

The fourth examination is the strength of the individual contributions of the independent variables upon the dependent variable. This represents an analysis of the unstandardized effects of independent variables on the dependent variable. The unstandardized effects of independent variables are represented in the *Coefficients* table as either b or B; and Std. Error is the standard error of that coefficient. The *unstandardized coefficient* is interpreted generally thus: "We can expect an (increase or decrease) of (the value of the b coefficient) in the (dependent variable) for a one-unit change in the (independent variable)." The increase or the decrease is determined by the sign of the b coefficient. If the sign is negative, it is a decrease; if the sign is positive, it is an increase.

For family income using the wording denoted above, we can expect a decrease of 0.00001 hour of television viewing for a one-unit change in the amount of family income ($b = -0.00001$ in Table 11-5). In other words, the greater the income, the fewer hours of television viewing by the respondent. For age, we can expect an increase of

0.014 hour of television viewing daily for every additional year of life. On average, as we get older, we watch more television.

Dealing with dichotomous independent variables is somewhat easier as there is only one of the two values an independent variable can take. It is important to remember how the variable was coded. In the example, the only dichotomous variable is the respondent's sex. In this example, we can expect a very small decrease (-0.347) in hours of television viewing based on being female. Males are likely to watch more television, on average, every day.

The final step is to examine the standardized effects of independent variables on the dependent variable. This process puts all values into a standard measure and examines which variables make a greater contribution to the model. The Beta (β) value is the standardized regression coefficient. This standardization allows β to measure the contribution of variables irrespective of the scale upon which they were measured. Standardized scores are created when the data is converted to Z scores. Standardization also sets the mean to 0 and the standard deviation to 1. This allows the β's to be directly comparable between variables. The beta is the effect of a change of 1 standard deviation in an independent variable on the standard deviation of the dependent variable. In reality, beta represents the relative contribution that a particular variable makes to explaining variation in the dependent variable when other variables in the model are controlled for. This standardization of coefficients allows you to be able to rank-order the variables that are most important to the model.

Beta (β) values are found in the Beta column in Table 11-5. To interpret the standardized effects of the independent variables, multiply the value in the Beta column by 100 to convert to a percentage. After this is done, the variable with the greatest influence is family income, predicting almost 20% of the variance in the model. This indicates that family income is the greatest predictor of number of hours of television watched during the day. Age and sex both contribute about 10% of the variance in the model. These are relatively low percentages of the variance. Note that it does not matter if the value is negative. The size of the beta weight is the most important thing. As a rule, the bigger the beta, the better.

11-4 Conclusion

This chapter introduced the basics of multivariate analyses. The first section introduced some of the concepts and issues that are important for the completion of multivariate analysis. Although these do not directly affect the interpretation of analyses, these concepts are important to any multivariate analysis. This chapter also explored ANOVA as an inferential analysis dealing with multiple samples to examine how well they compare to the population from which they were drawn. Finally, this chapter examined OLS regression analysis and some of the most common techniques of interpreting statistical output. The two basic purposes of regression are to indicate the combined effect of all of the independent variables on the dependent variable and to indicate the separate or individual effects of each of the independent variables on the dependent variable. The discussions of these multivariate techniques were brief. For a better understanding, you will need to read more on both topics, through other advanced textbooks and peer-reviewed journal articles.

11-5   Equations in This Chapter

Sum of squares within groups:

$$SS_w = \Sigma(n_i - 1)s_i^2$$

Sum of squares between groups:

$$SS_b = \Sigma n_i(\overline{X}_i - \overline{X})^2$$

Degrees of freedom (*F*-test):

$$df_{total} = df_{within} + df_{between} = (N - k) + (k - 1)$$

F-ratio:

$$F = \frac{SS_b / df_{between}}{SS_w / df_{within}} = \frac{MS_b}{MS_w}$$

11-6   For Further Reading

Berry, W. D. *Understanding regression assumption.* Newbury Park, CA: Sage Publications, 1993.

— & Feldman, S. *Multiple regression in practice.* Newbury Park, CA: Sage Publications, 1985.

Box, G. E. P. Non-normality and tests of variances. *Biometrika*, 1953, *40*, 318–335.

Cohen, J. Partialed products *are* interactions; partialed vectors *are* curve components. *Psychological Bulletin*, 1978, *85*, 858–866.

Galton, F. 1877. Typical laws of heredity. *Nature*, 1877, *15*, 492.

—. Opening address. *Nature*, 1885, *32*, 507–510.

Garnett, J. C. M. On certain independent factors in mental measurement. *Proceedings of the Royal Society of London*, 1919, *96*, 91–111.

Yule, G. U. On the theory of correlation. *Journal of the Royal Statistical Society*, 1897, *60*, 812–854.

11-7   Exercises

1. Find journal articles that address some of the key concepts associated with multi-variate analyses. You may be able to find a single article that addresses several of these issues; or you may be required to use several articles to address all of these concepts. Be sure to include articles that address the following:

   a. Variable interaction

   b. Temporal and causal ordering

   c. Robustness of a statistical procedure

   d. Error

   e. Parsimony

2. Using the General Social Survey 2010 database, conduct an ANOVA on several variables you are interested in or think would impact one another. Discuss what limitations your analyses indicate.

3. Using the following regression output, interpret the results by using the methods outlined in this chapter. The dependent variable for this example is the number of delinquent acts per census tract. Be sure to discuss the significance of the model, R^2, the significance of the variables in the model, the unstandardized coefficients, and the standardized coefficients.

Model Summary				
Model	R	R^2	Adjusted R^2	Std. Error of Estimate
1	0.751[a]	0.564	0.481	28.956

[a]Predictors: Constant, number of families receiving social assistance, owner-occupied housing units, black heads of household, vacant housing units rented or sold but not occupied, population change, 1980–1990, boarded up housing units, median rental value.

ANOVA[a]					
Model	Sum of Squares	df	Mean Square	F	Sig.
Regression	40,061.840	7	5,723.120	6.826	0.000
Residual	31,023.138	37	838.463		
Total	71,084.978	44			

[a]Dependent variable: delinquent incidents for the census tract.

[b]Predictors: Constant, number of families receiving social assistance, owner-occupied housing units, black heads of household, vacant housing units rented or sold but not occupied, population change, 1980–1990, boarded up housing units, median rental value.

Table 11-6   OLS Regression Results with SPSS Output

Coefficients[a]

Model	Unstandardized Coefficients		Standardized Coefficients		
	B	Std. Error	Beta	T	Sig.
Constant	19.434	29.510		0.659	0.514
Vacant housing units rented or sold but not occupied	−0.133	0.248	−0.066	−0.538	0.594
Boarded up housing units	0.198	0.207	0.146	0.956	0.345
Median rental value	−3.135e-02	0.094	−0.060	−0.334	0.740
Population change, 1980–1990	−0.105	0.098	−0.134	−1.075	0.289
Black heads of household	0.102	0.021	0.675	4.832	0.000
Owner-occupied housing units	6.077e-04	0.008	0.011	0.077	0.939
Number of families receiving social assistance	−5.910E-03	0.108	−0.006	−0.055	0.957

[a]Dependent variable: delinquent incidents for the census tract.

Table 11-6   OLS Regression Results with SPSS Output, *continued*

4. Select a journal article that uses OLS regression as its primary analysis.

   a. Trace the development of the concepts and variables to determine if they are appropriate for the analysis (why or why not?).

   b. Before you look at the results of the analysis, attempt to analyze the output and see if you can come to the same conclusion(s) as the article did.

   c. Discuss the results and conclusions found by the author.

   d. Discuss the limitations of the analysis and how it differed from that outlined in this chapter.

Chapter 12
Putting It All Together

Learning Objectives

- Understand the relationship among statistics, research methods, and theory.
- Determine the use of descriptive or inferential statistics.
- Identify the abuses of statistics.

Over the course of this text, the topics have included

- The different possible statistical procedures
- How the type of data affects the statistical procedure used
- The mathematical foundations of statistical procedures through their formulas
- How to analyze and interpret statistical output

The goal of this final chapter is to look at how these are related, how statistics fit into the research process along with theory and methodology, and how all of these are applied in *practical* scientific inquiry.

What you should have noticed by now is how so much of the material in this book is interrelated. Look at how much of the chapters on univariate and even bivariate descriptive statistics is included in the chapter on ANOVA. The foundations of statistical analysis are very closely interrelated—so much so that you almost must take a statistics course before you can really understand a statistics course. As you can see after finishing this book, you really need the understanding that comes from learning about inferential analysis to understand descriptive analysis; and you need the understanding of descriptive analysis before you can fully understand inferential analysis. This same kind of interrelation spills over into the relationship among statistics, theory, and methodology. It is to this relationship that the discussion now turns.

12-1   The Relationship Among Statistics, Methodology, and Theory

Never be fooled into thinking that statistics can answer all of the questions of research. As discussed in the beginning of this book, statistical analysis is only one part of the complex work of scientific discovery. Good statistical analysis must be based on a sound and carefully planned methodology; and sound methodology is driven by careful construction of a theoretical and conceptual model.

That does not mean that theory and methodology can stand on their own, however. Theory without some statistical analysis is little more than armchair philosophizing. You have surely read articles in which the author was putting forth a lot of ideas with little or no empirical support, and you came away thinking, "That was OK, but I don't see how it fits in with reality." These articles have no support for their conclusions. To use the examples from the first chapter, it is like building a house without a foundation. It may stand for a while, but the least bit of wind will probably tumble it, and even the natural shift of the ground will bring it down. So it is with theories without statistical support. They may sound as if they would hold true, but they are often easily refuted because the author has nothing to back up his or her arguments; and the natural shifting of human behavior may change enough that the theory is no longer useful—and we do not know why because there was never a foundation for the arguments.

The same can be said for methodology without statistical analysis or qualitative support. Methodology is brought to life with analysis. Having a good theory with sound methodology and no analysis is tantamount to having a great idea for an invention but never telling anyone. Without statistical analysis, many forms of methodology cannot be accomplished.

It is also essential to understand that researchers cannot wait until the analysis stage of a research project to begin to think about what procedures to use. Waiting until this point will probably result in the researcher's having a very difficult time finding a good match between the data and an appropriate statistical procedure. For example, the researcher may have some data that is nominal, other data that is ordinal, and still other data that is interval. Although this can be overcome (especially by using nominal level analyses), it is not making the best use of the data. It is true that sometimes a researcher cannot avoid collecting data at different levels. Through careful conceptualization and operationalization, however, a researcher can often collect data that is at the appropriate level or is compatible for statistical analysis. Some even propose that researchers construct dummy tables (empty tables with only the headings) to see what the data will look like in certain bivariate analyses.

From the very outset of the research, therefore, a researcher should be cognizant of the statistical analyses to be used. When developing the primary and research questions, the researcher should be aware of what the data might look like and what analysis procedures would be most appropriate. This will ensure that the best analyses are used for the research to be conducted.

Understanding the statistical procedure at the outset of the research is also important in determining the sample size to be used. For example, to use a Z test requires a sample size of 120 or more. It is important, then, to have a full understanding of sample size requirements for particular statistical procedures early in the research process.

12-2   Describe It or Make Inferences

One of the biggest questions that arises in deciding on a statistical analysis procedure for research is whether to use descriptive or inferential analyses. This, of course, assumes that the researcher is not attempting to use descriptive analyses and make inferences from them, as happens all too often (see the section on abuses of statistics, below). The issue of descriptive versus inferential analyses is appropriate, and it should be a conscious decision made early in the research process.

Even though inferential analyses are central to many fields, there are those in the social sciences who argue that the data available are not appropriate for inferential analyses. For example, Labovitz (1970, 1971) argues that there is very little in social science data that supports an argument that the population parameter can be estimated with any real confidence. He proposes, as discussed in the section on inferential analyses, that we cannot even *estimate* the population parameters for social science data sufficiently to use them in inferential analyses. Furthermore, Labovitz argues that even if the population parameter could be estimated mathematically such that inferential formulas could be used, we do not have a good enough grasp on the characteristics of the population to be able to make sound inferences from a sample to the population. Selvin (1957) also argues that inferential analyses should not be used with surveys. He proposes that surveys are not a sufficient method of sampling and that the data is insufficient to estimate population parameters.

Given these arguments, should inferential analyses be abandoned for social sciences in favor of only using descriptive analyses? That is a decision that only you can make for your own research; however, abandoning inferential analyses is probably a little strong. The line between making inferences to a population and describing the data drawn is actually much finer that many would like to admit. In fact, many readers of research do not notice the difference. For example, if there is published research on trial judges in the Northwest, in the purest sense of statistical analysis, the results can be used in one of two ways: either they can be used as a descriptive analysis of the judges chosen; or if the proper sampling methodology has been followed, inferences can be made to all judges in the Northwest. Most readers will not interpret the findings this way, however. A large number of readers will infer (either explicitly or unconsciously) the results of the analysis to all judges in the United States. Is this technically correct? No, but most will make this leap of inference even if the researcher did not.

As the editor of a journal, I have also had to referee between authors who wished to report only descriptive analyses and reviewers who wanted to see significance tests (adding a significance value to lambda or Pearson's r, for example). One group explicitly did not want to make inferences with the data; the other group used tests of significance as an estimate of what might be expected in the population. Who was wrong in this case? Probably neither. Experienced researchers do not let the results of statistical analyses themselves sway their thinking. The results do not make the decision—the researcher makes the decision. Using the old statistical adage that statistics are like a lamp post for a drunk—used more for support than for illumination—most statisticians simply use the results of analyses to guide their theoretical decisions. In this case, the group that wanted to see the significance results perhaps did not want to make inferences beyond what the data allowed, but they would have liked the additional information to support or not support a decision to generalize the results.

While they are of value, inferential analyses should not be elevated to the place of prominence that they have in many disciplines, however. As discussed in previous chapters, inferential analyses are only as good as the univariate and bivariate (and sometimes multivariate) analyses upon which the conclusions can be drawn. In essence, inferences are based only on the observation of the relationships that exist in the sample. As repeatedly stated, rejection of the null hypothesis only means that there is a small chance that there is no relationship between the variables studied and that whatever is happening with the sample may happen in the population. As such, the description of what is happening in the sample is at least as important as making the inference and maybe more important.

In the end, it will be up to you to decide when and if to use descriptive or inferential analyses, and the most important decision may not be which to use. The most important decision should be what procedure is most appropriate for the data and research being conducted. A correct decision here will provide you with the proper tool to make the most of the results of the research. Like any tool, however, statistics can be misused. It is the abuses and misuses of statistics that should be avoided.

12-3   Abuses of Statistics

Probably the greatest abuse of statistics is the one discussed above—researchers employing descriptive analyses and trying to use them to make inferences. This is not the same as when significance results are included to assist in examining how the sample might be related to the population. The abuse suggested here occurs when researchers use purely descriptive analyses and make explicit references to the population.

There is also the problem of using the wrong analysis procedure for the data available or for the level of data. It is acceptable to use certain lower-level data with certain higher-order analyses, such as using dichotomized nominal level data with Pearson's *r*. Often, however, using lower-level data is a violation of the assumptions of the procedure. Even when it is not an explicit violation of the assumptions, any departures from the assumptions of a statistical procedure should be thoroughly analyzed and justified. For example, if you wanted to use Pearson's *r* and the data was in a Likert scale (1–5, high to low), it is accepted by some to do so; but you need to make sure that there is a good underlying continuum such that the data can be said to be somewhat continuous, and you should justify your use of Pearson's *r* with this data.

Another abuse of statistics is to simply ignore the assumptions of the statistical procedure. As in the example above, there are people who conduct correlations (Pearson's *r*) with any and all levels of data. They simply ignore the levels of measurement requirements. Others will use regression when more than one of the assumptions is so violated as to make the analysis practically worthless. This is not to say, however, that all of the assumptions must be strictly adhered to. Before using a statistical procedure when the assumptions are violated, the researcher should know how robust the procedure is to the violation. If the procedure is robust for the violation, then it may be acceptable to use the procedure in that manner.

The final abuse of statistics is in using the latest fad just to use it. Statistics is an evolving field. New procedures and improvements to old procedures are added almost daily. Indeed, our statistical techniques have surpassed researchers' sampling abilities. With every new advancement, researchers are better able to analyze data and draw conclusions. Many researchers get wrapped up in what is current, however. They will use a new statistical procedure with data that is perfectly suited for an existing procedure just to attempt to appear current. This is not necessarily wrong, but it is an abuse of statistics because the researcher is not using the most appropriate statistical procedure and is using it for the wrong reason.

12-4   When You Are on Your Own

One thing that may have bothered you about this text is that there were not always direct and steadfast rules. A lot of statistical analysis is knowing what applies (differently) in certain situations, knowing what assumptions may be violated, and justifying the procedure or interpretation. That is the nature of statistical analysis. Although there are a lot of rules and procedures, the majority probably can be violated under certain (sometimes many) conditions. Also, the key to statistical analysis is in the analysis.

Anyone can be taught the formulas; but you earn your money as a statistician and social scientist with your ability to interpret the findings.

When you are on your own, you will have a lot of latitude in how you work and what procedures you use. Whether you choose a descriptive or inferential analysis procedure is almost entirely up to you, depending, of course, on the type of data. Also, the particular statistical procedure that you choose is your decision. The rules that have been laid out in this text are designed to provide you with guidelines to use in making your selections. Additionally, the example analyses and interpretations were included to provide you with illustrations of how one might analyze or interpret particular findings from particular data. That does not mean that you must follow these guidelines or examples to the letter. There is a great deal of room for "artistic license" in statistical analysis. You may decide that the data requires a particular statistical procedure and that the results should be interpreted one way, and someone else may argue something completely different. Your job at that point (and any time you conduct research) will be to successfully argue your point. Your success will come from your ability to articulate your position.

When you stay within the guidelines presented in this text, you will have the support of hundreds of years of statistical analysis behind you. This does not mean that you may not draw the ire of a reviewer or reader, but it does mean that you have something to fall back on. Furthermore, we have attempted to provide you with the original works and writings where possible, so that if you are challenged, you can invoke the words of the person who developed the statistical procedure to support your arguments. This does not mean that you cannot disagree with what has been written here, or that you cannot depart from the guidelines presented; it only means that these are the more accepted attitudes about statistical analysis and that they are supported by a wider portion of social science researchers. If you choose to depart from the guidelines and discussion in this text, you only have to be sure of your arguments and have support for them.

12-5   Conclusion

We want to end with a short discussion of how you can benefit from the information contained here. There are four ways that statistics in general, and the material in this text, can affect you, depending on where you are in your academic career and what you want to do with your life.

If you are a graduating senior and want to be unemployed all of the rest of your life, you will probably not be affected very much by this material, except that you will know more about how the world around you works (such as election polls). This probably is not your goal.

If you are graduating and you plan to go to work, you may see this material again. Do not be caught in the trap of thinking, "I'll never need this stuff!" It is not uncommon for a person who never thought he or she would work in the research area to find a great job where ability to do research and conduct rudimentary analyses is needed. Finally, even in the most unexpected places, you can be moved into a job that requires you to conduct statistical analyses, interpret research, and write grants simply because you've got a college education. Don't underestimate the future; it is better to be open-minded and prepared rather than closed-minded and behind the power curve when the opportunity arises.

If you still have some time to go before earning your bachelor's degree, the material in this text can help you read the articles and books that you will have to read in the rest of your courses and actually understand what they are talking about. If you have always skipped the sections on statistics and findings, you can now read them and get a better understanding of what the authors did. You may not be able to pick apart an article's statistical methods, but you can read it and find that the authors used, for example, a regression or hypothesis test. You can then add that information in a discussion or paper and have more complete information—and impress your professors if you do it right!

If you are going on to a graduate program, this material provides you a basis of understanding that will be essential to fully comprehend the material and successfully complete a graduate program.

The focus of this book was on the practical theory and application of statistics. If the goal was met, you now have a better understanding of how statistics works, you have seen the problems and pitfalls that you can expect when you begin to conduct research on your own, and you have an understanding of what will be expected when the output starts rolling out of a printer. Good luck, and have some fun with research!

12-6 For Further Reading

Labovitz, S. The nonutility of significance tests: The significance of significance tests reconsidered. *Pacific Sociological Review*, Summer 1970, *13*, 141–148.

—. The zone of rejection: Negative thoughts on statistical inference. *Pacific Sociological Review*, 1971, *14*(4), 373–381.

Selvin, H. A critique of tests of significance in survey research. *American Sociological Review*, 1957, *22*(5), 519–527.

Appendix A
Statistical Tables

	Probability (Top Row) and Significance (Bottom Row)					
df	0.999 0.0001	0.99 .01	0.95 .05	0.90 .10	0.80 .20	0.70 .30
1	10.827	6.635	3.841	2.706	1.642	1.074
2	13.815	9.210	5.991	4.605	3.219	2.408
3	16.268	11.345	7.815	6.251	4.624	3.665
4	18.465	13.277	9.488	7.779	5.989	4.878
5	20.517	15.086	11.070	9.236	7.289	6.064
6	22.457	16.812	12.592	10.645	8.558	7.231
7	24.322	18.475	14.067	12.017	9.803	8.383
8	26.125	20.090	15.507	13.362	11.030	9.524
9	27.877	21.666	16.919	14.684	12.242	10.656
10	29.588	23.209	18.307	15.987	13.442	11.781
11	31.264	24.725	19.675	17.275	14.631	12.899
12	32.909	26.217	21.026	18.549	15.812	14.011
13	34.528	27.688	22.362	19.812	16.985	15.119
14	36.123	29.141	23.685	21.064	18.151	16.222
15	37.697	30.578	24.996	22.307	19.311	17.322
16	39.252	32.000	26.296	23.542	20.465	18.418
17	40.790	33.409	27.587	24.769	21.615	19.511
18	42.312	34.805	28.869	25.989	22.760	20.601
19	43.820	36.191	30.144	27.204	23.900	21.689
20	45.315	37.566	31.410	28.412	25.038	22.775
21	46.797	38.932	32.671	29.615	26.171	23.858
22	48.268	40.289	33.924	30.813	27.301	24.939

| df | \multicolumn{6}{c}{**Probability (Top Row) and Significance (Bottom Row)**} | | | | | |

df	0.999 0.0001	0.99 .01	0.95 .05	0.90 .10	0.80 .20	0.70 .30
23	49.728	41.638	35.172	32.007	28.429	26.018
24	51.179	42.980	36.415	33.196	29.553	27.096
25	52.620	44.314	37.652	34.382	30.675	28.172
26	54.052	45.642	38.885	35.563	31.795	29.246
27	55.476	46.963	40.113	36.741	32.912	30.319
28	56.893	48.278	41.337	37.916	34.027	31.391
29	58.302	49.588	42.557	39.087	35.139	32.461
30	59.703	50.892	43.773	40.256	36.250	33.530

Appendix B

Area Under the Normal Curve

a Z	b Area between $\bar{X}$ and Z	c Area beyond Z	a Z	b Area between $\bar{X}$ and Z	c Area beyond Z	a Z	b Area between $\bar{X}$ and Z	c Area beyond Z	a Z	b Area between $\bar{X}$ and Z	c Area beyond Z
0.00	0.0000	0.5000	0.45	0.1736	0.3264	0.90	0.3159	0.1841	1.35	0.4115	0.0885
0.01	0.0040	0.4960	0.46	0.1772	0.3228	0.91	0.3186	0.1814	1.36	0.4131	0.0869
0.02	0.0080	0.4920	0.47	0.1808	0.3192	0.92	0.3212	0.1788	1.37	0.4147	0.0853
0.03	0.0120	0.4880	0.48	0.1844	0.3156	0.93	0.3238	0.1762	1.38	0.4162	0.0838
0.04	0.0160	0.4840	0.49	0.1879	0.3121	0.94	0.3264	0.1736	1.39	0.4177	0.0823
0.05	0.0199	0.4801	0.50	0.1915	0.3085	0.95	0.3289	0.1711	1.40	0.4192	0.0808
0.06	0.0239	0.4761	0.51	0.1950	0.3050	0.96	0.3315	0.1685	1.41	0.4207	0.0793
0.07	0.0279	0.4721	0.52	0.1985	0.3015	0.97	0.3340	0.1660	1.42	0.4222	0.0778
0.08	0.0319	0.4681	0.53	0.2019	0.2981	0.98	0.3365	0.1635	1.43	0.4236	0.0764
0.09	0.0359	0.4641	0.54	0.2054	0.2946	0.99	0.3389	0.1611	1.44	0.4251	0.0749
0.10	0.0398	0.4602	0.55	0.2088	0.2912	1.00	0.3413	0.1587	1.45	0.4265	0.0735
0.11	0.0438	0.4562	0.56	0.2123	0.2877	1.01	0.3438	0.1562	1.46	0.4279	0.0721
0.12	0.0478	0.4522	0.57	0.2157	0.2843	1.02	0.3461	0.1539	1.47	0.4292	0.0708
0.13	0.0517	0.4483	0.58	0.2190	0.2810	1.03	0.3485	0.1515	1.48	0.4306	0.0694
0.14	0.0557	0.4443	0.59	0.2224	0.2776	1.04	0.3508	0.1492	1.49	0.4319	0.0681
0.15	0.0596	0.4404	0.60	0.2257	0.2743	1.05	0.3531	0.1469	1.50	0.4332	0.0668
0.16	0.0636	0.4364	0.61	0.2291	0.2709	1.06	0.3554	0.1446	1.51	0.4345	0.0655
0.17	0.0675	0.4325	0.62	0.2324	0.2676	1.07	0.3577	0.1423	1.52	0.4357	0.0643
0.18	0.0714	0.4286	0.63	0.2357	0.2643	1.08	0.3599	0.1401	1.53	0.437	0.0630
0.19	0.0753	0.4247	0.64	0.2389	0.2611	1.09	0.3621	0.1379	1.54	0.4382	0.0618
0.20	0.0793	0.4207	0.65	0.2422	0.2578	1.10	0.3643	0.1357	1.55	0.4394	0.0606
0.21	0.0832	0.4168	0.66	0.2454	0.2546	1.11	0.3665	0.1335	1.56	0.4406	0.0594
0.22	0.0871	0.4129	0.67	0.2486	0.2514	1.12	0.3686	0.1314	1.57	0.4418	0.0582
0.23	0.0910	0.4090	0.68	0.2517	0.2483	1.13	0.3708	0.1292	1.58	0.4429	0.0571
0.24	0.0948	0.4052	0.69	0.2549	0.2451	1.14	0.3729	0.1271	1.59	0.4441	0.0559
0.25	0.0987	0.4013	0.70	0.2580	0.2420	1.15	0.3749	0.1251	1.60	0.4452	0.0548
0.26	0.1026	0.3974	0.71	0.2611	0.2389	1.16	0.377	0.1230	1.61	0.4463	0.0537
0.27	0.1064	0.3936	0.72	0.2642	0.2358	1.17	0.379	0.1210	1.62	0.4474	0.0526
0.28	0.1103	0.3897	0.73	0.2673	0.2327	1.18	0.381	0.1190	1.63	0.4484	0.0516
0.29	0.1141	0.3859	0.74	0.2704	0.2296	1.19	0.383	0.1170	1.64	0.4495	0.0505
0.30	0.1179	0.3821	0.75	0.2734	0.2266	1.20	0.3849	0.1151	1.65	0.4505	0.0495
0.31	0.1217	0.3783	0.76	0.2764	0.2236	1.21	0.3869	0.1131	1.66	0.4515	0.0485
0.32	0.1255	0.3745	0.77	0.2794	0.2206	1.22	0.3888	0.1112	1.67	0.4525	0.0475
0.33	0.1293	0.3707	0.78	0.2823	0.2177	1.23	0.3907	0.1093	1.68	0.4535	0.0465
0.34	0.1331	0.3669	0.79	0.2852	0.2148	1.24	0.3925	0.1075	1.69	0.4545	0.0455
0.35	0.1368	0.3632	0.80	0.2881	0.2119	1.25	0.3944	0.1056	1.70	0.4554	0.0446
0.36	0.1406	0.3594	0.81	0.2910	0.2090	1.26	0.3962	0.1038	1.71	0.4564	0.0436
0.37	0.1443	0.3557	0.82	0.2939	0.2061	1.27	0.398	0.1020	1.72	0.4573	0.0427
0.38	0.1480	0.3520	0.83	0.2967	0.2033	1.28	0.3997	0.1003	1.73	0.4582	0.0418
0.39	0.1517	0.3483	0.84	0.2995	0.2005	1.29	0.4015	0.0985	1.74	0.4591	0.0409
0.40	0.1554	0.3446	0.85	0.3023	0.1977	1.30	0.4032	0.0968	1.75	0.4599	0.0401
0.41	0.1591	0.3409	0.86	0.3051	0.1949	1.31	0.4049	0.0951	1.76	0.4608	0.0392
0.42	0.1628	0.3372	0.87	0.3078	0.1922	1.32	0.4066	0.0934	1.77	0.4616	0.0384
0.43	0.1664	0.3336	0.88	0.3106	0.1894	1.33	0.4082	0.0918	1.78	0.4625	0.0375
0.44	0.1700	0.3300	0.89	0.3133	0.1867	1.34	0.4099	0.0901	1.79	0.4633	0.0367

a Z	b Area between $\bar{X}$ and Z	c Area beyond Z	a Z	b Area between $\bar{X}$ and Z	c Area beyond Z	a Z	b Area between $\bar{X}$ and Z	c Area beyond Z	a Z	b Area between $\bar{X}$ and Z	c Area beyond Z
1.80	0.4641	0.0359	2.25	0.4878	0.0122	2.70	0.4965	0.0035	3.15	0.4992	0.0008
1.81	0.4649	0.0351	2.26	0.4881	0.0119	2.71	0.4966	0.0034	3.16	0.4992	0.0008
1.82	0.4656	0.0344	2.27	0.4884	0.0116	2.72	0.4967	0.0033	3.17	0.4992	0.0008
1.83	0.4664	0.0336	2.28	0.4887	0.0113	2.73	0.4968	0.0032	3.18	0.4993	0.0007
1.84	0.4671	0.0329	2.29	0.4890	0.0110	2.74	0.4969	0.0031	3.19	0.4993	0.0007
1.85	0.4678	0.0322	2.30	0.4893	0.0107	2.75	0.4970	0.0030	3.20	0.4993	0.0007
1.86	0.4686	0.0314	2.31	0.4896	0.0104	2.76	0.4971	0.0029	3.21	0.4993	0.0007
1.87	0.4693	0.0307	2.32	0.4898	0.0102	2.77	0.4972	0.0028	3.22	0.4994	0.0006
1.88	0.4699	0.0301	2.33	0.4901	0.0099	2.78	0.4973	0.0027	3.23	0.4994	0.0006
1.89	0.4706	0.0294	2.34	0.4904	0.0096	2.79	0.4974	0.0026	3.24	0.4994	0.0006
1.90	0.4713	0.0287	2.35	0.4906	0.0094	2.80	0.4974	0.0026	3.25	0.4994	0.0006
1.91	0.4719	0.0281	2.36	0.4909	0.0091	2.81	0.4975	0.0025	3.30	0.4995	0.0005
1.92	0.4726	0.0274	2.37	0.4911	0.0089	2.82	0.4976	0.0024	3.35	0.4996	0.0004
1.93	0.4732	0.0268	2.38	0.4913	0.0087	2.83	0.4977	0.0023	3.40	0.4997	0.0003
1.94	0.4738	0.0262	2.39	0.4916	0.0084	2.84	0.4977	0.0023	3.45	0.4997	0.0003
1.95	0.4744	0.0256	2.40	0.4918	0.0082	2.85	0.4978	0.0022	3.50	0.4998	0.0002
1.96	0.4750	0.0250	2.41	0.4920	0.0080	2.86	0.4979	0.0021	3.60	0.4998	0.0002
1.97	0.4756	0.0244	2.42	0.4922	0.0078	2.87	0.4979	0.0021	3.70	0.4999	0.0001
1.98	0.4761	0.0239	2.43	0.4925	0.0075	2.88	0.4980	0.0020	3.80	0.4999	0.0001
1.99	0.4767	0.0233	2.44	0.4927	0.0073	2.89	0.4981	0.0019	3.90	0.49995	0.00005
2.00	0.4772	0.0228	2.45	0.4929	0.0071	2.90	0.4981	0.0019	4.00	0.49997	0.00003
2.01	0.4778	0.0222	2.46	0.4931	0.0069	2.91	0.4982	0.0018	4.50	0.4999966	0.0000034
2.02	0.4783	0.0217	2.47	0.4932	0.0068	2.92	0.4982	0.0018	5.00	0.4999997	0.0000003
2.03	0.4788	0.0212	2.48	0.4934	0.0066	2.93	0.4983	0.0017	5.50	0.4999999	0.0000001
2.04	0.4793	0.0207	2.49	0.4936	0.0064	2.94	0.4984	0.0016			
2.05	0.4798	0.0202	2.50	0.4938	0.0062	2.95	0.4984	0.0016			
2.06	0.4803	0.0197	2.51	0.4940	0.0060	2.96	0.4985	0.0015			
2.07	0.4808	0.0192	2.52	0.4941	0.0059	2.97	0.4985	0.0015			
2.08	0.4812	0.0188	2.53	0.4943	0.0057	2.98	0.4986	0.0014			
2.09	0.4817	0.0183	2.54	0.4945	0.0055	2.99	0.4986	0.0014			
2.10	0.4821	0.0179	2.55	0.4946	0.0054	3.00	0.4987	0.0013			
2.11	0.4826	0.0174	2.56	0.4948	0.0052	3.01	0.4987	0.0013			
2.12	0.4830	0.0170	2.57	0.4949	0.0051	3.02	0.4987	0.0013			
2.13	0.4834	0.0166	2.58	0.4951	0.0049	3.03	0.4988	0.0012			
2.14	0.4838	0.0162	2.59	0.4952	0.0048	3.04	0.4988	0.0012			
2.15	0.4842	0.0158	2.60	0.4953	0.0047	3.05	0.4989	0.0011			
2.16	0.4846	0.0154	2.61	0.4955	0.0045	3.06	0.4989	0.0011			
2.17	0.4850	0.0150	2.62	0.4956	0.0044	3.07	0.4989	0.0011			
2.18	0.4854	0.0146	2.63	0.4957	0.0043	3.08	0.4990	0.0010			
2.19	0.4857	0.0143	2.64	0.4959	0.0041	3.09	0.4990	0.0010			
2.20	0.4861	0.0139	2.65	0.4960	0.0040	3.10	0.4990	0.0010			
2.21	0.4864	0.0136	2.66	0.4961	0.0039	3.11	0.4991	0.0009			
2.22	0.4868	0.0132	2.67	0.4962	0.0038	3.12	0.4991	0.0009			
2.23	0.4871	0.0129	2.68	0.4963	0.0037	3.13	0.4991	0.0009			
2.24	0.4875	0.0125	2.69	0.4964	0.0036	3.14	0.4992	0.0008			

Appendix C
Student's *t* Distribution

	Level of Significance for One-Tailed Test					
	.10	.05	.025	.01	.005	.0005
	Level of Significance for Two-Tailed Test					
df	.20	.10	.05	.02	.01	.001
1	3.078	6.314	12.706	31.821	63.657	636.62
2	1.886	2.920	4.303	6.965	9.925	31.598
3	1.638	2.353	3.182	4.541	5.841	12.941
4	1.533	2.132	2.776	3.747	4.604	8.610
5	1.476	2.015	2.571	3.365	4.032	6.859
6	1.440	1.943	2.447	3.143	3.707	5.959
7	1.415	1.895	2.365	2.998	3.499	5.405
8	1.397	1.860	2.306	2.896	3.355	5.041
9	1.383	1.833	2.262	2.821	3.250	4.781
10	1.372	1.812	2.228	2.764	3.169	4.587
11	1.363	1.796	2.201	2.718	3.106	4.437
12	1.356	1.782	2.179	2.681	3.055	4.318
13	1.350	1.771	2.160	2.650	3.012	4.221
14	1.345	1.761	2.145	2.624	2.977	4.140
15	1.341	1.753	2.131	2.602	2.947	4.073
16	1.337	1.746	2.120	2.583	2.921	4.015
17	1.333	1.740	2.110	2.567	2.898	3.965
18	1.330	1.734	2.101	2.552	2.878	3.922
19	1.328	1.729	2.093	2.539	2.861	3.883
20	1.325	1.725	2.086	2.528	2.845	3.850
21	1.323	1.721	2.080	2.518	2.831	3.819
22	1.321	1.717	2.074	2.508	2.819	3.792
23	1.319	1.714	2.069	2.500	2.807	3.767
24	1.318	1.711	2.064	2.492	2.797	3.745
25	1.316	1.708	2.060	2.485	2.787	3.725
26	1.315	1.706	2.056	2.479	2.779	3.707
27	1.314	1.703	2.052	2.473	2.771	3.690
28	1.313	1.701	2.048	2.467	2.763	3.674

		Level of Significance for One-Tailed Test				
	.10	**.05**	**.025**	**.01**	**.005**	**.0005**
		Level of Significance for Two-Tailed Test				
df	**.20**	**.10**	**.05**	**.02**	**.01**	**.001**
29	1.311	1.699	2.045	2.462	2.756	3.659
30	1.310	1.697	2.042	2.457	2.750	3.646
40	1.303	1.684	2.021	2.423	2.704	3.551
60	1.296	1.671	2.000	2.390	2.660	3.460
120	1.289	1.658	1.980	2.358	2.617	3.373
∞	1.282	1.645	1.960	2.326	2.576	3.291

Appendix D
Distribution of *F*; *p* = .05

df_{within}	$df_{between}$						
	1	**2**	**3**	**4**	**5**	**6**	**8**
1	161.4	199.5	215.7	224.6	230.2	234	238.9
2	18.51	19.00	19.16	19.25	19.3	19.33	19.37
3	10.13	9.55	9.28	9.12	9.01	8.94	8.85
4	7.71	6.94	6.59	6.39	6.26	6.16	6.04
5	6.61	5.79	5.41	5.19	5.05	4.95	4.82
6	5.99	5.14	4.76	4.53	4.39	4.28	4.15
7	5.59	4.74	4.35	4.12	3.97	3.87	3.73
8	5.32	4.46	4.07	3.84	3.69	3.58	3.44
9	5.12	4.26	3.86	3.63	3.48	3.37	3.23
10	4.96	4.10	3.71	3.48	3.33	3.22	3.07
11	4.84	3.98	3.59	3.36	3.20	3.09	2.95
12	4.75	3.89	3.49	3.26	3.11	3.00	2.85
13	4.67	3.81	3.41	3.18	3.03	2.92	2.77
14	4.60	3.74	3.34	3.11	2.96	2.85	2.70
15	4.54	3.68	3.29	3.06	2.90	2.79	2.64
16	4.49	3.63	3.24	3.01	2.85	2.74	2.59
17	4.45	3.59	3.20	2.96	2.81	2.70	2.55
18	4.41	3.55	3.16	2.93	2.77	2.66	2.51
19	4.38	3.52	3.13	2.90	2.74	2.63	2.48
20	4.35	3.49	3.10	2.87	2.71	2.60	2.45
21	4.32	3.47	3.07	2.84	2.68	2.57	2.42
22	4.30	3.44	3.05	2.82	2.66	2.55	2.40
23	4.28	3.42	3.03	2.80	2.64	2.53	2.37
24	4.26	3.40	3.01	2.78	2.62	2.51	2.36
25	4.24	3.39	2.99	2.76	2.60	2.49	2.34
16	4.23	3.37	2.98	27.4	2.59	2.47	2.32
27	4.21	3.35	2.96	2.73	2.57	2.46	2.31
18	4.20	3.34	2.95	2.71	2.56	2.45	2.29
29	4.18	3.33	2.93	2.70	2.55	2.43	2.28
30	4.17	3.32	2.92	2.69	2.53	2.42	2.27
40	4.08	3.23	2.84	2.61	2.45	2.34	2.18
60	4.00	3.05	2.76	2.53	2.37	2.25	2.10
80	3.96	3.11	2.72	2.48	2.33	2.21	2.05
120	3.92	3.07	2.68	2.45	2.29	2.17	2.02
∞	3.84	3.00	2.60	2.37	2.21	2.10	1.94

df_{within}	$df_{between}$							
	10	**15**	**20**	**30**	**40**	**60**	**120**	**∞**
1	241.9	245.9	248	250.1	251.1	252.2	253.3	254.3
2	19.4	19.43	19.45	19.46	19.47	19.48	19.49	16.5
3	8.79	8.70	8.66	8.62	8.59	8.57	8.55	8.53
4	5.96	5.86	5.80	5.75	5.72	5.69	5.66	5.63
5	4.74	4.62	4.56	4.50	4.46	4.43	4.40	4.36
6	4.06	3.94	3.87	3.81	3.77	3.74	3.70	3.67
7	3.64	3.51	3.44	3.38	3.34	3.30	3.27	3.23
8	3.35	3.22	3.15	3.08	3.04	3.01	2.97	2.93
9	3.14	3.01	2.94	2.86	2.83	2.79	2.75	2.71
10	2.98	2.85	2.77	2.70	2.66	2.62	2.58	2.54
11	2.85	2.72	2.65	2.57	2.53	2.49	2.45	2.40
12	2.75	2.62	2.54	2.47	2.43	2.38	2.35	2.30
13	2.67	2.53	2.46	2.38	2.34	2.30	2.25	2.21
14	2.60	2.46	2.39	2.31	2.27	2.22	2.18	2.13
15	2.54	2.40	2.33	2.25	2.20	2.16	2.11	2.07
16	2.49	2.35	2.28	2.19	2.15	2.11	2.06	2.01
17	2.45	2.31	2.23	2.15	2.10	2.06	2.01	1.96
18	2.41	2.27	2.19	2.11	2.06	2.02	1.97	1.92
19	2.38	2.23	2.16	2.07	2.03	1.98	1.93	1.88
20	2.35	2.20	2.12	2.04	1.99	1.95	1.90	1.84
21	2.32	2.18	2.10	2.01	1.96	1.92	1.87	1.81
22	2.30	2.15	2.07	1.98	1.94	1.89	1.84	1.78
23	2.27	2.13	2.05	1.96	1.91	1.86	1.81	1.76
24	2.25	2.11	2.03	1.94	1.89	1.84	1.79	1.73
25	2.24	2.09	2.01	1.92	1.87	1.82	1.77	1.71
16	2.22	2.07	1.99	1.90	1.85	1.80	1.75	1.69
27	2.20	2.06	1.97	1.88	1.84	1.79	1.73	1.67
18	2.19	2.04	1.96	1.87	1.82	1.77	1.71	1.65
29	2.18	2.03	1.94	1.85	1.81	1.75	1.70	1.64
30	2.16	2.01	1.93	1.84	1.79	1.74	1.68	1.62
40	2.08	1.92	1.84	1.74	1.69	1.64	1.58	1.51
60	1.99	1.84	1.75	1.65	1.59	1.53	1.47	1.39
80	1.95	1.80	1.70	1.60	1.54	1.49	1.41	1.32
120	1.91	1.75	1.66	1.55	1.50	1.43	1.35	1.25
∞	1.83	1.67	1.57	1.46	1.39	1.32	1.22	1.00

Glossary

Additive Effect: Each variable explains a part of the variation in the dependent variable.

Analysis of Variance (ANOVA): An inferential test of the measure of dispersion between group means; allows for the simultaneous comparison of the means of more than two samples. There are one- and two-way ANOVA's.

Bivariate Analysis: Analysis that compares two variables to see how they differ or are similar. Also, this analysis examines change in one variable that may be associated with change in another variable.

Bivariate Tables: Tables that display the intersection of two variables' values across cases.

Causation: The culmination of association, temporal ordering, and the elimination of confounding variables.

Cell: Each box in a bivariate table.

Cell Frequency: The number of occurrences of a pair of values from the independent and dependent variables.

Chi-square: The primary method of establishing the existence of a relationship between two nominal, and sometimes higher, level variables.

Central Limit Theorem: Theorem stating that given any population, as the sample size increases, the sampling distribution of the means approaches a normal distribution.

Central Tendency: Average, middle point, or most common value of the distribution.

Coefficient of Determination: The square of Pearson's r. This coefficient tells the proportion of the variance in the dependent variable that is accounted for by variation in the independent variable.

Concept: Abstract terms that are generally agreed upon as representing some characteristic or phenomena.

Conceptualization: The process of drawing out concepts from research questions or hypotheses.

Concordant Pairs: Pairs that are ranked in the same order on both variables.

Confidence Intervals: The range of values within which the true population means should fall.

Confounding Variables: Rival causal factors that can influence the explanation of a causal relationship by their omission from an analytic model.

Constant: A measure that has no variation across cases/characteristics.

Critical Value: A value from a chart that links degrees of freedom and the desired level of significance. The critical value selected is evaluated with regard to an obtained value to determine if the relationship among two variables is statistically significant.

Cross-Tabulation Table (Crosstab): The most common bivariate table that displays the intersection of two variables' values (cell frequency, column percentages, row percentages, and total percentages) across cases.

Deduction: Testing preconceived theory through observation and statistical analysis.

Degrees of Freedom: A statistical technique that compensates for error stemming from the use of samples rather than populations.

Delta: A more precise manner of examining the relationship between two nominal level variables than epsilon.

Dependent Variable: The variable we are most interested in. A dependent variable will be pitted against one or more independent variables to examine how the independent variable(s) impact the dependent variable.

Deviation: The difference between a single value or case and the measure of central tendency.

Direction of the Relationship: How scores on one variable are associated with scores on another variable. This statistic is focused on how high and low scores of variables are related in particular.

Discordant Pairs: Pairs that are ranked one way or another on one variable and the opposite way on the other variable.

Discovery: What statistics is about; discovering something previously unknown or something we thought we knew but we were not sure.

Dispersion: The overall difference between all cases or values and the measure of central tendency.

Epsilon: A statistic that allows the determination of difference among nominal level variables, which denotes the existence of a relationship.

Error: Problems with any statistical model; includes measurement error, observation error, random error, and systematic error.

Estimate: Results of an analysis on a sample when inferred to a larger population.

Existence: A determination of if there is a relationship between two variables.

Expected Value: The estimated population parameter.

Form of a Distribution: The symmetry, number of peaks, and flatness of a distribution of values.

Frequency Distribution: A distribution that summarizes data and provides a visualization of how scores are spread over categories.

_F_-Test: Hypothesis test that measures the possible magnitude of difference between two samples or groups.

Fully-Ordered Ordinal Level Data: Ordinal level data with more than five categories or characteristics.

Heteroskedasticity: When the variance of the error term is not constant over the entire length of the regression line.

Hypothesis: Statements whose answers will support or refute theoretical propositions in research.

Hypothesis Testing: A statistical decision-making process where assumptions are established through the creation of research and null hypotheses, sample characteristics are compared to population parameters, and a decision is made to reject or fail to reject the null hypothesis.

Independent Variable: Explanatory variables that we expect to have some impact on a dependent variable.

Induction: Turning observation and statistical analyses into theory.

Inference: Performing an analysis on the sample and then concluding that the findings apply to the population.

Inferential Statistics: Techniques that allow researchers to examine the characteristics of a sample and draw conclusions on the larger population from which the sample was drawn.

Interaction: Any change in one variable that produces, or is associated with, change in another variable.

Interval Level Data: Data whose categories can be rank-ordered, but the intervals between the categories are equal.

Kurtosis: The extent to which cases are piled up around the measure of central tendency or piled up around the tails of a distribution.

Lambda: An asymmetric measure of association which measures the proportional reduction in errors made in predicting modal values or categories of a dependent variable when information about an independent variable is used.

Leptokurtic: A distribution where the values are tightly clustered around the measure of central tendency.

Levels of Measurement: The level of mathematical sophistication a variable contains.

Marginals: Numbers on the outside of a table.

Measures of Central Tendency: Statistics that examine where the central value is in the distribution or the distribution's most typical value.

Mean: The average of the values in the distribution.

Median: The point of distribution that marks the 50th percentile; stands as the exact midpoint splitting the distribution into two identical parts.

Mesokurtic: A distribution where the values are evenly distributed around the measure of central tendency.

Mode: The distribution's most frequently occurring value or case.

Model of No Association: The distribution of expected frequencies.

Monotonicity: The general nature of association for nominal and ordinal level data. There are two types of monotonicity: Monotone-increasing and monotone-decreasing.

Multivariate Analysis: Analyses that compare three or more variables against each other or examine how several independent variables influence a dependent variable.

Nature of the Relationship: Indicates when the data is arranged in such a manner as to make bivariate analyses erroneous.

Negative Relationship: Relationships in which high values of one variable are associated with low values in the other variable.

Nominal Level Data: Measured data that is purely qualitative in nature; these variables' characteristics are typically word based. The color of a car is an example.

Normal Curve: A special distribution that is symmetrical and unimodal; the area under the curve is always the same (1 or 100%).

Null Hypothesis: A competing statement that is used to evaluate/disprove the merits of a research hypothesis.

Number of Modes: The total number of modes a variable's cases/characteristics contains.

Obtained Value: A value generated by a statistical procedure examining the relationship between two or more variables. The obtained value is compared to the critical value to determine if there is a statistically significant relationship between two variables.

One-Tailed Test: A test that evaluates difference between two groups and specifies the direction of the difference.

Operationalization: The process of translating a concept into a variable, or converting the abstract into the concrete.

Ordinal Level Data: Data that is still qualitative in nature, but the various categories can be rank-ordered. The order refers to categories that can be less than or greater than other categories, but not by how much. T-shirt size is an example.

Ordinary Least Squares (OLS) Regression: Shows the linear relational effects on a dependent variable of an independent variable, controlling for the effects of other independent variablesw, plus the combined effects of all the independent variables.

Parameter: A characteristic of a population.

Parsimony: The attempt to identify the smallest number of the most important influences on a dependent variable.

Pearson's _r_ (Product Moment Correlation): A bivariate measure of the existence, strength, and direction of a relationship for interval and ratio level data.

Percentage Table: A table that allows direct comparison between categories of two variables. There are three types of percentage table: Column, row, and total.

Platykurtic: A distribution where most of the values occur in the tails.

Population: The entire group of subjects in which we are interested in studying.

Positive Relationship: When high values or ranks on one variable are associated with high values or ranks in the other variable.

Primary Question: The one driving thought/question behind a research project by positing the relationship between two broad ideas.

Probability: The relative likelihood of the occurrence of an event or the number of times an event can occur relative to the number of times any event can occur.

Proportional Reduction of Errors: Process of calculating how much better your prediction of the dependent variable would be with knowledge of some independent variable over knowledge of the dependent variable alone.

Range: The difference between the highest and lowest values in a distribution.

Rank Order of Pairs: Process in which categories of a dependent variable such as high, medium, or low are compared to categories of another ordinal independent variable. A determination is then made of whether or not the rank ordering of cases of one variable is useful in predicting the rank ordering of cases of the other variable.

Ratio Level Data: Considered the highest order of data; this level of data is identical to interval level with the except that this level of measurement contains a true zero, where there is the possibility of a true absence of the characteristics of the variable.

Research Design: The method to be used (experiment, survey, etc.) and the approach to be taken in conducting a research study.

Research Hypothesis: A statement that indicates the expected outcome of a part of a research project.

Research Methods: A scientific, systematic way of examining and testing a theory.

Research Questions: Questions that break down the primary question into subproblems that are more manageable and more testable through research.

Robustness: The ability of a statistical technique to provide accurate results when assumptions are violated.

Sample: A small group of subjects (subset) drawn from a larger population.

Scientific Inquiry: A systematic method of examining things that interest us.

Skewness: The degree of symmetry of the distribution; distributions are identified as symmetrical, positively skewed, or negatively skewed.

Somer's *d*: An asymmetric measure of association for ordinal level data.

Spearman's Rho (Correlation): A bivariate measure of the existence of a relationship for fully ordered ordinal level data.

Standard Deviation: The square root of the variance; places the dispersion in the same units as the distribution.

Standard Error: A measure of the variation of the statistic around the parameter it is estimating.

Statistic: Characteristic of the sample for which researchers may make inferences to the population parameter.

Statistical Significance: Suggests that there is a relationship between two or more variables based on some bivariate or multivariate statistical technique.

Strength of Association: The degree to which two or more variables are related, i.e., a strong or weak relationship.

Sum of Squares between Groups: The sum of the squared deviations between each sample mean and the total mean for all observed values.

Sum of Squares within Groups: The sum of the squared deviations between each score and the mean.

Synergy Effect: Situation in which the sum of the variables' contribution is greater than their individual effects.

Temporal Ordering: The relationship in time between two variables.

Theory: Statements concerning the relationship among characteristics of people or things.

True Zero: A true absence of the characteristic in the variable.

t-**Test:** Examines whether a sample could have come from a known population or whether two samples come from the same population. Used with samples with sizes less than 120 cases.

Two-Tailed Test: Evaluates difference between two groups being tested without specifying the direction of the difference.

Type I Error: The rejection of the null hypothesis when the null hypothesis is actually true.

Type II Error: The failure to reject a null hypothesis when the null hypothesis is false.

Univariate Analysis: Analyses that deal with only a single variable.

Variable: A concrete, empirical measurement of a concept that can be seen and used in statistical analyses; contains variance across cases/characteristics.

Variance: The average of squared deviations of scores about the mean; the difference between the mean and each score.

Z Scores: Standard deviations put into a standard distance from the mean of a normal curve. A conversion of any value in the distribution into standard deviation units.

Z Test: A test that examines whether a sample could have come from a known population or whether two samples come from the same population. The z test is used primarily with large samples (>120).

Equation Glossary

Beta:

$$\beta = \frac{\mu_{H_o} - \mu_{\text{true}}}{\sigma}$$

Chi-Square:

$$\chi^2 = \sum \frac{(f_o - f_e)^2}{f_e}$$

Confidence Intervals:

$$\overline{X} \pm z_{CI}\left(\frac{\sigma}{\sqrt{N}}\right)$$

Degrees of Freedom for Chi-square:

$$df = (\text{number of rows} - 1) \times (\text{number of columns} - 1)$$

Degrees of Freedom (*F*-Test):

$$df_{\text{total}} = df_{\text{within}} + df_{\text{between}} = (N - k) + (k - 1)$$

Delta:

$$\Delta = (f_{o11} - f_{e11}), (f_{o12} - f_{e12}), \ldots$$

F-Ratio:

$$F = \frac{SS_b \,/\, df_{between}}{SS_w \,/\, df_{within}} = \frac{MS_b}{MS_w}$$

Lambda:

$$\lambda = \frac{(N - R_l) - \Sigma(C_t - f_l)}{N - R_l}$$

Mean:

$$\bar{X} = \frac{\Sigma fx}{N}$$

Median:

$$ME = \frac{N + 1}{2}$$

Pearson's r (Product Moment Correlation):

$$r = \frac{N\Sigma(XY) - (\Sigma X)(\Sigma Y)}{\sqrt{[N\Sigma(X^2) - (\Sigma X)^2][N(\Sigma Y^2) - (\Sigma Y)^2]}}$$

Somers' d:

$$d_{yx} = \frac{N_s + N_d}{N_s + N_d + T_y}$$

Standard Deviation:

$$\sigma = \sqrt{\frac{\Sigma(X - \bar{X})^2}{N}}$$

Sum of Squares within Groups:

$$SS_w = \Sigma(n_i - 1)s_i^2$$

Sum of Squares between Groups:

$$SS_b = \Sigma n_i(\bar{X}_i - \bar{X})^2$$

_t_-Test (obtained value):

$$t = \frac{\overline{X} - \mu}{\dfrac{s}{\sqrt{N-1}}}$$

_t_-Test (two-sample):

$$t = \frac{\overline{X}_1 - \overline{X}_2}{\sqrt{\dfrac{s_1^2}{N_1 - 1} + \dfrac{s_2^2}{N_2 - 1}}}$$

Variance:

$$\sigma^2 = \frac{\Sigma(X - \overline{X})^2}{N}$$

Z Score (sample):

$$Z = \frac{X - \overline{X}}{s}$$

Z Score (population):

$$Z = \frac{\overline{X} - \mu}{\sigma}$$

Z Test (population):

$$Z = \frac{\overline{X} - \mu}{\dfrac{\sigma}{\sqrt{N}}}$$

Z Test (sample):

$$Z = \frac{\overline{X} - \mu}{\dfrac{s}{\sqrt{N}}}$$

Index

Note: Italicized page locators indicate figures; tables are noted with *t*.